Other Books and Series by Jeff Bowen

Applications for Enrollment of Chickasaw Newborn Act of 1905
Volumes I thru VII

Cherokee Intermarried White 1906 Volume I thru X

Applications for Enrollment of Creek Newborn Act of 1905
Volumes I thru XIV

Applications for Enrollment of Choctaw Newborn Act of 1905
Volume I & II

Visit our website at **www.nativestudy.com** to learn more about these and other books and series by Jeff Bowen

APPLICATIONS FOR ENROLLMENT OF CHOCTAW NEWBORN ACT OF 1905

VOLUME III

TRANSCRIBED BY
JEFF BOWEN

NATIVE STUDY
Gallipolis, Ohio
USA

Other Books and Series by Jeff Bowen

1901-1907 Native American Census Seneca, Eastern Shawnee, Miami, Modoc, Ottawa, Peoria, Quapaw, and Wyandotte Indians (Under Seneca School, Indian Territory)

1932 Census of The Standing Rock Sioux Reservation with Births And Deaths 1924-1932

Census of The Blackfeet, Montana, 1897- 1901 Expanded Edition

Eastern Cherokee by Blood, 1906-1910, Volumes I thru XIII

Choctaw of Mississippi Indian Census 1929-1932 with Births and Deaths 1924-1931 Volume I
Choctaw of Mississippi Indian Census 1933, 1934 & 1937, Supplemental Rolls to 1934 & 1935 with Births and Deaths 1932-1938, and Marriages 1936-1938 Volume II

Eastern Cherokee Census Cherokee, North Carolina 1930-1939 Census 1930-1931 with Births And Deaths 1924-1931 Taken By Agent L. W. Page Volume I
Eastern Cherokee Census Cherokee, North Carolina 1930-1939 Census 1932-1933 with Births And Deaths 1930-1932 Taken By Agent R. L. Spalsbury Volume II
Eastern Cherokee Census Cherokee, North Carolina 1930-1939 Census 1934-1937 with Births and Deaths 1925-1938 and Marriages 1936 & 1938 Taken by Agents R. L. Spalsbury And Harold W. Foght Volume III

Seminole of Florida Indian Census, 1930-1940 with Birth and Death Records, 1930-1938

Texas Cherokees 1820-1839 A Document For Litigation 1921

Choctaw By Blood Enrollment Cards 1898-1914 Volumes I thru XVII

Starr Roll 1894 (Cherokee Payment Rolls) Districts: Canadian, Cooweescoowee, and Delaware Volume One
Starr Roll 1894 (Cherokee Payment Rolls) Districts: Flint, Going Snake, and Illinois Volume Two
Starr Roll 1894 (Cherokee Payment Rolls) Districts: Saline, Sequoyah, and Tahlequah; Including Orphan Roll Volume Three

Cherokee Intruder Cases Dockets of Hearings 1901-1909 Volumes I & II

Indian Wills, 1911-1921 Records of the Bureau of Indian Affairs Books One thru Seven;
Native American Wills & Probate Records 1911-1921

Other Books and Series by Jeff Bowen

Turtle Mountain Reservation Chippewa Indians 1932 Census with Births & Deaths, 1924-1932

Chickasaw By Blood Enrollment Cards 1898-1914 Volume I thru V

Cherokee Descendants East An Index to the Guion Miller Applications Volume I
Cherokee Descendants West An Index to the Guion Miller Applications Volume II (A-M)
Cherokee Descendants West An Index to the Guion Miller Applications Volume III (N-Z)

Applications for Enrollment of Seminole Newborn Freedmen, Act of 1905

Eastern Cherokee Census, Cherokee, North Carolina, 1915-1922, Taken by Agent James E. Henderson
    Volume I (1915-1916)
    Volume II (1917-1918)
    Volume III (1919-1920)
    Volume IV (1921-1922)

Complete Delaware Roll of 1898

Eastern Cherokee Census, Cherokee, North Carolina, 1923-1929, Taken by Agent James E. Henderson
    Volume I (1923-1924)
    Volume II (1925-1926)
    Volume III (1927-1929)

Applications for Enrollment of Seminole Newborn Act of 1905 Volumes I & II

North Carolina Eastern Cherokee Indian Census 1898-1899, 1904, 1906, 1909-1912, 1914 Revised and Expanded Edition

1932 Hopi and Navajo Native American Census with Birth & Death Rolls (1925-1931) Volume 1 - Hopi
1932 Hopi and Navajo Native American Census with Birth & Death Rolls (1930-1932) Volume 2 - Navajo

Western Navajo Reservation Navajo, Hopi and Paiute 1933 Census with Birth & Death Rolls 1925-1933

Cherokee Citizenship Commission Dockets 1880-1884 and 1887-1889 Volumes I thru V

Copyright © 2012
by Jeff Bowen

ALL RIGHTS RESERVED
No part of this publication may be reproduced
or used in any form or manner whatsoever
without previous written permission from the
copyright holder or publisher.

Originally published:
Baltimore, Maryland
2012

Reprinted by:

Native Study LLC
Gallipolis, OH
www.nativestudy.com
2020

Library of Congress Control Number: 2020918113

ISBN: 978-1-64968-096-9

Made in the United States of America.

This series is dedicated to the descendants of the
Choctaw newborn listed in these applications.

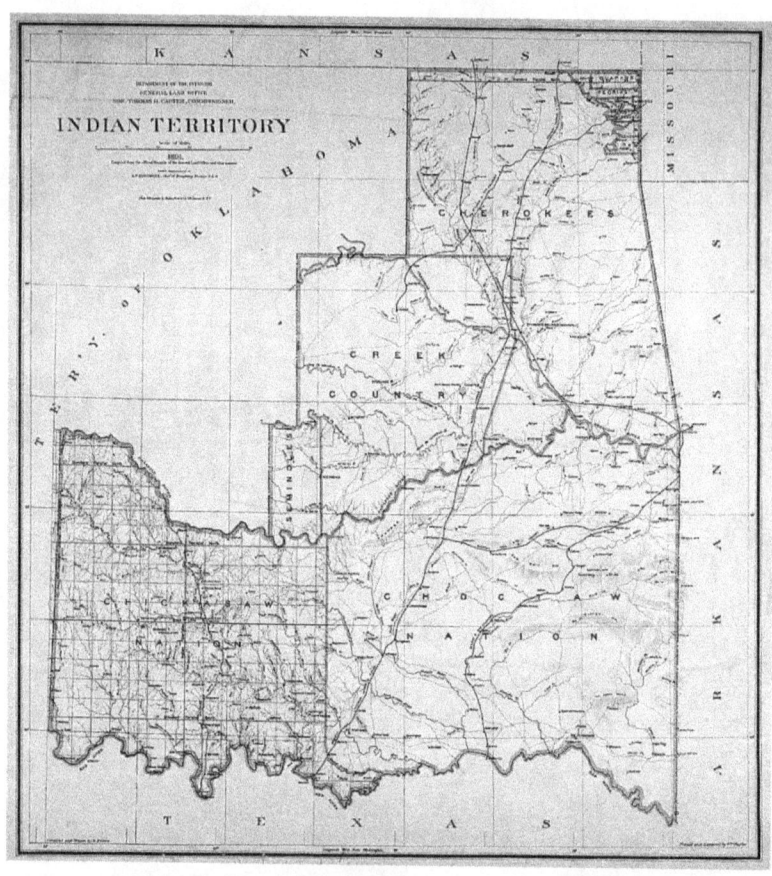

This map of Indian Territory shows how large the Choctaw and Chickasaw Nations' land base was that contained huge deposits of asphalt and coal. Just the size and territory involved was flooded with the "Grafters".

DEPARTMENT OF THE INTERIOR.
Commissioner to the Five Civilized Tribes.

NOTICE.

Opening of Land Office at Wewoka,
IN THE SEMINOLE NATION, INDIAN TERRITORY.

Notice is hereby given that on Monday, September 4, 1905, the Commissioner to the Five Civilized Tribes will establish a land office at Wewoka, in the Seminole Nation, Indian Territory, for the purpose of allowing citizens and freedmen of the Seminole Nation to select allotments of land for their minor children enrolled under the Act of Congress approved March 3, 1905 (33 Stat. L. 1060), and for the further purpose of allowing citizens and freedmen of the Seminole Nation, whose allotments are incomplete, to select additional land in order to bring the value of their allotments up to the standard of $309.09, as nearly as may be practicable.

Each child whose enrollment in accordance with the Act of March 3, 1905, has been duly approved by the Secretary of the Interior, is entitled to receive an alllotment of forty acres without regard to the character or value of the land selected.

Selection of allotments for minor children must be made by their citizen or freedmen parents or by a duly appointed guardian, or curator, or by a duly appointed administrator.

TAMS BIXBY,
Commissioner.

Muskogee, Indian Territory,
July 29, 1905.

This particular notice for the Seminole and Creek Newborn makes mention of the Act of 1905. It is likely that a similar notice was posted in the Choctaw and Chickasaw Nations for the registration of newborn children.

DEPARTMENT OF THE INTERIOR,
Commission to the Five Civilized Tribes.

Rules and Regulations Governing the Selection of Allotments and the Designation of Homesteads in the Choctaw and Chickasaw Nations.

1. Selections of allotments and designations of homesteads for adult citizens and selections of allotments for adult freedmen must be made in person except as herein otherwise provided.
2. Applications to have land set apart and homesteads designated for duly identified Mississippi Choctaws must be made personally before the Commission to the Five Civilized Tribes. Fathers may apply for their minor children and if the father be dead the mother may apply. Husbands may apply for wives. Applications for orphans, insane persons and persons of unsound mind may be made by duly appointed guardian or curator, and for aged and infirm persons and prisoners by agents duly authorized thereunto by power of attorney, in the discretion of said Commission.
3. At the time of the selection of allotment each citizen and duly identified Mississippi Choctaw shall designate as a homestead out of said selection land equal in value to one hundred and sixty acres of the average allottable land of the Choctaw and Chickasaw Nations, as nearly as may be.
4. Each Choctaw and Chickasaw freedman, at the time of selection shall designate as his or her allotment of the lands of the Choctaw and Chickasaw Nations, land equal in value to forty acres of the average allottable land of the Choctaw and Chickasaw Nations.
5. Citizens, freedmen and identified Mississippi Choctaws who are married, whether they have attained their majority or not, will be regarded as of age for the purpose of making selections.
6. Selections may be made by citizen and freedman parents for unmarried male children under twenty-one years of age and for unmarried female children under eighteen years of age, and a male citizen or freedman may make selection for his wife, if she is entitled to make selection, unless she shall, at the time or previously thereto, protest in writing.
7. Where the father of an unmarried minor citizen, freedman or identified Mississippi Choctaw is a non-citizen, the citizen, freedman or identified Mississippi Choctaw mother of such children must make selection in person in behalf of said children.
8. Selections of allotments and designations of homesteads for minor citizens and selections of allotments for minor freedmen may be made by the citizen father or mother or freedman father or mother, as the case may be, or by a guardian, curator, or an administrator having charge of their estate, in the order named.
9. Selections of allotments and designations of homesteads for citizen, and selections of allotment for freedmen, prisoners, convicts, aged and infirm persons and soldiers and sailors of the United States on duty outside of Indian Territory, may be made by duly appointed agents under power of attorney, and for incompetents by guardians, curators, or other suitable person akin to them.
10. Selections may be made and homesteads designated by duly identified Mississippi Choctaws, who have, within one year after the date of their identification as such, made satisfactory proof of bona fide settlement within the Choctaw-Chickasaw country, at any time within six months after the date of their said identification.
11. Persons authorized to make selections by power of attorney, as provided in rules 2 and 9 hereof, must be the husband or wife, or a relative not further removed than a cousin of the first degree of the person for whom such selection is made.
12. It shall be the duty of the Commission to the Five Civilized Tribes to see that selections of allotments and designations of homesteads for the classes of persons mentioned in rules 2, 6, 7, 8 and 9 hereof, are made for the best interests of such persons.
13. Selections of allotments for citizens, freedmen and identified Mississippi Choctaws who have died subsequent to September 25, 1902, and before making a selection of allotment, shall be made by a duly appointed administrator or executor. If, however, such administrator or executor be not duly and expeditiously appointed, or fails to act promptly when appointed, or for any other cause such selections be not so made within a reasonable and practicable time, the Commission to the Five Civilized Tribes shall designate the lands thus to be allotted.
14. In determining the value of a selection the appraised value of the land selected shall be increased by the appraised value of such pine timber on such land as has heretofore been estimated by the Commission to the Five Civilized Tribes.
15. Selections of allotments may be made only by citizens and freedmen whose enrollment has been approved by the Secretary of the Interior, and by persons duly identified by the Commission to the Five Civilized Tribes as Mississippi Choctaws, and by none others.
16. When a selection of land has been made by a citizen, freedman or identified Mississippi Choctaw, and the land so selected is claimed by a person whose rights as a citizen or freedman have not been finally determined, contest for the land so selected may be instituted by the person claiming the land, formal application for the land being first made as is required by the Rules of Practice in Choctaw and Chickasaw allotment contest cases.

THE COMMISSION TO THE FIVE CIVILIZED TRIBES.
TAMS BIXBY, Chairman.

Muskogee, Indian Territory, March 24, 1903.

The above statement published prior to 1905, was established for what was supposed to be a set of guidelines when it came to allotments. But with supplemental agreements and Congressional legislation, time frames as well as rules and regulations often changed and were not the same for every tribe.

INTRODUCTION

The *Applications for Enrollment of Choctaw Newborn Act of 1905*, National Archive film M-1301, Rolls 50-57, are found under the heading of Applications for Enrollment of the Commission to the Five Civilized Tribes. For this series, I have transcribed the application forms filled out by individuals applying for enrollment in the Five Civilized Tribes under the Dawes Commission. These applications contain considerably more information than stated on the census cards found in series M-1186. M-1301 possesses its own numerical sequence, separate from M-1186. To find each party's roll number you would have to reference M-1186.

The Choctaw as well as the Chickasaw allotments were likely some of the most sought after properties in Indian Territory. There was supposed to be a 25-year restriction on the sale or lease of any Indian lands so as to insure that the owners wouldn't be swindled, but that isn't what happened. This fact is borne out in the Dawes Commission General Allotment Act, of February 8, 1887, Section 5, which "Provides that after an Indian person is allotted land, the United States will hold the land 'in trust [1] for the sole use and benefit of the Indian' (or his heirs if the Indian landowner dies) for a period of 25 years. (Land held in trust by the United States government cannot be sold or in anyway alienated by the Indian landowner, since the United States government considers the underlying ownership of the land held by itself and not the tribe. After the period of trust ends, the Indian landowner is free to sell the land and is free from any encumbrance from the United States.)"[1] Instead, Native Americans were exploited by the devious. The Choctaw and Chickasaw Districts both had huge asphalt and coal deposits, so there was pressure from outsiders to acquire them from the minute they were discovered. After repeated attacks throughout the years and many legislative changes, President "Roosevelt finally signed the Five Tribes Bill at noon on April 26, 1906, the forces seeking to end all restrictions were disappointed. Section 19 removed restrictions from the sale of all inherited land but directed that no full-bloods could sell their land for twenty-five years. The Act also prohibited leases for more than one year without the approval of the Secretary of the Interior."[2]

Angie Debo described the opportunists that wanted these Native American allotments as, "Grafters". The parents of the newborns enumerated within this series would no sooner receive the approval for their child's allotment than there would be someone there with cash in hand holding a new deed or lease for the parents to sign their child's birthright away. Angie Debo said it best, "As the business incapacity of the allottees became apparent, a horde of despoilers fastened themselves upon their property." According to Debo, "The term 'grafter' was applied as a matter of course to dealers in Indian land, and was frankly accepted by them. The speculative fever also affected Government employees so that it was almost impossible to prevent them from making personal investments."[3]

---

[1] General Allotment Act, Act of Feb. 8, 1887 (24 Stat. 388, ch. 119, 25 USCA 331)
[2] The Dawes Commission and the Allotment of the Five Civilized Tribes, 1893-1914 by Kent Carter, pg. 173
[3] And Still the Waters Run, Angie Debo, p. 92.

INTRODUCTION

According to the Department of Interior in 1905, "It is estimated that there will be added to the final rolls of the citizens and freedmen of the Choctaw and Chickasaw nations the names of 2,000 persons, including 1,500 new-born children to be enrolled under the provisions of the act of Congress approved March 3, 1905."[4]

The quote below explains, in detail, the requirements for qualifying as a newborn Choctaw, "By the act of Congress approved March 3, 1905 (H.R. 17474), entitled 'An act making appropriations for the current and contingent expenses of the Indian Department and for fulfilling treaty stipulations with various Indian tribes for the fiscal year ending June 30, 1906, and for other purposes,' it was provided as follows:

'That the Commission to the Five Civilized Tribes is hereby authorized for sixty days after the date of the approval of this act to receive and consider applications for enrollment of infant children born prior to September twenty-fifth, nineteen hundred and two, and who were living on said date, to citizens by blood of the Choctaw and Chickasaw tribes of Indians whose enrollment has been approved by the Secretary of the Interior prior to the date of the approval of this act; and to enroll and make allotments to such children.'

'That the Commission to the Five Civilized Tribes is authorized for sixty days after the date of the approval of this act to receive and consider applications for enrollment of children born subsequent to September twenty-fifth, nineteen hundred and two, and prior to March fourth, nineteen hundred and five, and who were living on said latter date, to citizens by blood of the Choctaw and Chickasaw tribes of Indians whose enrollment has been approved by the Secretary of the Interior prior to the date of the approval of this act; and to enroll and make allotments to such children.'

"Notice is hereby given that the Commission to the Five Civilized Tribes will, up to and inclusive of midnight, May 2, 1905, receive applications for the enrollment of infant children born prior to September 25, 1902, and who were living on said date, to citizens by blood of the Choctaw and Chickasaw tribes of Indians whose enrollment has been approved by the Secretary of the Interior prior to March 3, 1905."[5]

Following is the scope of these transcriptions: Besides the applications themselves, researchers will find the identities of other individuals within these applications -- doctors, lawyers, mid-wives, and other relatives -- that may help with you genealogical research.

Jeff Bowen
Gallipolis, Ohio
NativeStudy.com

---

[4] Annual Reports of the Department of the Interior For the Fiscal Year Ended June 30, 1905, p. 609.
[5] Annual Reports of the Department of the Interior For the Fiscal Year Ended June 30, 1905, p. 593.

Applications for Enrollment of Choctaw Newborn
Act of 1905   Volume III

Choc New Born 130
   Eunice Cox
   (Born Nov. 1, 1902)

NEW-BORN AFFIDAVIT.

Number..............

...Choctaw Enrolling Commission...

IN THE MATTER OF THE APPLICATION FOR ENROLLMENT, as a citizen of the Choctaw Nation, of Eunice Cox

born on the _____ day of _____ 190__

Name of father   John E Cox   a citizen of   U.S.A.
Nation final enrollment No._____
Name of mother   Matilda Cox   a citizen of   Choctaw
Nation final enrollment No.   7-3064

Postoffice   Howe

AFFIDAVIT OF MOTHER.

UNITED STATES OF AMERICA
INDIAN TERRITORY
   Central   DISTRICT

I   Matilda Cox   , on oath state that I am 26 years of age and a citizen by blood of the Choctaw Nation, and as such have been placed upon the final roll of the Choctaw Nation, by the Honorable Secretary of the Interior my final enrollment number being 7-3064 ; that I am the lawful wife of   John E Cox   , who is a citizen of the U S A Nation, and as such has been placed upon the final roll of said Nation by the Honorable Secretary of the Interior, his final enrollment number being .... and that a (Eunice Cox) Female child was born to me on the 1st day of November 190 2 ; that said child has been named Eunice Cox , and is now living.

Matilda Cox

Witnesseth.
   Must be two ⎫   S J Folsom
   Witnesses who⎬
   are Citizens. ⎭   Maude Moore

1

Applications for Enrollment of Choctaw Newborn
Act of 1905   Volume III

Subscribed and sworn to before me this 6 day of February 190 5

A L Bennett
Notary Public.

My commission expires: Nov 1ˢᵗ 1905

AFFIDAVIT OF ATTENDING PHYSICIAN OR MIDWIFE

UNITED STATES OF AMERICA
INDIAN TERRITORY
Central   DISTRICT

I, B. D. Woodson   a   Physician on oath state that I attended on Mrs. Matilda Cox   wife of   John E Cox on the 1st day of November , 190 2 , that there was born to her on said date a Female child, that said child is now living, and is said to have been named Eunice Cox

B.D. Woodson   M.D.

WITNESSETH:

Must be two witnesses who are citizens and know the child.
{ S J Folsom
  Maude Moore }

Subscribed and sworn to before me this, the 23 day of February   190 5

C C Mathies
Notary Public.

My Com expires Oct 24 - 1908

We hereby certify that we are well acquainted with B D Woodson a Physician and know him to be reputable and of good standing in the community.

{ S J Folsom
  Maude Moore }

Applications for Enrollment of Choctaw Newborn
Act of 1905 Volume III

BIRTH AFFIDAVIT.

DEPARTMENT OF THE INTERIOR.
COMMISSION TO THE FIVE CIVILIZED TRIBES.

IN RE APPLICATION FOR ENROLLMENT, as a citizen of the Choctaw Nation, of Eunice Cox, born on the 1st day of November, 1902

Name of Father:	J E Cox	a citizen of the U.S.A.	Nation.
Name of Mother:	Maude Cox	a citizen of the Choctaw	Nation.

Postoffice   Howe I.T.

AFFIDAVIT OF MOTHER.

UNITED STATES OF AMERICA, Indian Territory,
Central DISTRICT.

I, Matilda Cox, on oath state that I am 27 years of age and a citizen by Blood, of the Choctaw Nation; that I am the lawful wife of John Cox, who is a citizen, by .... of the U.S.A. Nation; that a Female child was born to me on 1st day of November, 1902; that said child has been named Eunice Cox, and was living March 4, 1905.

Matilda Cox

Witnesses To Mark:
{

Subscribed and sworn to before me this 24 day of March, 1905

W N Estes
Notary Public.

AFFIDAVIT OF ATTENDING PHYSICIAN OR MID-WIFE.

UNITED STATES OF AMERICA, Indian Territory,
Central DISTRICT.

I, B. D. Woodson, a Physician, on oath state that I attended on Mrs. Matilda Cox, wife of J E Cox on the 1st day of Nov 1902, 1......; that there was born to her on said date a Female child; that said child was living March 4, 1905, and is said to have been named Eunice Cox

B. D. Woodson MD

Witnesses To Mark:
{

Applications for Enrollment of Choctaw Newborn
Act of 1905   Volume III

Subscribed and sworn to before me this 24 day of   Mch   , 1905

C. C. Mathies
Notary Public.
My Com. expires Oct 24- 1908

7-3064

Muskogee, Indian Territory, March 29, 1905.

J. E. Cox,
     Howe, Indian Territory.

Dear Sir:

Receipt is hereby acknowledged of the affidavits of Matilda Cox and E[sic]. B. Woodson to the birth of Ona Leo Cox, Constant E. Cox and Eunice Cox, children of J. E. and Matilda Cox, November 28, 1897, March 30, 1900 and November 1, 1902, and the same have been filed with our records as an application for the enrollment of said child.

Respectfully,

Chairman.

Choc New Born 131
     Elma Edith Spring
     (Born Sep. 27, 1903)

NEW BORN AFFIDAVIT

No ....

CHOCTAW ENROLLING COMMISSION

IN THE MATTER OF THE APPLICATION FOR ENROLLMENT as a citizen of the Choctaw Nation, of   Elma Edith Spring   born on the 27 day of September   1903

Name of father   Benjamin J Spring   a citizen of   Choctaw   Nation, final enrollment No.   7230   wife of B.J.Spring

Name of mother   Lue Conser   a citizen of   Choctaw   Nation, final enrollment No.   6606

Applications for Enrollment of Choctaw Newborn
Act of 1905 Volume III

Kinta I.T. Postoffice.

AFFIDAVIT OF MOTHER

UNITED STATES OF AMERICA
   INDIAN TERRITORY
DISTRICT _____

I Lue Conser, wife of B.J. Spring, on oath state that I am 21 years of age and a citizen by blood of the Choctaw Nation, and as such have been placed upon the final roll of the Choctaw Nation, by the Honorable Secretary of the Interior my final enrollment number being 6606; that I am the lawful wife of Benjamin J Spring, who is a citizen of the Choctaw Nation, and as such has been placed upon the final roll of said Nation by the Honorable Secretary of the Interior, his final enrollment number being 7230 and that a Female child was born to me on the 27 day of September 1903; that said child has been named Elma Edith Spring, and is now living.

Lue Conser
WITNESSETH: By Benjamin Spring
   Must be two witnesses { H M Moore
   who are citizens   S.W. McKinny

Subscribed and sworn to before me this, the 27 day of February 1905

James Bower
                      Notary Public.

My Commission Expires:
   Sept 23-1907

Affidavit of Attending Physician or Midwife

UNITED STATES OF AMERICA,
   INDIAN TERRITORY,
Central   DISTRICT

I, Emmett Johnson a Practicing Physician on oath state that I attended on Mrs. Lue Spring (nee Conser) wife of Benjamin J Spring on the 27 day of Sept, 1903, that there was born to her on said date a female child, that said child is now living, and is said to have been named Elma Edith Spring

Emmett Johnson   M. D.

Applications for Enrollment of Choctaw Newborn
Act of 1905   Volume III

Subscribed and sworn to before me this the   28   day of   February   1905

L. D. Allen
Notary Public.

WITNESSETH:
Must be two witnesses who are citizens and know the child.
{ H.M. Moore
  S.W. McKinny

We hereby certify that we are well acquainted with   Dr Emmett Johnson   a   Physician   and know   him   to be reputable and of good standing in the community.

Must be two citizen witnesses.
{ HM Moore
  S W McKinny

BIRTH AFFIDAVIT.

DEPARTMENT OF THE INTERIOR.
COMMISSION TO THE FIVE CIVILIZED TRIBES.

IN RE APPLICATION FOR ENROLLMENT, as a citizen of the   Choctaw   Nation, of   Elma Edith Spring , born on the   27th   day of   Sept , 1903

Name of Father: Benjamin J Spring   a citizen of the   Choctaw   Nation.
Name of Mother: Lou Spring, deceased   a citizen of the   Choctaw   Nation.

Postoffice   Kinta, I.T.

AFFIDAVIT OF MOTHER.

UNITED STATES OF AMERICA, Indian Territory,
Central DISTRICT.

I,   Benjamin J Spring , on oath state that I am   34   years of age and a citizen by   blood , of the   Choctaw   Nation; that I ~~am~~ was the lawful ~~wife~~ husband of   Lou (Conser) Spring, deceased , who ~~is~~ was a citizen, by   blood   of the   Choctaw   Nation; that a   female   child was born to ~~me~~ us on   27th   day of   September , 1903; that said child has been named   Elma Edith Spring , and was living March 4, 1905.

B J Spring

Witnesses To Mark:
{

6

Applications for Enrollment of Choctaw Newborn
Act of 1905   Volume III

Subscribed and sworn to before me this 17th day of March , 1905

> Wirt Franklin
> Notary Public.

AFFIDAVIT OF ATTENDING PHYSICIAN OR MID-WIFE.

UNITED STATES OF AMERICA, Indian Territory, }
  Western   DISTRICT. }

I, E Johnson , a physician , on oath state that I attended on Mrs. Lou Spring , wife of B J Spring on the 27th day of Sept , 1903; that there was born to her on said date a female child; that said child was living March 4, 1905, and is said to have been named Elma Edith Spring

> E Johnson M.D.

Witnesses To Mark:

{ Subscribed and sworn to before me this 20th day of March , 1905

> *(Name Illegible)*
> Notary Public.

My Commission expires March 4th 1907

Executive Office, Choctaw Nation
Green McCurtain, Principal Chief

Kinta, I.T. March 20, 1905 *190*___

Honorable Tams Bixby, Chairman,
  Muskogee, Ind. Ter.

Sir:--

I am familliar[sic] with the contents of the application made by B.J. Spring, for the enrollment, as a citizen of the Choctaw Nation of Elma Edith Spring, born on Sept. 27, 1904, and am personally acquainted with all the facts in replation[sic] thereto and know them to be true;

> Green McCurtain

Subscribed and sworn to before me this 20th day of March, 1905.

> *(Name Illegible)*
> Notary Public.

My Commission expires March 4, 1907.

Applications for Enrollment of Choctaw Newborn
Act of 1905   Volume III

7-2280

Muskogee, Indian Territory, March 23, 1905.

B. J. Spring,
    Kinta, Indian Territory.

Dear Sir:

    Receipt is hereby acknowledged of the affidavits of B. J. Spring, E. Johnson and Green McCurtain to the birth of Elma Edith Spring, child of B. J. and Lou Spring, deceased, September 27, 1903. and the same have been filed with our records as an application for the enrollment of said child.

        Respectfully,

                Chairman.

Choc New Born 132
    Vermelle Underwood
    (Born Apr. 30, 1903)

BIRTH AFFIDAVIT.

DEPARTMENT OF THE INTERIOR.
COMMISSION TO THE FIVE CIVILIZED TRIBES.

IN RE APPLICATION FOR ENROLLMENT, as a citizen of the Choctaw Nation, of Vermelle Underwood, born on the 30th day of April, 1903

Name of Father: John W Underwood   a citizen of the Choctaw Nation.
Name of Mother: Julia V Underwood   a citizen of the Choctaw Nation.

        Postoffice   Spiro Ind Ter

Applications for Enrollment of Choctaw Newborn
Act of 1905 Volume III

AFFIDAVIT OF MOTHER.

UNITED STATES OF AMERICA, Indian Territory, }
    Central   DISTRICT.

    I, Julia V. Underwood, on oath state that I am 25 years of age and a citizen by blood, of the Choctaw Nation; that I am the lawful wife of John W. Underwood, who is a citizen, by marriage of the Choctaw Nation; that a female child was born to me on 30th day of April, 1903; that said child has been named Vermelle Underwood, and was living March 4, 1905.

                                            Julia V Underwood

Witnesses To Mark:
{

    Subscribed and sworn to before me this 30th day of March, 1905

                                              Wirt Franklin
                                                  Notary Public.

AFFIDAVIT OF ATTENDING PHYSICIAN OR MID-WIFE.

UNITED STATES OF AMERICA, Indian Territory, }
    Central   DISTRICT.

    I, Frances E Burgevin, a Physician, on oath state that I attended on Mrs. Julia V Underwood, wife of John W Underwood on the 30th day of April, 1903; that there was born to her on said date a female child; that said child was living March 4, 1905, and is said to have been named Vermelle Underwood

                                       Frances E. Burgevin, M.D.

Witnesses To Mark:
{

    Subscribed and sworn to before me this 30th day of March, 1905

                                             Wirt Franklin
                                                Notary Public.

Applications for Enrollment of Choctaw Newborn
Act of 1905   Volume III

BIRTH AFFIDAVIT.

DEPARTMENT OF THE INTERIOR,
COMMISSION TO THE FIVE CIVILIZED TRIBES.

IN RE Application for Enrollment, as a citizen of the Choctaw Nation, of Vermell[sic] Underwood, born on the 30th day of April, 1903

Name of Father: John W Underwood   a citizen of the Choctaw Nation.
Name of Mother: Julia V Underwood   a citizen of the Choctaw Nation.

Post-office   Spiro I.T.

AFFIDAVIT OF MOTHER.

UNITED STATES OF AMERICA, }
INDIAN TERRITORY,
Central   District.

I, Julia V Underwood, on oath state that I am .... years of age and a citizen by blood, of the Choctaw Nation; that I am the lawful wife of John W Underwood, who is a citizen, by marriage of the Choctaw Nation; that a female child was born to me on 30th day of April, 1903, that said child has been named Vermell Underwood, and is now living.

Julia V Underwood

WITNESSES TO MARK:

Subscribed and sworn to before me this 24 day of July, 1903

Edwin L Hickman
NOTARY PUBLIC.

AFFIDAVIT OF ATTENDING PHYSICIAN OR MID-WIFE.

UNITED STATES OF AMERICA, }
INDIAN TERRITORY,
Central   District.

I, C E Jones, a Physician, on oath state that I attended on Mrs. Julia V Underwood, wife of John W Underwood on the 30th day of April, 1903; that there was born to her on said date a female child; that said child is now living and is said to have been named Vermell Underwood

C E Jones M.D.

Applications for Enrollment of Choctaw Newborn
Act of 1905 Volume III

WITNESSES TO MARK:

Subscribed and sworn to before me this 24 day of July, 1903

Edwin L Hickman
NOTARY PUBLIC.

NEW-BORN AFFIDAVIT.

Number..............

...Choctaw Enrolling Commission...

IN THE MATTER OF THE APPLICATION FOR ENROLLMENT, as a citizen of the Choctaw Nation, of Vermelle Underwood

born on the 30 day of ____April____ 190 3

Name of father   J W Underwood   a citizen of   Choctaw (by marriage)
Nation final enrollment No. not yet approved
Name of mother   Julia V Underwood   a citizen of   Choctaw
Nation final enrollment No. 7213

Postoffice   Spiro I.T.

AFFIDAVIT OF MOTHER.

UNITED STATES OF AMERICA
INDIAN TERRITORY
Central   DISTRICT

I   Julia V Underwood   , on oath state that I am 24 years of age and a citizen by blood of the Choctaw Nation, and as such have been placed upon the final roll of the Choctaw Nation, by the Honorable Secretary of the Interior my final enrollment number being 7213 ; that I am the lawful wife of J. W. Underwood , who is a citizen by marriage, not yet approved of the Choctaw Nation, and as such has not been placed upon the final roll of said Nation by the Honorable Secretary of the Interior, his final enrollment number being ———— and that a female child was born to me on the 30$^{\underline{th}}$ day of April 190 3 ; that said child has been named ~~Julia~~ Vermelle Underwood , and is now living.

Julia V Underwood

Witnesseth.

Must be two Witnesses who are Citizens.   *(Name Illegible)*
E.A. Moore

Applications for Enrollment of Choctaw Newborn
Act of 1905 Volume III

Subscribed and sworn to before me this 31 day of Dec 190 4

Edwin L Hickman
Notary Public.

My commission expires:

AFFIDAVIT OF ATTENDING PHYSICIAN OR MIDWIFE

UNITED STATES OF AMERICA
INDIAN TERRITORY
Central DISTRICT

I, F.E. Burgevin a Physician on oath state that I attended on Mrs. Julia V Underwood wife of J.W. Underwood on the 30th day of April , 190 3 , that there was born to her on said date a Female child, that said child is now living, and is said to have been named Vermelle Underwood

F.E. Burgevin M.D.

Subscribed and sworn to before me this, the 3rd day of Jan 190 5

WITNESSETH:
Must be two witnesses who are citizens

(Name Illegible)

E A Moore

Edwin L Hickman Notary Public.

We hereby certify that we are well acquainted with F.E. Burgevin a Physician and know him to be reputable and of good standing in the community.

(Name Illegible) Spiro Ind Ter

(Name Illegible) E.A. Moore

BIRTH AFFIDAVIT.

DEPARTMENT OF THE INTERIOR.
COMMISSION TO THE FIVE CIVILIZED TRIBES.

IN RE APPLICATION FOR ENROLLMENT, as a citizen of the Choctaw Nation, of Vermelle Underwood , born on the 30" day of April , 1903

Name of Father: John W. Underwood a citizen of the Choctaw Nation.
Name of Mother: Julia V. Underwood a citizen of the Choctaw Nation.

Applications for Enrollment of Choctaw Newborn
Act of 1905   Volume III

Postoffice   Spiro, I.T.

_____

AFFIDAVIT OF MOTHER.

UNITED STATES OF AMERICA, Indian Territory, ⎱
Central   DISTRICT.   ⎰

I, Julia V. Underwood, on oath state that I am 25 years of age and a citizen by blood, of the Choctaw Nation; that I am the lawful wife of John W. Underwood, who is a citizen, by marriage of the Choctaw Nation; that a female child was born to me on 30" day of April, 1903; that said child has been named Vermelle Underwood, and was living March 4, 1905.

Julia V Underwood

Witnesses To Mark:
{

Subscribed and sworn to before me this 7 day of April, 1905

Robt T Hickman
Notary Public.

MY COMMISSION EXPIRES
APRIL 18, 1908

_____

AFFIDAVIT OF ATTENDING PHYSICIAN OR MID-WIFE.

UNITED STATES OF AMERICA, Indian Territory, ⎱
Central   DISTRICT.   ⎰

I, Frances E Burgevin, a Physician, on oath state that I attended on Mrs. Julia V Underwood, wife of John W Underwood on the 30" day of April, 1903; that there was born to her on said date a female child; that said child was living March 4, 1905, and is said to have been named Vermell[sic] Underwood

Frances E. Burgevin, M.D.

Witnesses To Mark:
{

Subscribed and sworn to before me this 8th day of April, 1905

W.E. Harrell
Notary Public.

MY COMMISSION EXPIRES AUG. 6, 1908

Applications for Enrollment of Choctaw Newborn
Act of 1905 Volume III

COPY

N. B. 132

Muskogee, Indian Territory, April 4, 1905.

John W. Underwood,
    Spiro, Indian Territory.

Dear Sir:

    There is inclosed you herewith for execution application for the enrollment of your infant child, Vermell Underwood, born April 30, 1903.

    The affidavits heretofore filed with the Commission show the child was living on July 24, 1903. It is necessary, for the child to be enrolled, that she was living on March 4, 1905. You will please insert the age of the mother in the space left blank for that purpose.

    In having these affidavits executed care should be exercised to see that all names are written in full, as they appear in the body of the affidavit, and in the event that either of the persons signing the affidavit are unable to write, signatures by mark must be attested by two witnesses. Each affidavit must be executed before a Notary Public and the notarial seal and signature of the officer must be attached to each separate affidavit.

                                         Respectfully,
                                           SIGNED
                                       T. B. Needles.
LM 4-25.   Commissioner in Charge.

COPY   Choctaw N. B. 132.

Muskogee, Indian Territory, April 13, 1905.

John W. Underwood,
    Spiro, Indian Territory.

Dear Sir:

    Receipt is hereby acknowledged of your letter of April 8, transmitting the affidavits of Julia V. Underwood and Francis E. Burgevin to the birth of Vermell Underwood, daughter of John W. and Julia V. Underwood, April 30, 1903, and the same have been filed with our records in the matter of the enrollment of the above named child.

Applications for Enrollment of Choctaw Newborn
Act of 1905   Volume III

Respectfully,
SIGNED
T. B. Needles.
Commissioner in Charge.

7-NB-132

Muskogee, Indian Territory, July 24, 1905.

J. W. Underwood,
    Spiro, Indian Territory.

Dear Sir:

    Receipt is hereby acknowledged of your letter of July 17, 1905, in which you state that the correct spelling of your child's name is Vermelle instead of Vernelle and you ask if her name does not appear this way upon the rolls that the same be changed.

    In reply to your letter you are advised that the name of your child appears upon the approved roll of citizens by blood of the Choctaw Nation as Vermelle.

Respectfully,

Commissioner.

Applications for Enrollment of Choctaw Newborn
Act of 1905 Volume III

Choc New Born 133
    H. Gaines Mitchell
    (Born Nov. 18, 1903)

NEW-BORN AFFIDAVIT.

Number..................

Choctaw Enrolling Commission.

IN THE MATTER OF THE APPLICATION FOR ENROLLMENT, as a citizen of the Choctaw Nation, of   H. Gaines Mitchell

born on the 18 day of November 190 3

Name of father   William L Mitchell   a citizen of   Choctaw Nation final enrollment No   9940
Name of mother   Virginia P. Mitchell   a citizen of   Choctaw Nation final enrollment No   1215

                 Postoffice   Sterrett I T

AFFIDAVIT OF MOTHER.

UNITED STATES OF AMERICA,
    INDIAN TERRITORY,
    Central   DISTRICT

    I   Virginia P. Mitchell   , on oath state that I am   32   years of age and a citizen by   Intermarriage   of the   Choctaw   Nation, and as such have been placed upon the final roll of the   Choctaw   Nation, by the Honorable Secretary of the Interior my final enrollment number being   1215   ; that I am the lawful wife of   William L. Mitchell   , who is a citizen of the   Choctaw Nation, and as such has been placed upon the final roll of said Nation by the Honorable Secretary of the Interior, his final enrollment number being   9940   and that a   male child was born to me on the   18   day of   November   190 3   ; that said child has been named   H. Gaines Mitchell   , and is now living.

WITNESSETH: Virginia P. Mitchell
    Must be two   Jas Yarbrough
    Witnesses who
    are Citizens.   Green Thompson

    Subscribed and sworn to before me this   20   day of   January   190 5

                   G W Goodwin
                           Notary Public.

My commission expires   May 15th 1905

Applications for Enrollment of Choctaw Newborn
Act of 1905 Volume III

AFFIDAVIT OF ATTENDING PHYSICIAN OR MIDWIFE

UNITED STATES OF AMERICA
INDIAN TERRITORY
   Central   DISTRICT

I, G. M. Rushing a Practicing Physician on oath state that I attended on Mrs. Virginia P Mitchell wife of William L Mitchell on the 18 day of November , 190 3 , that there was born to her on said date a Male child, that said child is now living, and is said to have been named H Gaines Mitchell

                            G. M. Rushing,   M.D.

Subscribed and sworn to before me this, the 20 day of Jany 190 5

                            SH Kyle   Notary Public.

WITNESSETH:
Must be two witnesses who are citizens and know the child.   Jas Yarbrough

We hereby certify that we are well acquainted with G M Rushing a Practicing Physician and know him to be reputable and of good standing in the community.

                        Jas Yarbrough

                        Green Thompson

BIRTH AFFIDAVIT.

DEPARTMENT OF THE INTERIOR.
COMMISSION TO THE FIVE CIVILIZED TRIBES.

IN RE APPLICATION FOR ENROLLMENT, as a citizen of the Choctaw Nation, of H. Gaines Mitchell , born on the 18th day of November , 1903

Name of Father: William L. Mitchell   a citizen of the Choctaw Nation.
Name of Mother: Virginia P. Mitchell   a citizen of the Choctaw Nation.

                      Postoffice   Sterrett, Indian Territory

Applications for Enrollment of Choctaw Newborn
Act of 1905   Volume III

AFFIDAVIT OF MOTHER.

UNITED STATES OF AMERICA, Indian Territory, }
Central DISTRICT.

I, Virginia P. Mitchell, on oath state that I am 33 years of age and a citizen by marriage, of the Choctaw Nation; that I am the lawful wife of William L. Mitchell, who is a citizen, by blood of the Choctaw Nation; that a male child was born to me on 18th day of November, 1903; that said child has been named H. Gaines Mitchell, and was living March 4, 1905.

Virginia P. Mitchell

Witnesses To Mark:
{

Subscribed and sworn to before me this 23rd day of March, 1905

SH Kyle
Notary Public.

AFFIDAVIT OF ATTENDING PHYSICIAN OR MID-WIFE.

UNITED STATES OF AMERICA, Indian Territory, }
Central DISTRICT.

I, G.M. Rushing, a Physician, on oath state that I attended on Mrs. Virginia P. Mitchell, wife of William L. Mitchell on the 18th day of November, 1903; that there was born to her on said date a male child; that said child was living March 4, 1905, and is said to have been named H. Gaines Mitchell

G.M. Rushing M.D.

Witnesses To Mark:
{

Subscribed and sworn to before me this 23rd day of March, 1905

SH Kyle
Notary Public.

Applications for Enrollment of Choctaw Newborn
Act of 1905   Volume III

Choctaw 3491

Muskogee, Indian Territory, March 30, 1905.

William L. Mitchell,
    Sterrett, Indian Territory.

Dear Sir:

    Receipt is hereby acknowledged of your letter of March 25, inclosing affidavits of Virginia P. Mitchell and G. M. Rushing to the birth of H. Gaines Mitchell, son of William L. and Virginia P. Mitchell, November 18, 1903, and the same have been filed with our records as an application for the enrollment of said child.

Respectfully,

Chairman.

Choc New Born 134
    Douglas Newton Lankford
    (Born May 2, 1904)

BIRTH AFFIDAVIT.
DEPARTMENT OF THE INTERIOR.
COMMISSION TO THE FIVE CIVILIZED TRIBES.

    IN RE APPLICATION FOR ENROLLMENT, as a citizen of the Choctaw Nation, of Douglas Newton Lankford, born on the 2 day of May, 1904

Name of Father: Thomas N Lankford   a citizen of the Choctaw Nation.
Name of Mother: Mary Lankford   a citizen of the Choctaw Nation.

Postoffice   Cairo, I.T.

AFFIDAVIT OF MOTHER.

UNITED STATES OF AMERICA, Indian Territory,
    Central   DISTRICT.

    I, Mary Lankford, on oath state that I am 30 years of age and a citizen by blood, of the Choctaw Nation; that I am the lawful wife of Thomas N.

Applications for Enrollment of Choctaw Newborn
Act of 1905   Volume III

Lankford, who is a citizen, by intermarriage of the Choctaw Nation; that a male child was born to me on 2nd day of May, 1904; that said child has been named Douglas Newton Lankford, and was living March 4, 1905.

Mary Lankford

Witnesses To Mark:
{ W K Sumpter
 Henry Brock

Subscribed and sworn to before me this 20 day of March, 1905

W.B. Harl
Notary Public.

AFFIDAVIT OF ATTENDING PHYSICIAN OR MID-WIFE.

UNITED STATES OF AMERICA, Indian Territory,
Central DISTRICT.

I, W.A. Spindle, a physician, on oath state that I attended on Mrs. Mary Lankford, wife of Thomas N. Lankford on the 2nd day of May, 1904; that there was born to her on said date a male child; that said child was living March 4, 1905, and is said to have been named Douglas Newton Lankford

W.A. Spindle

Witnesses To Mark:
{ S W Allen
 Wm Guynes

Subscribed and sworn to before me this............ day of ...., 190....

Notary Public.

BIRTH AFFIDAVIT.

DEPARTMENT OF THE INTERIOR.
COMMISSION TO THE FIVE CIVILIZED TRIBES.

IN RE APPLICATION FOR ENROLLMENT, as a citizen of the Choctaw Nation, of Douglas Newton Lankford, born on the 2 day of May, 1904

Name of Father: Thomas N Lankford   a citizen of the Choctaw Nation.
Name of Mother: Mary Lankford   a citizen of the Choctaw Nation.

Postoffice   Cairo, I.T.

Applications for Enrollment of Choctaw Newborn
Act of 1905   Volume III

AFFIDAVIT OF MOTHER.

UNITED STATES OF AMERICA, Indian Territory, }
Central   DISTRICT.

I, Mary Lankford, on oath state that I am 30 years of age and a citizen by blood, of the Choctaw Nation; that I am the lawful wife of Thomas N. Lankford, who is a citizen, by intermarriage of the Choctaw Nation; that a male child was born to me on 2 day of May, 1904; that said child has been named Douglas Newton Lankford, and was living March 4, 1905.

                                Mary Lankford

Witnesses To Mark:
{

    Subscribed and sworn to before me this 8 day of April, 1905

                                W.B. Harl
                                      Notary Public.

AFFIDAVIT OF ATTENDING PHYSICIAN OR MID-WIFE.

UNITED STATES OF AMERICA, Indian Territory, }
Central   DISTRICT.

I, W.A. Spindle, a physician, on oath state that I attended on Mrs. Mary Lankford, wife of Thomas N. Lankford on the 2nd day of May, 1904; that there was born to her on said date a male child; that said child was living March 4, 1905, and is said to have been named Douglas Newton Lankford

                                W.A. Spindle

Witnesses To Mark:
{

    Subscribed and sworn to before me this 8 day of April, 1905

                                W.B. Harl
                                    Notary Public.

Applications for Enrollment of Choctaw Newborn
Act of 1905 Volume III

Choctaw 3273

Muskogee, Indian Territory, March 30, 1905.

Thomas N. Lankford,
    Cairo, Indian Territory.

Dear Sir:

    Receipt is hereby acknowledged of the affidavits of Mary Lankford and W. A. Spindle to the birth of Douglas Newton Lankford, son of Thomas N. and Mary Lankford, May 2, 1904, and the same have been filed with our records as an application for the enrollment of said child.

Respectfully,

Chairman.

COPY   N. B. 134

Muskogee, Indian Territory, April 5, 1905.

Thomas N. Lankford,
    Cairo, Indian Territory.

Dear Sir:

    There is inclosed you herewith for execution application for the enrollment of your infant child, Douglas Newton Lankford, born May 2, 1904.

    In having these affidavits executed care should be exercised to see that all names are written in full, as they appear in the body of the affidavit, and in the event that either of the persons signing the affidavit are unable to write, signatures by mark must be attested by two witnesses. Each affidavit must be executed before a Notary Public and the notarial seal and signature of the officer must be attached to each separate affidavit.

Respectfully,
SIGNED

T. B. Needles.
Commissioner in Charge.

LM 5-6

Applications for Enrollment of Choctaw Newborn
Act of 1905   Volume III

COPY   7 N B 134

Muskogee, Indian Territory, April 12, 1905.

Thomas A Lankford,
    Cairo, Indian Territory.

Dear Sir:

    Receipt is hereby acknowledged of the affidavits of Mary Lankford and W. A. Spindle to the birth of Douglas Newton Lankford son of Thomas N. and Mary Lankford, May 2, 1904, and the same have been filed with our records as an application for the enrollment of said child.

                  Respectfully,
                  SIGNED
                  T. B. Needles.
                  Commissioner in Charge.

Choc New Born 135
    Mitchell Singer
    (Born May 16, 1903)

NEW-BORN AFFIDAVIT.

        Number.............

...Choctaw Enrolling Commission...

    IN THE MATTER OF THE APPLICATION FOR ENROLLMENT, as a citizen of the Choctaw   Nation, of   Mitchell Singer

born on the 16th day of _____May_____ 190 2

Name of father   Alexander Singer   a non- a citizen of   Choctaw
Nation final enrollment No. _____
Name of mother   Mary Singer nee Mary Wilson   a citizen of   Choctaw
Nation final enrollment No. 9299

                  Postoffice   Hartshorne I.T.

Applications for Enrollment of Choctaw Newborn
Act of 1905 Volume III

AFFIDAVIT OF MOTHER.

UNITED STATES OF AMERICA
INDIAN TERRITORY
Central DISTRICT

I Mary Singer nee Mary Wilson, on oath state that I am 22 years of age and a citizen by blood of the Choctaw Nation, and as such have been placed upon the final roll of the Choctaw Nation, by the Honorable Secretary of the Interior my final enrollment number being 9299 ; that I am the lawful wife of Alexander Singer, who is a ~~citizen of the~~ non-citizen of the Choctaw Nation, and as such has not been placed upon the final roll of said Nation by the Honorable Secretary of the Interior, his final enrollment number being .... and that a Male child was born to me on the 16th day of May 190 3 ; that said child has been named Mitchell Singer, and is now living.

Witnesseth.

Mary Singer nee Mary Wilson

Must be two Witnesses who are Citizens.
JD Chastain
Jno W Robinson

Subscribed and sworn to before me this 23rd day of Jan 190 5

Geo W Walsh
Notary Public.

My commission expires: Oct 8th 1906

AFFIDAVIT OF ATTENDING PHYSICIAN OR MIDWIFE

UNITED STATES OF AMERICA
INDIAN TERRITORY
Central DISTRICT

I, W W Sames a Physician on oath state that I attended on Mrs. Mary Singer nee Mary Wilson wife of Alexander Singer on the 16th day of May, 190 3, that there was born to her on said date a Male child, that said child is now living, and is said to have been named Mitchell Singer

W W Sames M.D.

Subscribed and sworn to before me this, the 23rd day of Jan 190 5

Geo W Walsh Notary Public.
My commission will expire Oct 8th 1906

WITNESSETH:
Must be two witnesses who are citizens
J D Chastain
Jno W Robinson

Applications for Enrollment of Choctaw Newborn
Act of 1905   Volume III

We hereby certify that we are well acquainted with   W W Sames a   Physician   and know   him   to be reputable and of good standing in the community.

J D Chastain

Jno. W. Robinson

BIRTH AFFIDAVIT.

DEPARTMENT OF THE INTERIOR.
COMMISSION TO THE FIVE CIVILIZED TRIBES.

IN RE APPLICATION FOR ENROLLMENT, as a citizen of the   Choctaw   Nation, of Mitchell Singer   , born on the   16th   day of   May   , 1903

Name of Father: Alexander Singer   a non   a citizen of the   Choctaw   Nation.
Name of Mother: Mary Singer nee Mary Wilson   a citizen of the   Choctaw   Nation.

Postoffice   Hartshorne Ind. Ter.

AFFIDAVIT OF MOTHER.

UNITED STATES OF AMERICA, Indian Territory,
Central   DISTRICT.

I, Mary Singer nee Mary Wilson   , on oath state that I am   22   years of age and a citizen by   Blood   , of the   Choctaw   Nation; that I am the lawful wife of Alexander Singer   , who is a non citizen, ~~by~~ .... of the   Choctaw Nation; that a   male   child was born to me on   16th   day of   May   , 1903; that said child has been named   Mitchell Singer   , and was living March 4, 1905.

Mary Singer nee Mary Wilson

Witnesses To Mark:

Subscribed and sworn to before me this 22nd   day of   March   , 1905

Geo W Walshe[sic]
Notary Public.
My com will expire Oct 8th 1906

Applications for Enrollment of Choctaw Newborn
Act of 1905 Volume III

AFFIDAVIT OF ATTENDING PHYSICIAN OR MID-WIFE.

UNITED STATES OF AMERICA, Indian Territory,
Central DISTRICT.

I, W W Sames, a Physician, on oath state that I attended on Mrs. Mary Singer nee Mary Wilson, wife of Alexander Singer on the 16th day of May, 1903; that there was born to her on said date a male child; that said child was living March 4, 1905, and is said to have been named Mitchell Singer

W W Sames

Witnesses To Mark:
{

Subscribed and sworn to before me this 22nd day of March, 1905

Geo W Walshe[sic]
Notary Public.

Choc New Born 136
    Greenwood Mitchell McCurtain
    (Born Nov. 3, 1904)

BIRTH AFFIDAVIT.

DEPARTMENT OF THE INTERIOR.
COMMISSION TO THE FIVE CIVILIZED TRIBES.

IN RE APPLICATION FOR ENROLLMENT, as a citizen of the Choctaw Nation, of Greenwood Mitchell McCurtain, born on the 3rd day of November, 1904

Name of Father: David C. McCurtain   a citizen of the Choctaw Nation.
Name of Mother: Katherine N. McCurtain   a citizen of the Choctaw Nation.

Postoffice   South McAlester, Ind. Ter.

Applications for Enrollment of Choctaw Newborn
Act of 1905   Volume III

AFFIDAVIT OF MOTHER.

UNITED STATES OF AMERICA, Indian Territory,　}
　Central　　　　　　　　DISTRICT.

I, Katherine N McCurtain, on oath state that I am thirty years of age and a citizen by blood, of the Choctaw Nation; that I am the lawful wife of David C McCurtain, who is a citizen, by blood of the Choctaw Nation; that a male child was born to me on third day of November, 1904; that said child has been named Greenwood Mitchell McCurtain, and was living March 4, 1905.

　　　　　　　　　　　　　　　Katherine N McCurtain

Witnesses To Mark:
{

Subscribed and sworn to before me this 17th day of March, 1905

　　　　　　　　　　　　　　　E.P. Hill
　　　　　　　　　　　　　　　　Notary Public.

AFFIDAVIT OF ATTENDING PHYSICIAN OR MID-WIFE.

UNITED STATES OF AMERICA, Indian Territory,　}
　Central　　　　　　　　DISTRICT.

I, Le Roy Long, a Physician, on oath state that I attended on Mrs. Katherine N McCurtain, wife of David C McCurtain on the third day of November, 1904; that there was born to her on said date a male child; that said child was living March 4, 1905, and is said to have been named Greenwood Mitchell McCurtain

　　　　　　　　　　　　　　　LeRoy Long

Witnesses To Mark:
{

Subscribed and sworn to before me this 18th day of March, 1905

　　　　　　　　　　　　　　　E.P. Hill
　　　　　　　　　　　　　　　　Notary Public.

Applications for Enrollment of Choctaw Newborn
Act of 1905 Volume III

Choc New Born 137
    Marion Francis Merryman
    (Born May 28, 1903)

BIRTH AFFIDAVIT.

DEPARTMENT OF THE INTERIOR,
COMMISSION TO THE FIVE CIVILIZED TRIBES.

In Re Application for Enrollment, as a citizen of the Choctaw Nation, of Marriene[sic] Frances Marryman[sic], born on the 28 day of May, 1903

Name of Father: Abraham Merryman   a citizen of the Choctaw Nation.
Name of Mother: Ora Merryman   a citizen of the Choctaw Nation.

    Post-office   Bengal, I.T.

AFFIDAVIT OF MOTHER.

UNITED STATES OF AMERICA, }
  INDIAN TERRITORY,
  Central   District.

    I, Ora Merryman, on oath state that I am 17 years of age and a citizen by Marriage, of the Choctaw Nation; that I am the lawful wife of Abraham Merryman, who is a citizen, by blood of the Choctaw Nation; that a male child was born to me on 28 day of May, 1903, that said child has been named Marriene[sic] Frances Merryman, and is now living.

                              Ora Merryman

WITNESSES TO MARK:

    Subscribed and sworn to before me this 16 day of January, 1904.

                            Robert E Lee
My Com Ex Jan 11-1906   **NOTARY PUBLIC.**

Applications for Enrollment of Choctaw Newborn
Act of 1905   Volume III

AFFIDAVIT OF ATTENDING PHYSICIAN OR MID-WIFE.

UNITED STATES OF AMERICA,
   INDIAN TERRITORY,
  Central   District.

    I, Ruth Millus, a nurse, on oath state that I attended on Mrs. Ora Merryman, wife of Abraham Merryman on the 28 day of May, 1903; that there was born to her on said date a male child; that said child is now living and is said to have been named Marriene Frances Merryman.

                                                    her
                                        Ruth x Millus

WITNESSES TO MARK: mark
  { Cordilia E Merryman
    Mary Graham

    Subscribed and sworn to before me this 16 day of January, 1904.

                                      Robert E Lee
My Com Ex Jan 11-1906   NOTARY PUBLIC.

NEW BORN AFFIDAVIT

No ....

CHOCTAW ENROLLING COMMISSION

    IN THE MATTER OF THE APPLICATION FOR ENROLLMENT as a citizen of the Choctaw Nation, of Marion Francis Merryman born on the 28 day of May 190 3

    Name of father Abraham Merryman   a citizen of Choctaw Nation, final enrollment No. 8456
    Name of mother Ora Merryman   a citizen of _____ Nation, final enrollment No. _____

                                      Leflore I.T.   Postoffice.

Applications for Enrollment of Choctaw Newborn
Act of 1905   Volume III

AFFIDAVIT OF MOTHER

UNITED STATES OF AMERICA
   INDIAN TERRITORY
DISTRICT   Central

I   Ora Merryman   , on oath state that I am   27   years of age and a citizen by ——— of the ——— Nation, and as such have been placed upon the final roll of the ——— Nation, by the Honorable Secretary of the Interior my final enrollment number being   ——— ; that I am the lawful wife of   Abraham Merryman , who is a citizen of the   Choctaw   Nation, and as such has been placed upon the final roll of said Nation by the Honorable Secretary of the Interior, his final enrollment number being   8456   and that a   Male   child was born to me on the   28   day of May   190 3   ; that said child has been named   Marion Francis Merryman , and is now living.

WITNESSETH: Ora Merryman
Must be two witnesses { Jefferson Goin
who are citizens   Ned Sockey

Subscribed and sworn to before me this, the   17   day of   February   190 5

                              James *(Illegible)*
                                   Notary Public.

My Commission Expires:
        Sept 23-1907.

Affidavit of Attending Physician or Midwife

UNITED STATES OF AMERICA,
   INDIAN TERRITORY,
Central   DISTRICT

I,   Rutha Millus   a   midwife   on oath state that I attended on Mrs.   Ora Merryman   wife of   Abraham Merryman   on the   28   day of   May , 190 3 , that there was born to her on said date a   male   child, that said child is now living, and is said to have been named   Marion Francis Merryman
                                 <u>Midwife</u>
                        Rutha Millus   M. D.

Subscribed and sworn to before me this the   18   day of   March   1905

                          B J Johnson
My Commission Expires Jan 28-1909   Notary Public.

WITNESSETH:
Must be two witnesses { Ned Sockey
who are citizens and
know the child.   Jefferson Goin

Applications for Enrollment of Choctaw Newborn
Act of 1905   Volume III

We hereby certify that we are well acquainted with   Ruth Millus a   midwife   and know   her   to be reputable and of good standing in the community.

Must be two citizen witnesses. { Ned Sockey
Jefferson Goin

BIRTH AFFIDAVIT.

Enrollment No 8456

DEPARTMENT OF THE INTERIOR.
COMMISSION TO THE FIVE CIVILIZED TRIBES.

IN RE APPLICATION FOR ENROLLMENT, as a citizen of the   Choctaw   Nation, of Maron[sic] Francis Merryman   , born on the 28   day of May , 1903

Name of Father: Abraham Merryman   a citizen of the Choctaw   Nation.
Name of Mother: Ora Merryman   a citizen of the .... Nation.

Postoffice   Leflore I.T.

AFFIDAVIT OF MOTHER.

UNITED STATES OF AMERICA, Indian Territory,
Central   DISTRICT.

I,   Ora Merryman   , on oath state that I am 18   years of age and a citizen by ———— , of the   Choctaw   Nation; that I am the lawful wife of Abraham Merryman   , who is a citizen, by Blood   of the   Choctaw   Nation; that a male   child was born to me on 28   day of   May   , 1903; that said child has been named Marion Francis Merryman   , and was living March 4, 1905.

Ora Merryman

Witnesses To Mark:
{ L A Asher
Jno. B. Millus

Subscribed and sworn to before me this 18   day of   March   , 1905

B J Johnson
Notary Public.

Applications for Enrollment of Choctaw Newborn
Act of 1905 Volume III

AFFIDAVIT OF ATTENDING PHYSICIAN OR MID-WIFE.

UNITED STATES OF AMERICA, Indian Territory, }
    Central   DISTRICT.

I, Rutha Millus, a midwife, on oath state that I attended on Mrs. Ora Merryman, wife of Abraham Merryman on the 28 day of May, 1903; that there was born to her on said date a male child; that said child was living March 4, 1905, and is said to have been named Marion Francis Merryman

                      her
        Rutha Millus x
Witnesses To Mark: mark
  { L A Asher
    Jno B. Millus

Subscribed and sworn to before me this 18 day of March, 1905

        B J Johnson
          Notary Public.
My Commission Expires Jan 28-1909

7-NB-137

        Muskogee, Indian Territory, July 27, 1905.

Abraham Merryman,
    Leflore, Indian Territory.

Dear Sir:

    Receipt is hereby acknowledged of your letter of July 19, 1905, stating that you have received notice of the approval of the enrollment of your child and you wish to know how long before you will be entitled to draw your $40 payment.

    In reply to your letter you are advised that the payment of the townsite moneys to citizens of the Choctaw and Chickasaw Nations is within the jurisdiction of the United States Indian Agent and for information upon the subject you should address him at Muskogee, Indian Territory.

        Respectfully,

                Commissioner.

Applications for Enrollment of Choctaw Newborn
Act of 1905   Volume III

Choc New Born 138
    Kenney Muse Powell
    (Born July 1, 1903)

BIRTH AFFIDAVIT.

DEPARTMENT OF THE INTERIOR,
COMMISSION TO THE FIVE CIVILIZED TRIBES.

IN RE APPLICATION FOR ENROLLMENT, as a citizen of the   Choctaw   Nation, of   Kennie[sic] Muse Powell   , born on the   1st   day of   July   , 1903

Name of Father: Hubbard Powell   a citizen of the   Choctaw   Nation.
Name of Mother: Lizzie M Powell   a citizen of the   ———   Nation.

Post-Office :   Kingston I.T.

AFFIDAVIT OF MOTHER.

UNITED STATES OF AMERICA, ⎫
  INDIAN TERRITORY,   ⎬
  Southern   District. ⎭

    I,   Lizzie M Powell   , on oath state that I am   26   years of age and a citizen by ——, of the ———— Nation; that I am the lawful wife of   Hubbard Powell   , who is a citizen, by   blood   of the   Choctaw   Nation; that a   male   child was born to me on the   1st   day of   July   , 190 3, that said child has been named   Kennie Muse Powell   , and is now living.

                              Lizzie M. Powell

WITNESSES TO MARK:

    Subscribed and sworn to before me this   23d   day of   March   , 1905.

                              D R Johnston
                              NOTARY PUBLIC.

AFFIDAVIT OF ATTENDING PHYSICIAN OR MID-WIFE.

UNITED STATES OF AMERICA, ⎫   Washington Co.
  INDIAN TERRITORY,   ⎬
  State of Arkansas   District. ⎭   Winslow P.O.

    I,   C.E. Jones   , a   Physician   , on oath state that I attended on Mrs.   Lizzie M Powell   , wife of   Hubbard Powell   on the   first   day of   July   , 190 3; that there was born to her on said date a   male   child; that said child is now living and is said to have been named   Kinney Muse Powell

Applications for Enrollment of Choctaw Newborn
Act of 1905 Volume III

C. E. Jones M.D.

WITNESSES TO MARK:

Subscribed and sworn to before me this 20th day of March, 1905.

J H Smith
NOTARY PUBLIC.

My Com Expires Dec 7- 1908

BIRTH AFFIDAVIT.

DEPARTMENT OF THE INTERIOR.
COMMISSION TO THE FIVE CIVILIZED TRIBES.

IN RE APPLICATION FOR ENROLLMENT, as a citizen of the Choctaw Nation, of Kenney Muse Powell, born on the 1st day of July, 1903

Name of Father: Hubbard Powell   a citizen of the Choctaw Nation.
Name of Mother: Lizzie M. Powell   a citizen of the ——— Nation.

Postoffice   Kingston I.T.

AFFIDAVIT OF MOTHER.

UNITED STATES OF AMERICA, Indian Territory,
Southern DISTRICT.

I, Lizzie M Powell, on oath state that I am 26 years of age and a citizen by ———, of the ——— Nation; that I ~~am~~ was the lawful wife of Hubbard Powell, who is a citizen, by blood of the Choctaw Nation; that a male child was born to me on 1st day of July, 1903; that said child has been named Kenney Muse Powell, and was living March 4, 1905.

Lizzie M. Powell

Witnesses To Mark:

Subscribed and sworn to before me this 8th day of April, 1905

D.R. Johnston
Notary Public.

Applications for Enrollment of Choctaw Newborn
Act of 1905   Volume III

AFFIDAVIT OF ATTENDING PHYSICIAN OR MID-WIFE.

UNITED STATES OF AMERICA, Indian Territory,
Southern   DISTRICT.

  I,   Kentucky A Muse   , a   Midwife   , on oath state that I attended on Mrs. Lizzie M Powell   , wife of   Hubbard Powell   on the 1st day of   July , 1903; that there was born to her on said date a   male   child; that said child was living March 4, 1905, and is said to have been named   Kenney Muse Powell

                 Kentucky A Muse

Witnesses To Mark:

   Subscribed and sworn to before me this 8th day of   April   , 1905

                D.R. Johnston
                Notary Public.

                   7-2581

      Muskogee, Indian Territory, March 29, 1905.

Hubbard Powell,
  Kingston, Indian Territory.

Dear Sir:

  Receipt is hereby acknowledged of the affidavits of Lizzie M. Powell and C. E. Jones to the birth of Kannie[sic] Muse Powell, son of Hubbard Powell and Lizzie M. Powell, July 1, 1903, and the same have been filed with our records as an application for the enrollment of said child.

             Respectfully,

                Chairman.

Applications for Enrollment of Choctaw Newborn
Act of 1905 Volume III

COPY

N. B. 138

Muskogee, Indian Territory, April 4, 1905.

Hubbard Powell,
Kingston, Indian Territory.

Dear Sir:

There is inclosed you herewith for execution application for the enrollment of your infant child, --- Powell, born July 1, 1903.

In The affidavits heretofore filed with the Commission the christain[sic] name of the applicant was written as "Kemie", "Kannie" and "Kenney". You will please insert the correct names of the child in the inclosed application.

In having these affidavits executed care should be exercised to see that all names are written in full, as they appear in the body of the affidavit, and in the event that either of the persons signing the affidavit are unable to write, signatures by mark must be attested by two witnesses. Each affidavit must be executed before a Notary Public and the notarial seal and signature of the officer must be attached to each separate affidavit.

Respectfully,
SIGNED
T. B. Needles.

LM 4-12.   Commissioner in Charge.

138

COPY   Choctaw N. B. ~~38~~.

Muskogee, Indian Territory, April 13, 1905.

D. R. Johnston,
Kingston, Indian Territory.

Dear Sir:

Receipt is hereby acknowledged of your letter of April 8, enclosing the affidavits of Lizzie M. Powell and Kentucky A. Muse to the birth of Kenney Muse Powell, son of Hubbard and Lizzie M. Powell, July 1, 1903, and the same have been filed with our records in the matter of the enrollment of the above named child.

Respectfully,
SIGNED
T. B. Needles.
Commissioner in Charge.

Applications for Enrollment of Choctaw Newborn
Act of 1905   Volume III

1771-1907
7-NB-138

Muskogee, Indian Territory, July 20, 1907.

Edgar F. Powell,
    Bokoshe, Indian Territory.

Dear Sir:

    Receipt is hereby acknowledged of your letter of July 13, 1907, in which you ask if Kenny Muse Powell appears on the roll as a Choctaw by blood and as the son of Hubbard Powell as you state you understand he has a child on the roll.

    In reply to your letter you are advised that Kenney Muse Powell, son of Hubbard and Lizzie M. Powell, has been enrolled as a new born citizen of the Choctaw Nation under the Act of Congress approved March 3, 1905, and his enrollment as such approved by the Secretary of the Interior June 30, 1905.

                  Respectfully,

                              Acting Commissioner.

Choc New Born 139
    Everet F. Statham
    (Born August 30, 1904)

BIRTH AFFIDAVIT.

DEPARTMENT OF THE INTERIOR.
COMMISSION TO THE FIVE CIVILIZED TRIBES.

IN RE APPLICATION FOR ENROLLMENT, as a citizen of the Choctaw Nation, of Everet F. Statham, born on the 30th day of August, 1904

Name of Father: James F Statham   a citizen of the   x   Nation.
Name of Mother: Myrtle G Statham   a citizen of the   Choctaw Nation.

                  Postoffice   Bokoshe Ind Ter

Applications for Enrollment of Choctaw Newborn
Act of 1905   Volume III

AFFIDAVIT OF MOTHER.

UNITED STATES OF AMERICA, Indian Territory, }
Central   DISTRICT.

I, Myrtle G. Statham   , on oath state that I am Twenty years of age and a citizen by   blood   , of the   Choctaw   Nation; that I am the lawful wife of James F Statham   , who is a Choctaw citizen, by .... of the .... Nation; that a   male   child was born to me on   30th   day of August   , 1904, that said child has been named Everet F Sthatham[sic]   , and is now living.

                                                Myrtle G Statham

Witnesses To Mark:
{

Subscribed and sworn to before me this 10th day of   November   , 1905.

                                                Jno. R. Smoot
                                                Notary Public.

AFFIDAVIT OF ATTENDING PHYSICIAN OR MID-WIFE.

UNITED STATES OF AMERICA, Indian Territory, }
Central   DISTRICT.

I, F C Parrott   , a   Physician   , on oath state that I attended on Mrs. Myrtle G Statham   , wife of James F Statham   on the   30th   day of Aug , 1904; that there was born to her on said date a   male   child; that said child is now living and is said to have been named Everet F Statham

                                                F. C. Parrott, M.D.

Witnesses To Mark:
{

Subscribed and sworn to before me this 10th day of   November   , 1905.

                                                Jno. R. Smoot
                                              Notary Public.

Applications for Enrollment of Choctaw Newborn
Act of 1905   Volume III

NEW-BORN AFFIDAVIT.

Number..................

...Choctaw Enrolling Commission...

IN THE MATTER OF THE APPLICATION FOR ENROLLMENT, as a citizen of the Choctaw Nation, of Everett F Statham

born on the 30 day of August 190 4

Name of father   James F Statham   a citizen of   the United States
Nation final enrollment No.   x
Name of mother   Myrtle G Statham   a citizen of   Choctaw
Nation final enrollment No.   7490

Postoffice   Bokoshe Ind Ty.

AFFIDAVIT OF MOTHER.

UNITED STATES OF AMERICA
INDIAN TERRITORY
   Central   DISTRICT

I   Myrtle G Statham   , on oath state that I am   21   years of age and a citizen by   Blood   of the   Choctaw   Nation, and as such have been placed upon the final roll of the   Choctaw   Nation, by the Honorable Secretary of the Interior my final enrollment number being   7490 ; that I am the lawful wife of   James F Statham   , who is a citizen of the   x   x   Nation, and as such has been placed upon the final roll of said Nation by the Honorable Secretary of the Interior, his final enrollment number being _____ and that a   Male   child was born to me on the   30th   day of   August   190 4 ; that said child has been named   Everet F Statham   , and is now living.

Witnesseth.   Myrtle G Statham
   Must be two ⎤ C. B. Ward
   Witnesses who⎦
   are Citizens.   James Taylor

Subscribed and sworn to before me this   10   day of   Jan   190 5

John R. Smoot
Notary Public.

My commission expires:
   July 21st 1906.

Applications for Enrollment of Choctaw Newborn
Act of 1905 Volume III

AFFIDAVIT OF ATTENDING PHYSICIAN OR MIDWIFE

UNITED STATES OF AMERICA
INDIAN TERRITORY
Central DISTRICT

I, F C Parrott a Physician on oath state that I attended on Mrs. Myrtle G Statham wife of James F Statham on the 30 day of August , 190 4 , that there was born to her on said date a Male child, that said child is now living, and is said to have been named Everet F Statham

F C Parrott M.D.
Subscribed and sworn to before me this, the 10th day of January 190 5

WITNESSETH: who know child John R Smoot Notary Public.
Must be two witnesses C.B. Wood
who are citizens
James Taylor

We hereby certify that we are well acquainted with James F Statham a intermarried citizen and know him to be reputable and of good standing in the community.

C. B. Wood John R Smoot
Notary Public.
James Taylor

Applications for Enrollment of Choctaw Newborn
Act of 1905   Volume III

No. 1934

Certificate of Record of Marriages.

DEPARTMENT OF THE INTERIOR,
Commission to the Five Civilized Tribes.

FILED

APR -8 1905   Tams Bixby CHAIRMAN.

UNITED STATES OF AMERICA, ⎫
INDIAN TERRITORY, ⎬ SCT:
Central   DISTRICT. ⎭

I,   E.J. Fannin   , Clerk of the United States Court in the Indian Territory and District aforesaid, do hereby CERTIFY, that the License for and Certificate of the Marriage of

Mr.   James F Statham   and

M   Myrtle G Powell   was

filed in my office in said Territory and District the 30 day of November A.D., 1903 and duly recorded in Book 2 of Marriage Record, Page 349.

WITNESS my hand and seal of said Court, at   Poteau   , this 30 day of   November   , A.D. 190 3

E. J. Fannin
Clerk.

By   T.T. Varner   *Deputy.*

No. 1934

FORM NO. 598.

MARRIAGE LICENSE.

UNITES STATES OF AMERICA, ⎫
THE INDIAN TERRITORY, ⎬ ss:
Central   DISTRICT. ⎭

To any Person Authorized by Law to Solemnize Marriage—Greeting:

You are hereby commanded to solemnize the Rite and publish the Banns of Matrimony *between* Mr.   James F Statham   *of*   Bokoshe in the Indian Territory, aged 26- years, and Miss Myrtle G. Powell   *of*   Bokoshe

41

Applications for Enrollment of Choctaw Newborn
Act of 1905 Volume III

in the Indian Territory, aged 19 years, according to law, and do you officially sign and return this License to the parties therein named.

WITNESS my hand and official seal, this 9" day of November A. D. 190 3

EJ Fannin
Clerk of the United States Court.

By T.T. Varner
Deputy

CERTIFICATE OF MARRIAGE.

UNITES STATES OF AMERICA,
THE INDIAN TERRITORY, } ss: I,   Rev J. C. Fowler
DISTRICT.
a ———— ————

do hereby CERTIFY, that on the 22nd day of November A, D. 190 ; I did duly and according to law, as commanded in the foregoing License, solemnize the Rite and publish the BANNS OF MATRIMONY between the parties therein named.

Witness my hand this 22nd day of November , A. D. 1903

My credentials are recorded in the office of the Clerk of the United States Court in the Indian Territory, Central District, Book A Page 120

Rev J. C. Fowler

a ———— ————

NOTE. -The License and Certificate of Marriage must be returned to the Office of the Clerk of the United States Court of the Indian Territory, from whence it was issued, within sixty days from the date thereof, or the party to whom the License was issued will be liable in the amount of One Hundred Dollars ($100.00).

7-7490   card No. 7-2581
BIRTH AFFIDAVIT.
DEPARTMENT OF THE INTERIOR.
COMMISSION TO THE FIVE CIVILIZED TRIBES.

IN RE APPLICATION FOR ENROLLMENT, as a citizen of the   Choctaw   Nation, of Everett F. Statham   , born on the 30th   day of August , 1904

Name of Father: James F. Statham   a citizen of the United States Nation.
Name of Mother: Myrtle G. Statham(nee Powell) a citizen of the   Choctaw   Nation.

Applications for Enrollment of Choctaw Newborn
Act of 1905   Volume III

Postoffice   Bokoshe, Ind. Ter.

AFFIDAVIT OF MOTHER.

UNITED STATES OF AMERICA, Indian Territory, }
Central   DISTRICT.

I, Myrtle G. Statham, on oath state that I am 21 years of age and a citizen by blood, of the Choctaw Nation; that I am the lawful wife of James F. Statham, xxx xx x xxxxxxx, xx .... of the United States Nation; that a male child was born to me on 30th day of August, 1904; that said child has been named Everett F. Statham, and was living March 4, 1905.

Myrtle G. Statham

Witnesses To Mark:
{

Subscribed and sworn to before me this 3rd day of April, 1905

O.L. Johnson
Notary Public.

AFFIDAVIT OF ATTENDING PHYSICIAN OR MID-WIFE.

UNITED STATES OF AMERICA, Indian Territory, }
Central   DISTRICT.

I, F. C. Parrott, a physician, on oath state that I attended on Mrs. Myrtle G. Statham, wife of James F. Statham on the 30th day of August, 1904; that there was born to her on said date a male child; that said child was living March 4, 1905, and is said to have been named Everett F. Statham

F C Parrott

Witnesses To Mark:
{

Subscribed and sworn to before me this 3rd day of April, 1905

O.L. Johnson
Notary Public.

Applications for Enrollment of Choctaw Newborn
Act of 1905   Volume III

COPY   N. B. 139

Muskogee, Indian Territory, April 4, 1905.

James F. Statham,
    Bokoshe, Indian Territory.

Dear Sir:

    There is inclosed you herewith for execution application for the enrollment of your infant child, Everet F. Statham, born August 30, 1904.

    The affidavits heretofore filed with the Commission show the child was living on November 10, 1904. It is necessary, for the child to be enrolled, that he was living on March 4, 1905.

    In having these affidavits executed care should be exercised to see that all names are written in full, as they appear in the body of the affidavit, and in the event that either of the persons signing the affidavit are unable to write, signatures by mark must be attested by two witnesses. Each affidavit must be executed before a Notary Public and the notarial seal and signature of the officer must be attached to each separate affidavit.

                         Respectfully,
                           SIGNED

                          T. B. Needles.
LM 4-13.   Commissioner in Charge.

7-NB-139

                    Muskogee, Indian Territory, May 28, 1907.

James F. Statham,
    Bokoshe, Indian Territory.

Dear Sir:

    Receipt is hereby acknowledged of your letter of May 16, 1907, asking for the return of the marriage certificate between James F. Statham and Myrtle G. Powell which was filed in the matter of the enrollment of Everett F. Statham.

    In reply you are advised that this office has been directed by the Department to retain all papers filed in enrollment matters, and it is therefore impracticable to comply with your request.

                           Respectfully,

                                      Commissioner.

Applications for Enrollment of Choctaw Newborn
Act of 1905   Volume III

Choc New Born 140
    David Reagan Welch
    (Born September 12, 1903)
    Pauline Welch
    (Born Nov. 16, 1904)

NEW-BORN AFFIDAVIT.

        Number..................

...Choctaw Enrolling Commission...

IN THE MATTER OF THE APPLICATION FOR ENROLLMENT, as a citizen of the Choctaw Nation, of David Reagan Welch

born on the 12 day of September 190 3

Name of father   Robert A. Welch   a citizen of   Choctaw
Nation final enrollment No.   7302
Name of mother   Lula M. Welch   a citizen of   Choctaw
Nation final enrollment No.   109

                                            Postoffice   Red Oak, I.T.

AFFIDAVIT OF MOTHER.

UNITED STATES OF AMERICA
INDIAN TERRITORY
   Central   DISTRICT

       I   Lula M. Welch   , on oath state that I am 26   years of age and a citizen by   Intermarriage   of the   Choctaw Nation, and as such have been placed upon the final roll of the   Choctaw Nation, by the Honorable Secretary of the Interior my final enrollment number being   109 ; that I am the lawful wife of   Robert A. Welch   , who is a citizen of the   Choctaw Nation, and as such has been placed upon the final roll of said Nation by the Honorable Secretary of the Interior, his final enrollment number being   7302   and that a Male   child was born to me on the   12   day of September   190 3   ; that said child has been named   David Reagan Welch   , and is now living.

Witnesseth.   Lula M. Welch
   Must be two ⎤ Phebe Reagan
   Witnesses who ⎬
   are Citizens. ⎦ Robert L Reagan

Applications for Enrollment of Choctaw Newborn
Act of 1905   Volume III

Subscribed and sworn to before me this   25   day of   Feb   190 5

J. D. Yandell
Notary Public.

My commission expires:
Jan. 1907

AFFIDAVIT OF ATTENDING PHYSICIAN OR MIDWIFE

UNITED STATES OF AMERICA
INDIAN TERRITORY
Central   DISTRICT

I,   Jno. J. Gill   a   Physician on oath state that I attended on Mrs. Lula M. Welch   wife of   Robert A. Welch on the   12   day of   September   , 190 3 , that there was born to her on said date a Male child, that said child is now living, and is said to have been named David Reagan Welch

Jno J Gill   M.D.

WITNESSETH:
Must be two witnesses who are citizens and know the child.
Phebe Reagan
Robert L Reagan

Subscribed and sworn to before me this, the   25   day of   Feb.   190 5

J. D. Yandell   Notary Public.

We hereby certify that we are well acquainted with   Jno J. Gill   a   Physician   and know   him   to be reputable and of good standing in the community.

Phebe Reagan
Robert L Reagan

Applications for Enrollment of Choctaw Newborn
Act of 1905   Volume III

NEW-BORN AFFIDAVIT.

    Number..............

...Choctaw Enrolling Commission...

IN THE MATTER OF THE APPLICATION FOR ENROLLMENT, as a citizen of the Choctaw Nation, of Pauline Welch

born on the 17 day of November 1904

Name of father   Robert A. Welch   a citizen of   Choctaw
Nation final enrollment No.   7302
Name of mother   Lula M. Welch   a citizen of   Choctaw
Nation final enrollment No.   109

                    Postoffice   Red Oak, I.T.

AFFIDAVIT OF MOTHER.

UNITED STATES OF AMERICA
INDIAN TERRITORY
   Central   DISTRICT

I   Lula M. Welch   , on oath state that I am 26 years of age and a citizen by   Intermarriage   of the   Choctaw Nation, and as such have been placed upon the final roll of the   Choctaw Nation, by the Honorable Secretary of the Interior my final enrollment number being   109 ; that I am the lawful wife of   Robert A. Welch   , who is a citizen of the   Choctaw Nation, and as such has been placed upon the final roll of said Nation by the Honorable Secretary of the Interior, his final enrollment number being   7302   and that a   Female   child was born to me on the   17   day of November   1904 ; that said child has been named   Pauline Welch   , and is now living.

Witnesseth.   Lula M. Welch
   Must be two ⎫   Phebe Reagan
   Witnesses who ⎬
   are Citizens. ⎭   Robert L Reagan

Subscribed and sworn to before me this   25   day of   Feb   1905

                                        J. D. Yandell
                                                Notary Public.

My commission expires:
   Jan. 1907

Applications for Enrollment of Choctaw Newborn
Act of 1905   Volume III

AFFIDAVIT OF ATTENDING PHYSICIAN OR MIDWIFE

UNITED STATES OF AMERICA
INDIAN TERRITORY
Central   DISTRICT

I, Jno. J. Gill a Physician on oath state that I attended on Mrs. Lula M. Welch wife of Robert A. Welch on the 17 day of November , 190 4 , that there was born to her on said date a Female child, that said child is now living, and is said to have been named Pauline Welch

Jno J Gill   M.D.

WITNESSETH:
Must be two witnesses who are citizens and know the child.
{ Phebe Reagan
  Robert L Reagan

Subscribed and sworn to before me this, the 25 day of Feb. 190 5

J. D. Yandell   Notary Public.

We hereby certify that we are well acquainted with Jno J. Gill a Physician and know him to be reputable and of good standing in the community.

{ Phebe Reagan
  Robert L Reagan

BIRTH AFFIDAVIT.

DEPARTMENT OF THE INTERIOR.
COMMISSION TO THE FIVE CIVILIZED TRIBES.

IN RE APPLICATION FOR ENROLLMENT, as a citizen of the Choctaw Nation, of David Reagan Welch , born on the 12th day of Sept , 1903

Name of Father: Robert A. Welch   a citizen of the Choctaw Nation.
Name of Mother: Lula M. Welch   a citizen of the Choctaw Nation.

Postoffice   Redoak, I.T.

Applications for Enrollment of Choctaw Newborn
Act of 1905   Volume III

AFFIDAVIT OF MOTHER.

UNITED STATES OF AMERICA, Indian Territory,
Central   DISTRICT.

I, Lula M Welch, on oath state that I am 27 years of age and a citizen by marriage, of the Choctaw Nation; that I am the lawful wife of Robert A Welch, who is a citizen, by blood of the Choctaw Nation; that a male child was born to me on 12th day of September, 1903; that said child has been named David Reagan Welch, and was living March 4, 1905.

Lula M. Welch

Witnesses To Mark:
{

Subscribed and sworn to before me this 23rd day of March, 1905

Wirt Franklin
Notary Public.

AFFIDAVIT OF ATTENDING PHYSICIAN OR MID-WIFE.

UNITED STATES OF AMERICA, Indian Territory,
Central   DISTRICT.

I, John J Gill, a physician, on oath state that I attended on Mrs. Lula M Welch, wife of Robert A Welch on the 12th day of September, 1903; that there was born to her on said date a male child; that said child was living March 4, 1905, and is said to have been named David Reagan Welch

Jno J Gill M.D.

Witnesses To Mark:
{

Subscribed and sworn to before me this 23rd day of March, 1905

Wirt Franklin
Notary Public.

Applications for Enrollment of Choctaw Newborn
Act of 1905 Volume III

BIRTH AFFIDAVIT.

DEPARTMENT OF THE INTERIOR.
COMMISSION TO THE FIVE CIVILIZED TRIBES.

IN RE APPLICATION FOR ENROLLMENT, as a citizen of the Choctaw Nation, of Pauline Welch, born on the 17th day of November, 1904

Name of Father: Robert A. Welch   a citizen of the Choctaw Nation.
Name of Mother: Lula M. Welch   a citizen of the Choctaw Nation.

Postoffice   Redoak, I.T.

AFFIDAVIT OF MOTHER.

UNITED STATES OF AMERICA, Indian Territory, }
Central   DISTRICT.

I, Lula M Welch, on oath state that I am 27 years of age and a citizen by marriage, of the Choctaw Nation; that I am the lawful wife of Robert A Welch, who is a citizen, by blood of the Choctaw Nation; that a female child was born to me on 17th day of November, 1904; that said child has been named Pauline Welch, and was living March 4, 1905.

Lula M. Welch

Witnesses To Mark:
{

Subscribed and sworn to before me this 23rd day of March, 1905

Wirt Franklin
Notary Public.

AFFIDAVIT OF ATTENDING PHYSICIAN OR MID-WIFE.

UNITED STATES OF AMERICA, Indian Territory, }
Central   DISTRICT.

I, John J Gill, a physician, on oath state that I attended on Mrs. Lula M Welch, wife of Robert A Welch on the 17th day of November, 1904; that there was born to her on said date a female child; that said child was living March 4, 1905, and is said to have been named Pauline Welch

Jno J Gill M.D.

Witnesses To Mark:
{

Applications for Enrollment of Choctaw Newborn
Act of 1905   Volume III

Subscribed and sworn to before me this 23rd day of March , 1905

Wirt Franklin
Notary Public.

7-2518

Muskogee, Indian Territory, April 4, 1905.

R. A. Welch,
 Redoak, Indian Territory.

Dear Sir:

Receipt is hereby acknowledged of your letter of March 23, 1905, in which you state that you have registered your children and wish to know how long it will be before you can go to the land office and file for them.

In reply to your letter you are informed that the affidavits heretofore forwarded to the birth of David Reagan Welch and Pauline Welch have been filed with our records as an application for the enrollment of said children.

You are advised, however, that no selection of allotment can be permitted for children enrolled under the Act of Congress approved March 3, 1905, as number provisions of the act of Congress approved March 3, 1905, until their enrollment has been approved by the Secretary of the Interior.

Respectfully,

Commissioner in Charge.

Applications for Enrollment of Choctaw Newborn
Act of 1905   Volume III

Choc New Born 141
    Martha Ann Potts
    (Born Nov. 30, 1902)
    Margaret Jane Potts
    (Born Nov. 30, 1902)

BIRTH AFFIDAVIT.

Department of the Interior,
COMMISSION TO THE FIVE CIVILIZED TRIBES.

IN RE APPLICATION FOR ENROLLMENT, as a citizen of the Choctaw Nation, of Martha A. Potts, born on the 30 day of November, 1902

Name of Father: Forbis Potts   a citizen of the Choctaw Nation.
                                                                             marriage
Name of Mother: Ada Potts   a citizen of the " by Nation.

Post-Office: Howe, I.T.

AFFIDAVIT OF ~~MOTHER~~.
father

UNITED STATES OF AMERICA, ⎫
   INDIAN TERRITORY,   ⎬
   Central   District.   ⎭

I, Forbis Potts, on oath state that I am 42 years of age and a citizen by blood, of the Choctaw Nation; that I am the lawful ~~wife~~ husband of Ada Potts, who is a citizen, by marriage of the Choctaw Nation; that a Female child was born to ~~me~~ her on 30 day of November, 1902, that said child has been named Martha A Potts, and is now living.

                                      Forbis Potts
WITNESSES TO MARK:
{

Subscribed and sworn to before me this 15 day of December, 1902.

                                      H.C. Risteen
                                          Notary Public.

Applications for Enrollment of Choctaw Newborn
Act of 1905 Volume III

BIRTH AFFIDAVIT.

Department of the Interior,
COMMISSION TO THE FIVE CIVILIZED TRIBES.

IN RE APPLICATION FOR ENROLLMENT, as a citizen of the Choctaw Nation, of Margaret J. Potts, born on the 30 day of Nov, 190 2

Name of Father: Forbis Potts   a citizen of the Choctaw Nation.
                                                                                                                         marriage
Name of Mother: Ada Potts   a citizen of the " by Nation.

Post-Office: Howe, I.T.

AFFIDAVIT OF ~~MOTHER~~. father

UNITED STATES OF AMERICA,
    INDIAN TERRITORY,
Central   District.

I, Forbis Potts, on oath state that I am 42 years of age and a citizen by blood, of the Choctaw Nation; that I am the lawful ~~wife~~ husband of Ada Potts, who is a citizen, by marriage of the Choctaw Nation; that a Female child was born to ~~me~~ her on 30 day of Nov, 190 2, that said child has been named Margaret J. Potts, and is now living.

                                                          Forbis Potts

WITNESSES TO MARK:

Subscribed and sworn to before me this 15 day of December, 190 2.

                                                 H.C. Risteen
                                                     Notary Public.

State of Indian Territory.
    Central District.

Before me Sam T Roberts Jr, a Notary Public within and for the Central District Indian Territory, at My Office at Talihina I T personall[sic] appeared Raymond Bryant to me well known who after being duly sworn deposes and says, my name is Raymond Bryant my age is 45 my Post Office is Talihina Ind Ty I am personally acquainted with Forbis Potts and Ada Potts his wife I know that Ada Potts is the mother of Margaret Jane Potts born November 30 1902 and that the said Child Margaret Jane Potts was liveing[sic] March 4 1905.

                                                 Raymond Bryant

Applications for Enrollment of Choctaw Newborn
Act of 1905   Volume III

Subscribed and sworn to before me this the 11 day of April 1905.

My commission expires Feb. 4, 1908
Commission from U.S. Court, So. McAlester I.T.
MY OFFICE TALIHINA, I.T.

Sam T Roberts Jr
Notary Public

State of Indian Territory.
Central District

Before me Sam T Roberts Jr a Notary Public within and for the Central District Indian Territory, at my Office in Talihina I T personally appeared D C Merryman to me well known who first being duly sworn deposes and says [sic] name is D C Merryman, my age is 52 years, my Post Office is Bengal I T, I am personally acquainted with Forbis Potts and Ada Potts his wife. I know that Ada Potts is the mother of Margaret Jane Potts born November 30 1902 and that the said child Margaret Jane Potts was liveing[sic] March 4, 1905.

David C Merryman

Subscribed and sworn to before me this the 11 day of April 1905.

My commission expires Feb. 4, 1908
Commission from U.S. Court, So. McAlester I.T.
MY OFFICE TALIHINA, I.T.

Sam T Roberts Jr
Notary Public

BIRTH AFFIDAVIT.

DEPARTMENT OF THE INTERIOR.
COMMISSION TO THE FIVE CIVILIZED TRIBES.

IN RE APPLICATION FOR ENROLLMENT, as a citizen of the Choctaw Nation, of Margaret Jane Potts, born on the 30 day of November, 1902
Martha Ann Potts   30   November   1902
Name of Father: Forbis Potts   a citizen of the   Choctaw   Nation.
Name of Mother: Ada B Potts   a citizen of the   Choctaw   Nation.

Postoffice   Talihina I.T.

AFFIDAVIT OF MOTHER.

UNITED STATES OF AMERICA, Indian Territory,
Central   DISTRICT.

I, Ada B Potts, on oath state that I am 33 years of age and a citizen by Intermarriage, of the Choctaw Nation; that I am the lawful wife of Forbis Potts, who is a citizen, by Blood of the Choctaw Nation; that a 2 Female child was born to me on 30 day of November, 1902; that said

Applications for Enrollment of Choctaw Newborn
Act of 1905   Volume III

children Twins has been named Margaret Jane Potts   , and ~~was~~ were living March 4, 1905.   Martha Ann Potts

              Ada B Potts

Witnesses To Mark:
{   My commission expires Feb. 4, 1908
   Commission from U.S. Court, So. McAlester I.T.
    MY OFFICE TALIHINA, I.T.

  Subscribed and sworn to before me this   27 day of   March   , 1905

            Sam T Roberts Jr
            Notary Public.

AFFIDAVIT OF ATTENDING PHYSICIAN OR MID-WIFE.

UNITED STATES OF AMERICA, Indian Territory, ⎫
 Central   DISTRICT.   ⎬
           ⎭

  I,   Forbis Potts   , a husband of Ada Potts , on oath state that I attended on My. wife Ada B. Potts   , ~~wife of~~ ———— on the 30 day of November , 1902; that there was born to her on said date a   Female Twins   children; that said children ~~was~~ were living March 4, 1905, and is said to have been named Margaret Jane Potts and Martha Ann Potts

          Forbis B Potts

Witnesses To Mark:
{

  Subscribed and sworn to before me this 27 day of March , 1905
    My commission expires Feb. 4, 1908
    Commission from U.S. Court, So. McAlester I.T.
     MY OFFICE TALIHINA, I.T. Sam T Roberts Jr
           Notary Public.

BIRTH AFFIDAVIT.

DEPARTMENT OF THE INTERIOR.
COMMISSION TO THE FIVE CIVILIZED TRIBES.

  IN RE APPLICATION FOR ENROLLMENT, as a citizen of the   Choctaw   Nation, of Margaret Jane Potts   , born on the 30th day of November , 1902

Name of Father: Forbis Potts   a citizen of the   Choctaw   Nation.
Name of Mother: Ada Potts   a citizen of the   Choctaw   Nation.

       Postoffice Talihina I.T.

Applications for Enrollment of Choctaw Newborn
Act of 1905   Volume III

AFFIDAVIT OF MOTHER.

UNITED STATES OF AMERICA, Indian Territory, } ....DISTRICT.

    I, Ada Potts, on oath state that I am 33 years of age and a citizen by Intermarriage, of the Choctaw Nation; that I am the lawful wife of Forbis Potts, who is a citizen, by blood of the Choctaw Nation; that a female child was born to me on 30th day of November, 1902; that said child has been named Margaret Jane Potts, and was living March 4, 1905.

Ada Potts

Witnesses To Mark:
{

    Subscribed and sworn to before me this 11 day of April, 1905

Sam T Roberts Jr
Notary Public.

AFFIDAVIT OF ATTENDING PHYSICIAN OR MID-WIFE.

UNITED STATES OF AMERICA, Indian Territory, } ....DISTRICT.

    I,.., a ...., on oath state that I attended on Mrs. Ada Potts, wife of Forbis Potts on the 30th day of November, 1902; that there was born to her on said date a female child; that said child was living March 4, 1905, and is said to have been named Margaret Jane Potts

Witnesses To Mark:
{

    Subscribed and sworn to before me this .... day of ...., 1905

Notary Public.

Applications for Enrollment of Choctaw Newborn
Act of 1905   Volume III

State of Indian Territory.
Central District.

    Before me Sam T Roberts Jr a Notary Public within and for the Central District Indian Territory at my Office in Talihina I T personally appeared Raymond Bryant to me well known who first being duly sworn deposes and says, My name is Raymond Bryant I am 45 years of age, my Post Office is Talihina I T, I am personally acquainted with Forbis Potts and Ada Potts his wife I know that Ada Potts is the mother of Martha Ann Potts born November 30, 1902, and that the said Child Martha Ann Potts was liveing[sic] March 4 1905.

                                          Raymond Bryant

Subscribed and sworn to before me this the 11 day of April 1905.
        My commission expires Feb. 4, 1908
        Commission from U.S. Court, So. McAlester I.T.
            MY OFFICE TALIHINA, I.T.   Sam T Roberts Jr
                                                Notary Public.

State of Indian Territory
Central District

    Before me Sam T Roberts Jr a notary[sic] Public within and for the Central District, at my office in Talihina I T personally appeared D C Merryman to me well known who first being duly sworn deposes and says My name is D C Merryman I am 52 years of age, my Post Office is Bengal I T   I am personally acquainted with Forbis Potts and Ada Potts his wife I know that Ada Potts is the mother of Martha Ann Potts born November 30 1902 and that the said child Martha Ann Potts was liveing[sic] March 4, 1905.

                                          David C Merryman

Subscribed and sworn to before me this the 11 day of April 1905.
        My commission expires Feb. 4, 1908
        Commission from U.S. Court, So. McAlester I.T.
            MY OFFICE TALIHINA, I.T.   Sam T Roberts Jr
                                                Notary Public.

BIRTH AFFIDAVIT.

DEPARTMENT OF THE INTERIOR.
COMMISSION TO THE FIVE CIVILIZED TRIBES.

    IN RE APPLICATION FOR ENROLLMENT, as a citizen of the   Choctaw   Nation, of Martha Ann Potts   , born on the 30th day of November , 1902

Name of Father: Forbis Potts   a citizen of the   Choctaw   Nation.
Name of Mother: Ada Potts   a citizen of the   Choctaw   Nation.

Applications for Enrollment of Choctaw Newborn
Act of 1905   Volume III

Postoffice   Talihina I.T.

AFFIDAVIT OF MOTHER.

UNITED STATES OF AMERICA, Indian Territory, } DISTRICT.

I, Ada Potts, on oath state that I am 33 years of age and a citizen by intermarriage, of the Choctaw Nation; that I am the lawful wife of Forbis Potts, who is a citizen, by blood of the Choctaw Nation; that a female child was born to me on 30th day of November, 1902; that said child has been named Martha Ann Potts, and was living March 4, 1905.

Ada Potts

Witnesses To Mark:

Subscribed and sworn to before me this 11 day of April, 1905

Sam T Roberts Jr
Notary Public.

AFFIDAVIT OF ATTENDING PHYSICIAN OR MID-WIFE.

UNITED STATES OF AMERICA, Indian Territory, } DISTRICT.

I, ..., a ...., on oath state that I attended on Mrs. Ada Potts, wife of Forbis Potts on the 30th day of November, 1902; that there was born to her on said date a female child; that said child was living March 4, 1905, and is said to have been named Martha Ann Potts

Witnesses To Mark:

Subscribed and sworn to before me this .... day of ...., 1905

Notary Public.

Applications for Enrollment of Choctaw Newborn
Act of 1905   Volume III

7-2382.

Muskogee, Indian Territory, January 8, 1903.

Forbis Potts,
    Howe, Indian Territory.

Dear Sir:

    Referring the applications for enrollment as citizens of the Choctaw Nation of Martha A. and Margaret J. Potts, twin children of Forbis and Ada Potts, born November 30, 1902; you are advised that the Commission is without authority to enroll these children as citizens of the Choctaw Nation, it appearing that they were born November 30, 1902, subsequent to the ratification by the citizens of the Choctaw and Chickasaw Nations September 25, 1902, of an act of Congress approved July 1, 1902 (32 Stats., 641). Section twenty-eight thereof provides as follows:

    "The names of all persons living on the date of the final ratification of this agreement entitled to be enrolled as provided in section 27 hereof shall be placed upon the rolls made by said Commission; and no child born thereafter to a citizen or freedman and no person intermarried thereafter to a citizen shall be entitled to enrollment or to participate in the distribution of the tribal property of the Choctaws and Chickasaws."

Respectfully,

Acting Chairman.

Choctaw 2382.

Muskogee, Indian Territory, April 4, 1905.

Forbis Potts,
    Talihina, Indian Territory.

Dear Sir:

    Receipt is hereby acknowledged of the affidavits of Ada B. Potts and Forbis B. Potts to the birth of Margaret Jane Potts and Martha Ann Potts, twin children of Forbis and Ada B. Potts, November 30, 1902, and the same have been filed with our records as an application for the enrollment of said children.

Respectfully,

Commissioner in Charge.

Applications for Enrollment of Choctaw Newborn
Act of 1905 Volume III

COPY N.B. 141.

Muskogee, Indian Territory, April 7, 1905.

Forbis Potts,
    Talihina, Indian Territory.

Dear Sir:

    There is enclosed you herewith for execution application for the enrollment of your infant children, Martha Ann Potts and Margaret Jane Potts, born November 30, 1902.

    The affidavits of the attending physician or mid-wife was ommitted[sic] from the application heretofore submitted to this office. In case there was no physician or mid-wife in attendance it will be necessary that you secure the affidavits of two persons who know that the applicants were born, that they were living on March 4, 1905 and that Ada Potts was their mother. It will also be noted that separate affidavits are required for each applicant.

    In having these affidavits executed care should be exercised to see that all names are written in full, as they appear in the body of the affidavit, and in the event that either of the persons signing the affidavit are unable to write, signatures by mark must be attested by two witnesses. Each affidavit must be executed before a Notary Public and the notarial seal and signature of the officer must be attached to each separate affidavit.

                                   Respectfully,
                                     SIGNED
                                   T. B. Needles.

LM 7-6   Commissioner in Charge.

COPY

Choctaw N.B. 141.

Muskogee, Indian Territory, April 14, 1905.

Forbis Potts,
    Talihina, Indian Territory.

Dear Sir:

    Receipt is hereby acknowledged of the affidavits of Raymond Bryant, David C. Merryman and Ada Potts to the birth of Martha Ann Potts and Margaret Jane Potts, twin daughters of Forbis and Ada Potts, November 30, 1902, and the same have been filed with our records in the matter of the enrollment of the above named child.

Applications for Enrollment of Choctaw Newborn
Act of 1905 Volume III

Respectfully,
SIGNED

T. B. Needles.
Commissioner in Charge.

Choc New Born 141
    Martha Eloise Wall
    (Born August 3, 1903)

BIRTH AFFIDAVIT.

DEPARTMENT OF THE INTERIOR,
COMMISSION TO THE FIVE CIVILIZED TRIBES.

In Re Application for Enrollment, as a citizen of the Choctaw Nation, of Martha Eloise Wall , born on the 3 rd day of August , 1903

Name of Father: Thomas B. Wall   a citizen of the Choctaw Nation.
Name of Mother: Ida Lee Wall, nee   a citizen of the Choctaw Nation.
                   Ida Lee Griffith
                           Post-office   Poteau, I. T.

AFFIDAVIT OF MOTHER.

UNITED STATES OF AMERICA,
   INDIAN TERRITORY,
Central   District.

    I, Ida Lee Wall , on oath state that I am twenty years of age and a citizen by blood , of the Choctaw Nation; that I am the lawful wife of Thomas B. Wall , who is a citizen, by blood of the Choctaw Nation; that a female child was born to me on third day of August, 1903 , 1......, that said child has been named Martha Eloise Wall , and is now living.

                                   Ida Lee Wall

WITNESSES TO MARK:

    Subscribed and sworn to before me this 14th day of March , 1904.

                                 W.H. Harrison
My Commission expires March 19-1907   NOTARY PUBLIC.

Applications for Enrollment of Choctaw Newborn
Act of 1905   Volume III

AFFIDAVIT OF ATTENDING PHYSICIAN OR MID-WIFE.

UNITED STATES OF AMERICA, }
INDIAN TERRITORY,
Central   District.

I,   A.S. Pollock   , a   Physician   , on oath state that I attended on Mrs.   Ida Lee Wall   , wife of Thos. B Wall   on the   3rd. day of August , 1903 ; that there was born to her on said date a   Female   child; that said child is now living and is said to have been named   Martha Eloise Wall

A. S. Pollock, MD

WITNESSES TO MARK:
{ R.F. Stinson
{ G.H. Ward

Subscribed and sworn to before me 15th   day of   March   1904 , 190.....

My Commission expires Apr 12 1907   A B Davis
                                   NOTARY PUBLIC.

BIRTH AFFIDAVIT.
DEPARTMENT OF THE INTERIOR.
COMMISSION TO THE FIVE CIVILIZED TRIBES.

IN RE APPLICATION FOR ENROLLMENT, as a citizen of the   Choctaw Nation   Nation, of   Martha Eloise Wall   , born on the   third   day of   August   , 1905[sic]

Name of Father: Thomas B. Wall   a citizen of the   Choctaw   Nation.
Name of Mother: Ida L Wall, nee Ida L Griffith   a citizen of the   Choctaw   Nation.

Postoffice   Poteau, I.T.

AFFIDAVIT OF MOTHER.

UNITED STATES OF AMERICA, Indian Territory, }
Central   **DISTRICT.** }

I,   Ida L. Wall, nee Ida L. Griffith   , on oath state that I am   22   years of age and a citizen by   blood   , of the   Choctaw   Nation; that I am the lawful wife of   Thomas B. Wall   , who is a citizen, by   blood   of the   Choctaw   Nation; that a   female   child was born to me on   third   day of   August   , 1903; that said child has been named   Martha Eloise Wall   , and was living March 4, 1905.

Applications for Enrollment of Choctaw Newborn
Act of 1905   Volume III

                                      Ida L Wall, nee Ida L Griffith

Witnesses To Mark:
{

      Subscribed and sworn to before me this   5th   day of   April, 1905   , 190...

                                       P C Bolger
                                         Notary Public.

My commission expires Nov. 1, 1905

AFFIDAVIT OF ATTENDING PHYSICIAN OR MID-WIFE.

~~UNITED STATES OF AMERICA, Indian Territory,~~
State of Texas.   ~~DISTRICT.~~
Upshur   County.

    I,   A. S. Pollock   , a   physician   , on oath state that I attended on Mrs. Thos. B. Wall   , wife of   Thomas B. Wall   on the third   day of August, 1903; that there was born to her on said date a   female   child; that said child was living March 4, 1905, and is said to have been named   Martha Eloise Wall

                                    A. S. Pollock, M.D.

Witnesses To Mark:
{ W.L. *(Illegible)*
  J.M. *(Illegible)*

      Subscribed and sworn to before me this   25   day of   April   , 1905

                            W Smith   **J. P. and Ex-Officio**
                            N~~otary~~ ***Public***
                            IN AND FOR UPSHUR COUNTY TEX.

                                      7-2282
                                      7-2305

              Muskogee, Indian Territory, March 28, 1904.

Thomas B. Wall,
     Poteau, Indian Territory.

Dear Sir:

    Receipt is hereby acknowledged of your letter of the 16th inst., enclosing the affidavits of Ida Lee Wall and A. S. Pollock, relative to the birth of your infant daughter, Martha Eloise Wall, August 3, 1903, which it is presumed have been forwarded to this office as an application for enrollment of said child as a citizen by blood of the Choctaw Nation.

Applications for Enrollment of Choctaw Newborn
Act of 1905   Volume III

You are informed that under the provisions of the Act of Congress, approved July 1, 1902, the Commission is now without authority to receive or consider the original application for enrollment of any person whomsoever as a citizen of the Choctaw or Chickasaw Nation.

Respectfully,

Commissioner in Charge.

COPY   N. B. 142

Muskogee, Indian Territory, April 4, 1905.

Thomas B. Wall,
   Poteau, Indian Territory.

Dear Sir:

There is inclosed you herewith for execution application for the enrollment of your infant child, Matha[sic] Eloise Wall, born August 3, 1903.

The affidavits heretofore filed with the Commission show the child was living on March 15, 1904. It is necessary, for the child to be enrolled, that she was living on March 4, 1905.

In having these affidavits executed care should be exercised to see that all names are written in full, as they appear in the body of the affidavit, and in the event that either of the persons signing the affidavit are unable to write, signatures by mark must be attested by two witnesses. Each affidavit must be executed before a Notary Public and the notarial seal and signature of the officer must be attached to each separate affidavit.

Respectfully,
SIGNED
T. B. Needles.

LM 4-5   Commissioner in Charge.

Applications for Enrollment of Choctaw Newborn
Act of 1905   Volume III

COPY

7 NB 142
7-2305

Muskogee, Indian Territory, May 5, 1905.

Thomas B. Wall,
    Poteau, Indian Territory.

Dear Sir:

    Receipt is hereby acknowledged of your letter of April 27, 1905, enclosing affidavits of Ida L. Wall nee Ida L. Griffith and A. S. Pollock to the birth of Martha Eloise Wall daughter of Thomas B. and Ida L. Griffith, August 3, 1903, and the same have been filed with our records as an application for the enrollment of said child.

    You state that you have heretofore forwarded marriage license and certificate between Thomas B. Wall and Ida L. Griffith but your wife still appears upon the rolls as Ida L. Griffith and you request that the same be changed and that your marriage license and certificate be returned to you.

    In reply to your letter you are advised that it appears from our records that the marriage license and certificate referred to were received at this office January 2, 1903, and that the name of your wife Ida L. Griffith had prior to that time been placed upon a schedule of citizens by blood of the Choctaw Nation which had been forwarded to the Secretary of the Interior and on *(The end of this file stops here.)*

Applications for Enrollment of Choctaw Newborn
Act of 1905   Volume III

Choc New Born 143
    Leviney Peter
    (Born Nov. 23, 1903)

NEW BORN AFFIDAVIT

No ....

CHOCTAW ENROLLING COMMISSION

IN THE MATTER OF THE APPLICATION FOR ENROLLMENT as a citizen of the Choctaw Nation, of **Levina Peter** born on the **23** day of **November** 190 **3**

Name of father **Barnabus Peter** a citizen of **Choctaw** Nation, final enrollment No. **6418**
Name of mother **Emaline Peter** a citizen of **Choctaw** Nation, final enrollment No. **6835**

                        Wister I.T.   Postoffice.

AFFIDAVIT OF MOTHER

UNITED STATES OF AMERICA }
   INDIAN TERRITORY   }
DISTRICT   Central   }

    I **Emaline Peter**, on oath state that I am **27** years of age and a citizen by **blood** of the **Choctaw** Nation, and as such have been placed upon the final roll of the **Choctaw** Nation, by the Honorable Secretary of the Interior my final enrollment number being **6835** ; that I am the lawful wife of **Barnabus Peter**, who is a citizen of the **Choctaw** Nation, and as such has been placed upon the final roll of said Nation by the Honorable Secretary of the Interior, his final enrollment number being **6418** and that a **female** child was born to me on the **23** day of **November** 190 **3** ; that said child has been named **Levina Peter**, and is now living.

                                      her
                        Emaline x Peter
WITNESSETH: mark
  Must be two witnesses { **Levine Peter**
  who are citizens   { **Charley Jones**

Applications for Enrollment of Choctaw Newborn
Act of 1905 Volume III

Subscribed and sworn to before me this, the 17 day of February 190 5

James Bower
Notary Public.

My Commission Expires:
Sept 23-1907

Affidavit of Attending Physician or Midwife

UNITED STATES OF AMERICA, ⎫
   INDIAN TERRITORY, ⎬
 Central   DISTRICT ⎭

   I,   Lousie[sic] Jones   a   Midwife on oath state that I attended on Mrs. Emaline Peter   wife of Barnabus Peter on the 23 day of November , 190 3 , that there was born to her on said date a female child, that said child is now living, and is said to have been named Levina Peter

          her
Lwena[sic] x Jones   M. D.
          mark

Subscribed and sworn to before me this the 18 day of February 1905

James Bower
Notary Public.

WITNESSETH:

Must be two witnesses ⎰ Levina Peter
who are citizens and ⎱ Charley Jones
know the child.

   We hereby certify that we are well acquainted with Louise Jones a   Midwife   and know   her   to be reputable and of good standing in the community.

Must be two citizen ⎰ Levina Peter
witnesses. ⎱ Charley Jones

BIRTH AFFIDAVIT.

DEPARTMENT OF THE INTERIOR.
COMMISSION TO THE FIVE CIVILIZED TRIBES.

   IN RE APPLICATION FOR ENROLLMENT, as a citizen of the   Choctaw   Nation, of Vina Peters , born on the 23 day of Nov , 1903

Name of Father: Barnabas Peters   a citizen of the Choctaw Nation.
Name of Mother: Emaline Peters   a citizen of the Choctaw Nation.

Applications for Enrollment of Choctaw Newborn
Act of 1905   Volume III

                              Postoffice   Wister I.T

AFFIDAVIT OF MOTHER.

UNITED STATES OF AMERICA, Indian Territory, }
   Central   DISTRICT.

     I, Emaline Peters , on oath state that I am 25 years of age and a citizen by Blood , of the Choctaw Nation; that I am the lawful wife of Barnabas Peters, who is a citizen, by Blood of the Choctaw Nation; that a female child was born to me on 23 day of Nov , 1903, that said child has been named Vina , and is now living.

                                               her
                                      Emaline x Peters
Witnesses To Mark: mark
 { John W Kinsey
   M Baldwin

     Subscribed and sworn to before me this 27 day of   Aug   , 1904

                                   J J Rigg
                                          Notary Public.

AFFIDAVIT OF ATTENDING PHYSICIAN OR MID-WIFE.

UNITED STATES OF AMERICA, Indian Territory, }
   Central   DISTRICT.

     I,   Ester Hill   , a   midwife   , on oath state that I attended on Mrs. Emaline Peters , wife of Barnabas Peters   on the 23 day of Nov , 1903; that there was born to her on said date a   female   child; that said child is now living and is said to have been named   Vina
                                         her
                                   Ester x Hill
Witnesses To Mark: mark
 { John W Kinsey
   M Baldwin

     Subscribed and sworn to before me this 27 day of   Aug   , 1904

                                   J J Rigg
                                          Notary Public.

Applications for Enrollment of Choctaw Newborn
Act of 1905   Volume III

BIRTH AFFIDAVIT.

DEPARTMENT OF THE INTERIOR.
COMMISSION TO THE FIVE CIVILIZED TRIBES.

IN RE APPLICATION FOR ENROLLMENT, as a citizen of the Choctaw Nation, of Leviney Peter, born on the 23rd day of November, 1904[sic]

Name of Father: Barnabas Peter   a citizen of the Choctaw Nation.
Name of Mother: Emeline Peter   a citizen of the Choctaw Nation.

Postoffice   Wister, Ind. Ter.

AFFIDAVIT OF MOTHER.

UNITED STATES OF AMERICA, Indian Territory,
Central   DISTRICT.

I, Emeline Peter, on oath state that I am 25 years of age and a citizen by blood, of the Choctaw Nation; that I am the lawful wife of Barnabas Peter, who is a citizen, by blood of the Choctaw Nation; that a female child was born to me on 23rd day of November, 1904; that said child has been named Leviney Peter, and was living March 4, 1905.

her
Emeline x Peter
mark

Witnesses To Mark:
 { Victor M Locks Jr
 { James Mills

Subscribed and sworn to before me this 25th day of March, 1905

Wirt Franklin
Notary Public.

AFFIDAVIT OF ATTENDING PHYSICIAN OR MID-WIFE.

UNITED STATES OF AMERICA, Indian Territory,
Central   DISTRICT.

I, Louina Jones, a midwife, on oath state that I attended on Mrs. Emeline Peter, wife of Barnabas Peter on the 23rd day of November, 1904; that there was born to her on said date a female child; that said child was living March 4, 1905, and is said to have been named Leviney Peter

her
Louina x Jones
mark

Applications for Enrollment of Choctaw Newborn
Act of 1905 Volume III

Witnesses To Mark:
- Victor M Locks Jr
- James Mills

Subscribed and sworn to before me this 25th day of March, 1905

Wirt Franklin
Notary Public.

BIRTH AFFIDAVIT.

DEPARTMENT OF THE INTERIOR.
COMMISSION TO THE FIVE CIVILIZED TRIBES.

IN RE APPLICATION FOR ENROLLMENT, as a citizen of the Choctaw Nation, of Leviney Peter, born on the 23 day of November, 1903

Name of Father: Barnabas Peter   a citizen of the Choctaw Nation.
Name of Mother: Emeline Peter   a citizen of the Choctaw Nation.

Postoffice   Wister, Ind. Ter.

AFFIDAVIT OF MOTHER.

UNITED STATES OF AMERICA, Indian Territory,
Central DISTRICT.

I, Emeline Peter, on oath state that I am 25 years of age and a citizen by blood, of the Choctaw Nation; that I am the lawful wife of Barnabas Peter, who is a citizen, by blood of the Choctaw Nation; that a female child was born to me on 23rd day of November, 1903; that said child has been named Leviney Peter, and was living March 4, 1905.

her
Emeline x Peter
mark

Witnesses To Mark:
- S D Collins
- George *(Illegible)*

Subscribed and sworn to before me this 20 day of May, 1905

J J Riggs
Notary Public.

Applications for Enrollment of Choctaw Newborn
Act of 1905   Volume III

AFFIDAVIT OF ATTENDING PHYSICIAN OR MID-WIFE.

UNITED STATES OF AMERICA, Indian Territory,
....DISTRICT.

I,   Loeni Jones   , a   midwife   , on oath state that I attended on Mrs.   Emeline Peter   , wife of   Barnabas Peter   on the   23rd   day of   November   , 1903; that there was born to her on said date a   female   child; that said child was living March 4, 1905, and is said to have been named Leviney Peter

                                                         her
                                                         Loeni x Jones
Witnesses To Mark: mark
   { S D Collins
   { George *(Illegible)*

Subscribed and sworn to before me this 20 day of   May   , 1905

                                   J J Riggs
                                        Notary Public.

                                                                                     7-N.B. 143.

                        Muskogee, Indian Territory, May 12, 1905.

Barnabas Peter,
       Wister, Indian Territory.

Dear Sir:

       There is enclosed you herewith for execution application for the enrollment of your infant child, Leviney Peter, born November 23, 1903.

       The mother's affidavit of August 27, 1904, heretofore filed with the Commission, gives the date of the child's birth as November 23, 1903, while in the affidavit of March 25, 1905, it is given as November 23, 1904. The former is apparently correct, but as this affidavit does not show that the child was living on March 4, 1905, it will be necessary for you to execute new affidavits.

       In having these affidavits executed care should be exercised to see that all names are written in full, as they appear in the body of the affidavit, and in the event that either of the persons signing the affidavit are unable to write, signatures by mark must be attested by two witnesses. Each affidavit must be executed before a Notary Public and the notarial seal and signature of the officer must be attached to each separate affidavit.

Applications for Enrollment of Choctaw Newborn
Act of 1905   Volume III

Respectfully,

(No name given.)

7-N.B. 143.

Muskogee, Indian Territory, May 25, 1905.

Barnabas Peter,
    Wister, Indian Territory.

Dear Sir:

    Receipt is hereby acknowledged of the affidavits of Emeline Peter and Leoni Jones to the birth of Leviney Peter, daughter of Barnabas and Emeline peter, November 23, 1903, and the same have been filed in the matter of the enrollment of said child.

Respectfully,

Chairman.

Muskogee, Indian Territory, July 25, 1905.

Chief Clerk,
    Choctaw Land Office,
        Atoka, Indian Territory.

Dear Sir:

    Refer to duplicate Choctaw New Born Roll Card No. 143, in the possession of your office, Levina Peter, and change the date of the birth of applicant thereon to read, "Born November 23, 1903", and the age of applicant, "One year."

Respectfully,

Commissioner.

(The above letter given again.)

Applications for Enrollment of Choctaw Newborn
Act of 1905 Volume III

Choc New Born 144
    William McCurtain
    (Born April 29, 1903)

BIRTH AFFIDAVIT.

DEPARTMENT OF THE INTERIOR,
COMMISSION TO THE FIVE CIVILIZED TRIBES.

In Re Application for Enrollment, as a citizen of the Choctaw Nation, of William McCurtain, born on the 29 day of April, 1903

Name of Father: Thomas McCurtain   a citizen of the Choctaw Nation.
Name of Mother: Louisa McCurtain   a citizen of the Choctaw Nation.

Post-office   Red Oak, I.T.

AFFIDAVIT OF MOTHER.

UNITED STATES OF AMERICA,
  INDIAN TERRITORY,
Central   District.

I, Louisa McCurtain, on oath state that I am 24 years of age and a citizen by Blood, of the Choctaw Nation; that I am the lawful wife of Thomas McCurtain, who is a citizen, by Blood of the Choctaw Nation; that a male child was born to me on 29 day of April, 190 3, that said child has been named William McCurtain, and is now living.

                              Louisa McCurtain

WITNESSES TO MARK:
  { John Williams
    Watson Wright

Subscribed and sworn to before me this 16 day of March, 1904.

                              Robert E Lee
                              NOTARY PUBLIC.
              My com ex Jan. 11- 1904[sic].

Applications for Enrollment of Choctaw Newborn
Act of 1905 Volume III

AFFIDAVIT OF ATTENDING PHYSICIAN OR MID-WIFE.

UNITED STATES OF AMERICA,
INDIAN TERRITORY,
Central District.

I, Sallie McCurtain , a mid-wife , on oath state that I attended on Mrs. Louisa McCurtain , wife of Thomas McCurtain on the 29 day of April , 1903 ; that there was born to her on said date a male child; that said child is now living and is said to have been named William McCurtain

Sallie McCurtain

WITNESSES TO MARK:
 John Williams
 Watson Wright

Subscribed and sworn to before me this 16 day of March , 1904.

Robert E Lee
NOTARY PUBLIC.
My com ex Jan. 11- 1904[sic].

NEW BORN AFFIDAVIT

No ....

CHOCTAW ENROLLING COMMISSION

IN THE MATTER OF THE APPLICATION FOR ENROLLMENT as a citizen of the Choctaw Nation, of William McCurtain born on the 28[sic] day of April 190 3

Name of father Thomas McCurtain a citizen of Choctaw Nation, final enrollment No. 8612
Name of mother Louisa Wright a citizen of Choctaw Nation, final enrollment No. 6967

Leflore I.T. Postoffice.

Applications for Enrollment of Choctaw Newborn
Act of 1905   Volume III

AFFIDAVIT OF MOTHER

UNITED STATES OF AMERICA
   INDIAN TERRITORY
DISTRICT   Central

I   Louisa Wright   , on oath state that I am   27   years of age and a citizen by   blood   of the   Choctaw   Nation, and as such have been placed upon the final roll of the   Choctaw   Nation, by the Honorable Secretary of the Interior my final enrollment number being   6967   ; that I am ~~the lawful wife of~~ not married to   Thomas McCurtain   , who is a citizen of the   Choctaw   Nation, and as such has been placed upon the final roll of said Nation by the Honorable Secretary of the Interior, his final enrollment number being   8612   and that a   Male   child was born to me on the   28   day of   April   190 3   ; that said child has been named   William McCurtain   , and is now living.

                                               her
WITNESSETH: Louisa x Wright
Must be two witnesses { Mitchell McCurtain   mark
who are citizens   Henry Burns

Subscribed and sworn to before me this, the   18   day of   February   190 5

                                        James Bower
                                                     Notary Public.

My Commission Expires:
Sept 23-1907.

Affidavit of Attending Physician or Midwife

UNITED STATES OF AMERICA,
   INDIAN TERRITORY,
Central   DISTRICT

I,   Sallie McCurtain   a   midwife on oath state that I attended on Mrs. Louisa Wright (mother of child) ~~wife of~~ Thomas McCurtain   on the   28   day of April   , 190 3   , that there was born to her on said date a   male   child, that said child is now living, and is said to have been named William McCurtain

                                     Sallie McCurtain   Midwife

Subscribed and sworn to before me this the   20   day of   February   1905

                                        Robert E Lee
My Com. expires Jan. 11-1906   Notary Public.

Applications for Enrollment of Choctaw Newborn
Act of 1905   Volume III

WITNESSETH:

Must be two witnesses who are citizens and know the child.   { Mitchell McCurtain
Henry Burns

We hereby certify that we are well acquainted with   Sallie McCurtain   a   Midwife   and know   her   to be reputable and of good standing in the community.

Must be two citizen witnesses.   { Mitchell McCurtain
Henry Burns

BIRTH AFFIDAVIT.

DEPARTMENT OF THE INTERIOR.
COMMISSION TO THE FIVE CIVILIZED TRIBES.

IN RE APPLICATION FOR ENROLLMENT, as a citizen of the   Choctaw   Nation, of   William McCurtain   , born on the .... day of ...., 1......

Name of Father: Thomas McCurtain - roll #8612   a citizen of the   Choctaw   Nation.
                                                       6967
Name of Mother: Louisa Wright - roll #~~8612~~   a citizen of the   "   Nation.

Postoffice   Leflore I.T.

AFFIDAVIT OF MOTHER.

UNITED STATES OF AMERICA, Indian Territory,   }
Central   DISTRICT.

I, Louisa McCurtain-nee Wright , on oath state that I am 26 years of age and a citizen by blood , of the Choctaw Nation; that I am the lawful wife of Thomas McCurtain , who is a citizen, by blood of the Choctaw Nation; that a male child was born to me on 29 day of April , 1902; that said child has been named William McCurtain , and was living March 4, 1905.

    her
Louisa x McCurtain
    mark

Witnesses To Mark:
{ W.L. West
  W.L Harris

Subscribed and sworn to before me this 22 day of April , 1905

My Com Exp 7/8/08   W L Harris
                              Notary Public.

Applications for Enrollment of Choctaw Newborn
Act of 1905   Volume III

AFFIDAVIT OF ATTENDING PHYSICIAN OR MID-WIFE.

UNITED STATES OF AMERICA, Indian Territory, }
Central   DISTRICT.

    I, Salley McCurtain, a woman, on oath state that I attended on Mrs. Louisa McCurtain, wife of Thomas McCurtain on the 29 day of April, 1902; that there was born to her on said date a male child; that said child was living March 4, 1905, and is said to have been named William McCurtain

                                                her
                                  Salley x McCurtain

Witnesses To Mark: mark
  { W.L. West
    W.L Harris

    Subscribed and sworn to before me this 22 day of April, 1905

    My Com Exp 7/8/08   W L Harris
                                                Notary Public.

                                                                  7-2928

                Muskogee, Indian Territory, March 28, 1904.

Thomas McCurtain,
    Redoak, Indian Territory.

Dear Sir:

    Receipt is hereby acknowledged of the affidavits of Louisa and Sallie McCurtain, relative to the birth of William McCurtain, April 29, 1903, which it is presumed have been forwarded to this office as an application for enrollment of said child as a citizen by blood of the Choctaw Nation.

    Under the provisions of the Act of Congress, approved July 1, 1902, the Commission is now without authority to receive or consider the original application for enrollment of any person whomsoever as a citizen of the Choctaw or Chickasaw Nation.

                                    Respectfully,

                                                  Commissioner in Charge.

Applications for Enrollment of Choctaw Newborn
Act of 1905   Volume III

COPY

7-N.B. 144.

Muskogee, Indian Territory, April 26, 1905.

Thomas McCurtain,
    Leflore, Indian Territory.

Dear Sir:

    Receipt is hereby acknowledged of the affidavits of Louisa McCurtain and Salley McCurtain to the birth of William McCurtain, son of Thomas and Louisa McCurtain, April 29, 1903, and the same have been filed with our records in the matter of the enrollment of the above named child.

          Respectfully,
          SIGNED

          Tams Bixby
          Chairman.

Choc New Born 145
    Freida I. Ward
    (Born March 10, 1903)

BIRTH AFFIDAVIT.

DEPARTMENT OF THE INTERIOR.
COMMISSION TO THE FIVE CIVILIZED TRIBES.

IN RE APPLICATION FOR ENROLLMENT, as a citizen of the Choctaw Nation, of Freida I. Ward, born on the 10 day of March, 1903

Name of Father: Jefferson D. Ward   a citizen of the Choctaw Nation.
Name of Mother: Helen I. Ward   a citizen of the Choctaw Nation.

        Postoffice   Atoka Ind. Ter.

Applications for Enrollment of Choctaw Newborn
Act of 1905   Volume III

AFFIDAVIT OF MOTHER.

UNITED STATES OF AMERICA, Indian Territory,
Central   DISTRICT.

I, Helen I. Ward, on oath state that I am 34 years of age and a citizen by Intermarriage, of the Choctaw Nation; that I am the lawful wife of Jefferson D. Ward, who is a citizen, by Blood of the Choctaw Nation; that a Female child was born to me on 10 day of March, 1903; that said child has been named Freida I. Ward, and was living March 4, 1905.

Helen I. Ward

Witnesses To Mark:

{

Subscribed and sworn to before me this 22 day of March, 1905

W.S. Fannin
Notary Public.

AFFIDAVIT OF ATTENDING PHYSICIAN OR MID-WIFE.

UNITED STATES OF AMERICA, Indian Territory,
Central   DISTRICT.

I, Lucy A Ferguson, a Midwife, on oath state that I attended on Mrs. Helen I Ward, wife of Jefferson D. Ward on the 29 day of April, 1903; that there was born to her on said date a Female child; that said child was living March 4, 1905, and is said to have been named Freida I Ward

Lucy A Ferguson

Witnesses To Mark:

{

Subscribed and sworn to before me this 15th day of March, 1905

Frank Lewis
My commission expires Jan. 20, 1908.   Notary Public.

Applications for Enrollment of Choctaw Newborn
Act of 1905 Volume III

Choc New Born 146
    Betsey King
    (Born Feb. 15, 1904)

BIRTH AFFIDAVIT.

DEPARTMENT OF THE INTERIOR,
COMMISSION TO THE FIVE CIVILIZED TRIBES.

In Re Application for Enrollment, as a citizen of the Choctaw Nation, of Betsey King, born on the 15th day of February, 1904

Name of Father: Nicodemas King   a citizen of the Choctaw Nation.
Name of Mother: Annie King   a citizen of the Choctaw Nation.

                Post-office   Iron Bridge I.T.

AFFIDAVIT OF MOTHER.

UNITED STATES OF AMERICA,
   INDIAN TERRITORY,
   Central   District.

    I, Anne[sic] King, on oath state that I am 45 years of age and a citizen by Blood, of the Choctaw Nation; that I am the lawful wife of Nicodemas King, who is a citizen, by Blood of the Choctaw Nation; that a Female child was born to me on 15th day of February, 1904, that said child has been named Betsey King, and is now living.

                              her
                        Annie x King
WITNESSES TO MARK: mark
    Adam Watson
    Tom Jones

    Subscribed and sworn to before me this 27th day of Sept, 1904

                        M. W. Newman
                            NOTARY PUBLIC.

Applications for Enrollment of Choctaw Newborn
Act of 1905   Volume III

AFFIDAVIT OF ATTENDING PHYSICIAN OR MID-WIFE.

UNITED STATES OF AMERICA,
   INDIAN TERRITORY,
Central   District.

I, Hannah Sucky, a Midwife, on oath state that I attended on Mrs. Annie King, wife of Nicodemas King on the 15th day of Feb, 1904; that there was born to her on said date a Female child; that said child is now living and is said to have been named Betsey King

                        her
                  Hannah x Sucky

WITNESSES TO MARK: mark
   Adam Watson
   Tom Jones

Subscribed and sworn to before me this 27th day of Sept, 1904

                      M. W. Newman
                            NOTARY PUBLIC.

NEW-BORN AFFIDAVIT.

        Number............

...Choctaw Enrolling Commission...

IN THE MATTER OF THE APPLICATION FOR ENROLLMENT, as a citizen of the Choctaw Nation, of Betsey King

born on the 15 day of Feb 190 4

Name of father N M King	a citizen of	Choctaw
Nation final enrollment No. 7181		
Name of mother Annie King	a citizen of	Choctaw
Nation final enrollment No. 8652		

                                        Postoffice   Iron Bridge IT

Applications for Enrollment of Choctaw Newborn
Act of 1905 Volume III

AFFIDAVIT OF MOTHER.

UNITED STATES OF AMERICA
INDIAN TERRITORY
Central DISTRICT

I, Annie King, on oath state that I am 40 years of age and a citizen by Blood of the Choctaw Nation, and as such have been placed upon the final roll of the Choctaw Nation, by the Honorable Secretary of the Interior my final enrollment number being 8652; that I am the lawful wife of N M King, who is a citizen of the Choctaw Nation, and as such has been placed upon the final roll of said Nation by the Honorable Secretary of the Interior, his final enrollment number being 7181 and that a Female child was born to me on the 15th day of February 1904; that said child has been named Betsey King, and is now living.

Witnesseth.
    Must be two Witnesses who are Citizens.
    James Isaac
    Josh Lucus

Annie x King (her mark)

Subscribed and sworn to before me this 15 day of Feb 1905

M W Newman
Notary Public.

My commission expires:

AFFIDAVIT OF ATTENDING PHYSICIAN OR MIDWIFE

UNITED STATES OF AMERICA
INDIAN TERRITORY
Central DISTRICT

I, Hannah Sockey a Midwife on oath state that I attended on Mrs. Annie King wife of N M King on the 15th day of Feb, 1904, that there was born to her on said date a Female child, that said child is now living, and is said to have been named Betsey King

Hannah x Sockey (her mark) M.D.

Subscribed and sworn to before me this, the day of 15 Feb 1905

WITNESSETH:
James Isaac
Josh Lucus
    Must be two witnesses who are citizens

M W Newman Notary Public.

Applications for Enrollment of Choctaw Newborn
Act of 1905   Volume III

We hereby certify that we are well acquainted with   Hannah Sockey   a   Midwife   and know   her   to be reputable and of good standing in the community.

_____   James Isaac

_____   Josh Lucus

BIRTH AFFIDAVIT.

DEPARTMENT OF THE INTERIOR.
COMMISSION TO THE FIVE CIVILIZED TRIBES.

IN RE APPLICATION FOR ENROLLMENT, as a citizen of the   Choctaw   Nation, of   Betsey King   , born on the 15" day of   Feby   , 1904

Name of Father: Nichodemas M King   a citizen of the   Choctaw   Nation.
Name of Mother: Annie King   a citizen of the   Choctaw   Nation.

Postoffice   Iron Bridge Ind Tey

AFFIDAVIT OF MOTHER.

UNITED STATES OF AMERICA, Indian Territory,
Central   DISTRICT.

I, Annie King , on oath state that I am 42 years of age and a citizen by Blood , of the Choctaw Nation; that I am the lawful wife of Nichodemas M King , who is a citizen, by Blood of the Choctaw Nation; that a Female child was born to me on 15" day of February , 1904; that said child has been named Betsey King , and was living March 4, 1905.

her
Annie x King
Witnesses To Mark: mark
 { Kizzie Isaac
 { Linnie Sakiki

Subscribed and sworn to before me this 1st day of   April   , 1905

N W Newman
Notary Public.

Applications for Enrollment of Choctaw Newborn
Act of 1905   Volume III

AFFIDAVIT OF ATTENDING PHYSICIAN OR MID-WIFE.

UNITED STATES OF AMERICA, Indian Territory,　}
　　Central　　　　　　　　DISTRICT.

I, Hanah Sockey, a Midwife, on oath state that I attended on Mrs. Annie King, wife of Nichodemas M King on the 15" day of February, 1904; that there was born to her on said date a .... child; that said child was living March 4, 1905, and is said to have been named Betsey King

　　　　　　　　　　　　　　　　　　　　　　her
　　　　　　　　　　　　　　　　Hanah x Sockey
Witnesses To Mark:　　　　　　　　mark
{ Kizzie Isaac
{ Linnie Sakiki

Subscribed and sworn to before me this 1st day of April, 1905

　　　　　　　　　　　　N W Newman
　　　　　　　　　　　　　　Notary Public.

BIRTH AFFIDAVIT.

DEPARTMENT OF THE INTERIOR.
COMMISSION TO THE FIVE CIVILIZED TRIBES.

IN RE APPLICATION FOR ENROLLMENT, as a citizen of the Choctaw Nation, of Betsey King, born on the 15" day of February, 1904

Name of Father:　Nicodemus King　　　a citizen of the Choctaw Nation.
Name of Mother:　Annie King (　　)　a citizen of the Choctaw Nation.

　　　　　　　Postoffice　　Iron Bridge I.T.

AFFIDAVIT OF MOTHER.

UNITED STATES OF AMERICA, Indian Territory,　}
....DISTRICT.

I, Annie King *(Illegible)*, on oath state that I am 46 years of age and a citizen by blood, of the Choctaw Nation; that I am the lawful wife of Nicodemus King, who is a citizen, by blood of the Choctaw Nation; that a female child was born to me on 15" day of February, 1904; that said child has been named Betsey King, and was living March 4, 1905.

　　　　　　　　　　　　her
　　　　　　　　Annie x King　　　Ne[sic]
　　　　　　　　　　mark　　　　　(Tokkwbbee

Applications for Enrollment of Choctaw Newborn
Act of 1905   Volume III

Witnesses To Mark:
{ Alex Johnson
{ John Williams

  Subscribed and sworn to before me this 6th day of May , 1905

        N W Newman
        Notary Public.

AFFIDAVIT OF ATTENDING PHYSICIAN OR MID-WIFE.

UNITED STATES OF AMERICA, Indian Territory, }
 Central   DISTRICT. }

  I, Hannah Sockey , a Midwife , on oath state that I attended on Mrs. Annie King ( ) , wife of Nicodemus M King on the 15" day of February , 1904; that there was born to her on said date a female child; that said child was living March 4, 1905, and is said to have been named Betsey King

          her
        Hannah x Sockey
          mark

Witnesses To Mark:
{ Alex Johnson
{ John Williams

  Subscribed and sworn to before me this 6th day of May , 1905

        N W Newman
        Notary Public.

          7-2475

    Muskogee, Indian Territory, October 6, 1904.

Nicodemus King,
 Ironbridge, Indian Territory.

Dear Sir:

  Receipt is hereby acknowledged of the affidavits of Annie King and Hannah Sucky relative to the birth of your infant daughter Betsey King February 15, 1904, which it is presumed have been forwarded to this office as an application for enrollment of said child as a citizen by blood of the Choctaw Nation.

Applications for Enrollment of Choctaw Newborn
Act of 1905   Volume III

The act of Congress approved July 1, 1902, which was ratified by the citizens of the Choctaw and Chickasaw Nations September 25, 1902, among other things provides that no child born to a citizen of the Choctaw or Chickasaw Nation subsequent to the date of said ratification shall be entitled to enrollment.

                Respectfully,

                        Chairman.

COPY

N. B. 146

Muskogee, Indian Territory, April 7, 1905.

Nicodemus King,
    Ironbridge, Indian Territory.

Dear Sir:

There is inclosed you herewith for execution application for the enrollment of your infant child, Betsey King, born February 15, 1904.

The affidavits heretofore filed with the Commission show the applicant was living on September 27, 1904. It is necessary, for the child to be enrolled, that he was living on March 4, 1905. You will please insert the maiden name of the mother in the space provided for that purpose.

Referring to the affidavits heretofore forwarded to the birth of Betsey King stated in the affidavit of the mother, Annie King, that she is a citizen by blood of the Choctaw Nation.

If this is correct you are requested to state when, where and under what name she was listed for enrollment, the names of her parents and other members of her family for whom application was made at the same time.

In having these affidavits executed care should be exercised to see that all names are written in full, as they appear in the body of the affidavit, and in the event that either of the persons signing the affidavit are unable to write, signatures by mark must be attested by two witnesses. Each affidavit must be executed before a Notary Public and the notarial seal and signature of the officer must be attached to each separate affidavit.

                Respectfully,
                SIGNED
                T. B. Needles.

LM 7-6   Commissioner in Charge.

Applications for Enrollment of Choctaw Newborn
Act of 1905 Volume III

7-N.B. 146.

Muskogee, Indian Territory, May 10, 1905.

Nicodemus King,
    Ironbridge, Indian Territory.

Dear Sir:

    Receipt is hereby acknowledged of the affidavits of Annie King and Hannah Sockey to the birth of Betsey King, daughter of Nicodemus and Annie King, February 15, 1904, and the same have been filed in the matter of the enrollment of this child.

        Respectfully,

            Chairman.

Annie King   Ne
        Annie Tokkwbbee
Allotment No Homestead 8652
Fathers Name was Tokkwbbee *(or Tokkubbee)*
        Annie King

Choc New Born 147
    Dawie Ophelie Lane
    (Born Feb. 8, 1903)

BIRTH AFFIDAVIT.

DEPARTMENT OF THE INTERIOR.
COMMISSION TO THE FIVE CIVILIZED TRIBES.

    IN RE APPLICATION FOR ENROLLMENT, as a citizen of the   Choctaw   Nation, of Dawie Ophelie Lane   , born on the 8 day of Feb , 1903

Name of Father: J. P. Lane   a citizen of the   U.S.   Nation.
Name of Mother: Allie Lane   a citizen of the   Choctaw   Nation.

        Postoffice   Chant, I.T.

Applications for Enrollment of Choctaw Newborn
Act of 1905   Volume III

AFFIDAVIT OF MOTHER.

UNITED STATES OF AMERICA, Indian Territory, ⎱
Central   DISTRICT.   ⎰

    I,   Allie Lane   , on oath state that I am   29   years of age and a citizen by Blood   , of the   Choctaw   Nation; that I am the lawful wife of   J. P. Lane   , who is a citizen, ~~by~~   of the U.S. of the ——— Nation; that a   Fehmale[sic]   child was born to me on   8th   day of   February   , 1903, that said child has been named Dawie Ophelie Lane, and is now living.

                                    Allie Lane

Witnesses To Mark:
  ⎰ A Lauderman
  ⎱ H Swanson

    Subscribed and sworn to before me this   26th   day of   Dec   , 1904.

                                Jos A Rogers
                                Notary Public.

AFFIDAVIT OF ATTENDING PHYSICIAN OR MID-WIFE.

UNITED STATES OF AMERICA, Indian Territory, ⎱
Central   DISTRICT.   ⎰

    I,   Susan Vaughan   , a   Midwife   , on oath state that I attended on Mrs.   Allie Lane   , wife of   J.P. Lane   on the   8th   day of February , 1903; that there was born to her on said date a   Female   child; that said child is now living and is said to have been named Dawie Ophelie Lane

                                Susie Vaughan

Witnesses To Mark:
  ⎰ A Lauderman
  ⎱ H Swanson

    Subscribed and sworn to before me this   26th   day of   Dec   , 1904.

                                Jos A Rogers
                                Notary Public.

Applications for Enrollment of Choctaw Newborn
Act of 1905   Volume III

NEW-BORN AFFIDAVIT.

Number ....

...Choctaw Enrolling Commission...

IN THE MATTER OF THE APPLICATION FOR ENROLLMENT, as a citizen of the Choctaw Nation, of Dawie Ophelie Lane

born on the 8 day of February 190 3

Name of father   J. P. Lane   a citizen of   white
Nation final enrollment No. _____
Name of mother   Allie Lane   a citizen of   Choctaw
Nation final enrollment No. 7204

Postoffice   Stigler Ind Ter

AFFIDAVIT OF MOTHER.

UNITED STATES OF AMERICA
INDIAN TERRITORY
Central   DISTRICT

I   Allie Lane   , on oath state that I am 29 years of age and a citizen by Blood of the Choctaw Nation, and as such have been placed upon the final roll of the Choctaw Nation, by the Honorable Secretary of the Interior my final enrollment number being 7204 ; that I am the lawful wife of   J P Lane   , who is a citizen of the White Nation, and as such has been placed upon the final roll of said Nation by the Honorable Secretary of the Interior, his final enrollment number being _____ and that a Female child was born to me on the 8 day of Feb 190 3 ; that said child has been named   Dawie Ophelie Lane   , and is now living.

Witnesseth.   Allie Lane

Must be two Witnesses who are Citizens.
J S Stigler
Henry Cooper

Subscribed and sworn to before me this 5 day of Jan 190 5

G. A. Holley
Notary Public.

My commission expires: Nov. 7, 1907.

Applications for Enrollment of Choctaw Newborn
Act of 1905   Volume III

AFFIDAVIT OF ATTENDING PHYSICIAN OR MIDWIFE

UNITED STATES OF AMERICA
INDIAN TERRITORY
  Central   DISTRICT

I, Susie Vaughan   a   Midwife on oath state that I attended on Mrs. Allie Lane   wife of   J P Lane on the 8 day of Feb , 190 3 , that there was born to her on said date a Female child, that said child is now living, and is said to have been named   Dawie Ophelie Lane

Susie Vaughan

Subscribed and sworn to before me this, the   21st day of Jan   190 5

(Name Illegible)

Notary Public.

WITNESSETH:
Must be two witnesses who are citizens { H Brown
Eliza Brown

We hereby certify that we are well acquainted with   Susie Vaughan   a midwife   and know   her   to be reputable and of good standing in the community.

H Brown   Chas W. *(Illegible)*

Eliza Brown

BIRTH AFFIDAVIT.

DEPARTMENT OF THE INTERIOR.
COMMISSION TO THE FIVE CIVILIZED TRIBES.

IN RE APPLICATION FOR ENROLLMENT, as a citizen of the   Choctaw   Nation, of Dawie Ophelie Lane   , born on the 8th day of February , 1903

Name of Father: J. P. Lane   a citizen of the   U. S.   Nation.
Name of Mother: Allie Lane   a citizen of the   Choctaw   Nation.

Postoffice   Chant Ind Ter

AFFIDAVIT OF MOTHER.

UNITED STATES OF AMERICA, Indian Territory,
  Central   DISTRICT.

I, Allie Lane , on oath state that I am   29   years of age and a citizen by blood , of the   Choctaw   Nation; that I am the lawful wife of   J. P. Lane   ,

Applications for Enrollment of Choctaw Newborn
Act of 1905   Volume III

who is a citizen, ~~by~~ ——— of the United States   Nation; that a   female   child was born to me on   8th   day of   February   , 1903; that said child has been named Dawie Ophelie Lane   , and was living March 4, 1905.

Allie Lane

Witnesses To Mark:
{

    Subscribed and sworn to before me this 26   day of   June   , 1905

E M (Illegible)
Notary Public.

    My commission expires Oct. 10, 1908

AFFIDAVIT OF ATTENDING PHYSICIAN OR MID-WIFE.

UNITED STATES OF AMERICA, Indian Territory, ⎫
    Central   DISTRICT. ⎬

    I,   Susie Vaughan   , a   Mid Wife   , on oath state that I attended on Mrs. Allie Lane   , wife of   J P Lane   on the 8th   day of   February   , 1903; that there was born to her on said date a   female   child; that said child was living March 4, 1905, and is said to have been named Dawie Ophelie Lane

Susie Vaughan

Witnesses To Mark:
{

    Subscribed and sworn to before me this 22nd   day of   June   , 1905

Stewart F Green
Notary Public.

Choctaw 2483

Muskogee, Indian Territory, December 28, 1904.

Allie Lane,
    Chant, Indian Territory.

Dear Madam:

    Receipt is hereby acknowledged of your affidavit and the affidavit of Susie Vaughan to the birth of Damie[sic] Ophelie Lane, infant daughter of Allie and J. P. Lane,

Applications for Enrollment of Choctaw Newborn
Act of 1905 Volume III

February 8, 1903, which it is presumed have been forwarded as an application for enrollment of the above named child.

You are advised that under the provisions of the act of Congress approved July 1, 1902, no child born to a recognized and enrolled citizen of the Choctaw or Chickasaw Nation subsequent to September 25, 1902, the date of the final ratification is entitled to enrollmen[sic] and allotment.

Respectfully,

Chairman.

N. B. 147

Muskogee, Indian Territory, April 5, 1905.

J. P. Lane,
    Chant, Indian Territory.

Dear Sir:

There is inclosed you herewith for execution application for the enrollment of your infant child, Dannie[sic] Ophelie Lane, born February 8, 1903.

The affidavits heretofore filed with the Commission show the child was living on December 26, 1904. It is necessary, for the child to be enrolled, that she was living on March 4, 1905. You will please insert the age of the mother in space provided for the purpose.

In having these affidavits executed care should be exercised to see that all names are written in full, as they appear in the body of the affidavit, and in the event that either of the persons signing the affidavit are unable to write, signatures by mark must be attested by two witnesses. Each affidavit must be executed before a Notary Public and the notarial seal and signature of the officer must be attached to each separate affidavit.

Respectfully,
Commissioner in Charge.

LM 5-5

Applications for Enrollment of Choctaw Newborn
Act of 1905   Volume III

7-N.B. 147.

Muskogee, Indian Territory, May 11, 1905.

J. P. Lane,
    Chant, Indian Territory.

Dear Sir:

There is enclosed you herewith for execution application for the enrollment of your infant child, Damie[sic] Ophelia[sic] Lane, born February 8, 1903.

Your attention is called to the Commission's letter of the 5th ultimo, in which is enclosed application similar to the one above mentioned, to which you have failed to reply.

Before this matter can be finally disposed of it will be necessary for you to file these affidavits with the Commission.

In having these affidavits executed care should be exercised to see that all names are written in full, as they appear in the body of the affidavit, and in the event that either of the persons signing the affidavit are unable to write, signatures by mark must be attested by two witnesses. Each affidavit must be executed before a Notary Public and the notarial seal and signature of the officer must be attached to each separate affidavit.

                Respectfully,

(End of letter.)

Choctaw NB 147

Muskogee, Indian Territory, June 28, 1905.

J. P. Lane,
    Stigler, Indian Territory.

Dear Sir:

Receipt is hereby acknowledged of your letter of June 26 transmitting affidavits of Allie Lane and Susie Vaughan to the birth of Dawie Ophelie Lane, daughter of J. P. and Allie Lane, February 8, 1903, and the same have been filed with our records in the matter of the enrollment of said child.

                Respectfully,

                        Chairman.

Applications for Enrollment of Choctaw Newborn
Act of 1905   Volume III

Muskogee, Indian Territory, July 25, 1905.

Chief Clerk,
    Choctaw Land Office,
        Atoka, Indian Territory.

Dear Sir:

    Refer to duplicate Choctaw New Born Roll Card No. 147, in the possession of your office and change the given name of applicant thereon to read, "Dawie Ophelie Lane" instead of "Damie Ophelie Lane."

        Respectfully,

                Commissioner.

Muskogee, Indian Territory, July 25, 1905.

Chief Clerk,
    Chickasaw Land Office,
        Ardmore, Indian Territory.

Dear Sir:

    Refer to duplicate Choctaw New Born Roll Card No. 147, in the possession of your office and change the given name of applicant thereon to read, "Dawie Ophelie Lane" instead of "Damie Ophelie Lane."

        Respectfully,

                Commissioner.

Applications for Enrollment of Choctaw Newborn
Act of 1905   Volume III

Choc New Born 148
    Herbert Luce
    (Born Nov. 21, 1902)
    Lester Luce
    (Born July 20, 1904)

BIRTH AFFIDAVIT.

DEPARTMENT OF THE INTERIOR,
COMMISSION TO THE FIVE CIVILIZED TRIBES.

In Re Application for Enrollment, as a citizen of the Choctaw Nation, of Herbert Luce, born on the 21st day of Nov, 1902

Name of Father: Thos Luce   a citizen of the Choctaw Nation.
Name of Mother: Saline Luce   a citizen of the Choctaw Nation.

Post-office   Iron Bridge, I.T.

AFFIDAVIT OF MOTHER.

UNITED STATES OF AMERICA,
    INDIAN TERRITORY,
    Central   District.

    I, Saline Luce, on oath state that I am 26 years of age and a citizen by Blood, of the Choctaw Nation; that I am the lawful wife of Thos Luce, who is a citizen, by Blood of the Choctaw Nation; that a Male child was born to me on 21st day of Nov, 1902, that said child has been named Herbert Luce, and is now living.

                          Selina[sic] Luce

WITNESSES TO MARK:

    Subscribed and sworn to before me this 18 day of Dec, 1905.

                          M. W. Newman
                              NOTARY PUBLIC.

Applications for Enrollment of Choctaw Newborn
Act of 1905   Volume III

AFFIDAVIT OF ATTENDING PHYSICIAN OR MID-WIFE.

UNITED STATES OF AMERICA,
INDIAN TERRITORY,
Central   District.

I, Swkey[sic] Whistler   , a Midwife   , on oath state that I attended on Mrs. Saline Luce , wife of   Thos Luce on the 21st day of November , 1902; that there was born to her on said date a   Male   child; that said child is now living and is said to have been named Herbert Luce

                                 her
                         Swkey x Whistler
WITNESSES TO MARK: mark
   Austin Chubber
   Noel Leflore

Subscribed and sworn to before me this   18   day of   Dec , 1905.

                             M. W. Newman
                                   NOTARY PUBLIC.

NEW-BORN AFFIDAVIT.

             Number............

...Choctaw Enrolling Commission...

IN THE MATTER OF THE APPLICATION FOR ENROLLMENT, as a citizen of the Choctaw   Nation, of   Herbert Luce

born on the 21   day of   Nov   190 2

Name of father   Thos Luce   a citizen of   Choctaw
Nation final enrollment No. 7373
Name of mother   Selina Luce   a citizen of   Choctaw
Nation final enrollment No.   7272

                         Postoffice   Iron Bridge I T

Applications for Enrollment of Choctaw Newborn
Act of 1905 Volume III

AFFIDAVIT OF MOTHER.

UNITED STATES OF AMERICA
INDIAN TERRITORY
Central   DISTRICT

I   Selina Luce   , on oath state that I am 29 years of age and a citizen by   Blood   of the   Choctaw Nation, and as such have been placed upon the final roll of the Choctaw Nation, by the Honorable Secretary of the Interior my final enrollment number being   7272 ; that I am the lawful wife of   Thomas Luce   , who is a citizen of the   Choctaw Nation, and as such has been placed upon the final roll of said Nation by the Honorable Secretary of the Interior, his final enrollment number being   7373   and that a Male   child was born to me on the   21st day of   November   190 2 ; that said child has been named   Herbert Luce   , and is now living.

Witnesseth.   Selina Luce

Must be two Witnesses who are Citizens.   Mitchell Weston
Sarah Weston

Subscribed and sworn to before me this   6   day of   Feb   190 5

M. W. Newman
Notary Public.

My commission expires:

AFFIDAVIT OF ATTENDING PHYSICIAN OR MIDWIFE

UNITED STATES OF AMERICA
INDIAN TERRITORY
Central   DISTRICT

I,   Thos Luce   a _____
on oath state that I attended on Mrs.   Selina Luce   My wife of (Mrs Swkey Whistler who is dead being the only one present at the time) on the   21st day of   November , 190 2, that there was born to her on said date a   Male   child, that said child is now living, and is said to have been named   Herbert Luce

Thomas Luce   ~~M.D.~~

WITNESSETH:

Must be two witnesses who are citizens and know the child.   Mitchell Weston
Sarah Weston

Subscribed and sworn to before me this, the   6th day of   November   190 5

M W Newman   Notary Public.

Applications for Enrollment of Choctaw Newborn
Act of 1905 Volume III

We hereby certify that we are well acquainted with _____
a   Thos Luce[sic]   and know   him   to be reputable and of good standing in the community.

$\left\{\begin{array}{l}\text{Mitchell Weston}\\ \text{Sarah Weston}\end{array}\right.$

BIRTH AFFIDAVIT.

DEPARTMENT OF THE INTERIOR.
COMMISSION TO THE FIVE CIVILIZED TRIBES.

IN RE APPLICATION FOR ENROLLMENT, as a citizen of the   Choctaw   Nation, of Herbert Luce   , born on the 21st day of Nov   , 1902

Name of Father: Thos Luce   a citizen of the   Choctaw   Nation.
Name of Mother: Selina Luce   a citizen of the   Choctaw   Nation.

Postoffice   Iron Bridge I.T.

AFFIDAVIT OF MOTHER.

UNITED STATES OF AMERICA, Indian Territory, ⎫
Central   DISTRICT. ⎭

I,   Selina Luce   , on oath state that I am 29   years of age and a citizen by Blood   , of the   Choctaw   Nation; that I am the lawful wife of   Thos Luce   , who is a citizen, by Blood   of the   Choctaw   Nation; that a   Male   child was born to me on 21st day of   Nov   , 1902; that said child has been named Herbert Luce   , and was living March 4, 1905.

Selina Luce

Witnesses To Mark:
$\left\{\begin{array}{l}\text{Mitchell Weston}\\ \text{Sarah Weston}\end{array}\right.$

Subscribed and sworn to before me this 29" day of   March   , 1905

M. W. Newman
Notary Public.

Applications for Enrollment of Choctaw Newborn
Act of 1905   Volume III

AFFIDAVIT OF ATTENDING PHYSICIAN OR MID-WIFE.

UNITED STATES OF AMERICA, Indian Territory,
Central   DISTRICT.

    I,   Thos Luce   , a ...., on oath state that I attended on Mrs. Selina Luce   my , wife of .... on the 21st day of Nov , 1902; that there was born to her on said date a   Male   child; that said child was living March 4, 1905, and is said to have been named   Herbert Luce

                                        his
                               Thos x Luce
Witnesses To Mark: mark
  { Mitchell Weston
    Sarah Weston

    Subscribed and sworn to before me this 29" day of   March   , 1905

                            M. W. Newman
                                Notary Public.

BIRTH AFFIDAVIT.

DEPARTMENT OF THE INTERIOR.
COMMISSION TO THE FIVE CIVILIZED TRIBES.

    IN RE APPLICATION FOR ENROLLMENT, as a citizen of the   Choctaw   Nation, of Herbert Luce   , born on the 21" day of Nov , 1902

Name of Father: Thos Luce   a citizen of the   Choctaw   Nation.
Name of Mother: Selina Luce   a citizen of the   Choctaw   Nation.

                Postoffice   Iron Bridge I.T.

AFFIDAVIT OF MOTHER.

UNITED STATES OF AMERICA, Indian Territory,
Central   DISTRICT.

    I,   Selina Luce   , on oath state that I am   29   years of age and a citizen by blood   , of the   Choctaw   Nation; that I am the lawful wife of   Thos Luce   , who is a citizen, by blood   of the   Choctaw   Nation; that a   male   child was born to me on 21" day of   Nov   , 1902; that said child has been named Herbert Luce   , and was living March 4, 1905.

                              Selina Luce

Applications for Enrollment of Choctaw Newborn
Act of 1905   Volume III

Witnesses To Mark:
- Nicodemus King
- Mitchell Weston

Subscribed and sworn to before me this 15th day of   April   , 1905

M. W. Newman
Notary Public.

AFFIDAVIT OF ATTENDING PHYSICIAN OR MID-WIFE.

UNITED STATES OF AMERICA, Indian Territory,
Central DISTRICT.

I,   Thomas Luce   , a ...., on oath state that I attended on Mrs. Selina Luce   , wife of   Thos Luce   on the   21" day of   Nov   , 1902; that there was born to her on said date a   male   child; that said child was living March 4, 1905, and is said to have been named   Herbert Luce

his
Thos x Luce
mark

Witnesses To Mark:
- Nicodemus King
- Mitchell Weston

Subscribed and sworn to before me this 15th day of   April   , 1905

M. W. Newman
Notary Public.

My Com Expires Jan the 17" 1907

BIRTH AFFIDAVIT.

DEPARTMENT OF THE INTERIOR,
COMMISSION TO THE FIVE CIVILIZED TRIBES.

IN RE Application for Enrollment, as a citizen of the   Choctaw   Nation, of Lester Luce   , born on the   20"   day of   July   , 1904

Name of Father: Thomas Luce   a citizen of the   Choctaw   Nation.
Name of Mother: Saline Luce   a citizen of the   Choctaw   Nation.

Post-office   Iron Bridge, I.T.

Applications for Enrollment of Choctaw Newborn
Act of 1905   Volume III

AFFIDAVIT OF MOTHER.

UNITED STATES OF AMERICA, }
   INDIAN TERRITORY,
   Central   District.

    I, Seline Luce, on oath state that I am 27 years of age and a citizen by Blood, of the Choctaw Nation; that I am the lawful wife of Thomas Luce, who is a citizen, by Blood of the Choctaw Nation; that a Male child was born to me on 20th day of July, 1904, that said child has been named Lester Luce, and is now living.

                                Selina Luce

WITNESSES TO MARK:

    Subscribed and sworn to before me this 23rd day of Sept, 1904

                                M. W. Newman
                                  NOTARY PUBLIC.

AFFIDAVIT OF ATTENDING PHYSICIAN OR MID-WIFE.

UNITED STATES OF AMERICA, }
   INDIAN TERRITORY,
   Central   District.

    I, Martha McGilbery, a Midwife, on oath state that I attended on Mrs. Seline Luce, wife of Thos Luce on the 20th day of July, 1904; that there was born to her on said date a Male child; that said child is now living and is said to have been named Lester Luce

                                her
                          Martha x McGilbery

WITNESSES TO MARK: mark
    Nicodemus King
    James Isaac

    Subscribed and sworn to before me this 23rd day of Sept, 1904

                                M. W. Newman
                                  NOTARY PUBLIC.

Applications for Enrollment of Choctaw Newborn
Act of 1905 Volume III

NEW-BORN AFFIDAVIT.

Number...............

...Choctaw Enrolling Commission...

IN THE MATTER OF THE APPLICATION FOR ENROLLMENT, as a citizen of the Choctaw Nation, of Lester Luce

born on the 20 day of July 190 4

Name of father Tom Luce a citizen of Choctaw Nation final enrollment No. 7373
Name of mother Selina Luce a citizen of Choctaw Nation final enrollment No. 7272

Postoffice Ironbridge I.T.

AFFIDAVIT OF MOTHER.

UNITED STATES OF AMERICA
INDIAN TERRITORY
Central DISTRICT

I Selina Luce, on oath state that I am 29 years of age and a citizen by Blood of the Choctaw Nation, and as such have been placed upon the final roll of the Choctaw Nation, by the Honorable Secretary of the Interior my final enrollment number being 7272 ; that I am the lawful wife of Tom Luce, who is a citizen of the Choctaw Nation, and as such has been placed upon the final roll of said Nation by the Honorable Secretary of the Interior, his final enrollment number being 7373 and that a Male child was born to me on the 20 day of July 190 4 ; that said child has been named Lester Luce, and is now living.

Witnesseth.   Selina Luce
Must be two ⎫ Stephen Perry
Witnesses who⎬
are Citizens. ⎭ Dan Perry

Subscribed and sworn to before me this 1 day of feb[sic] 190 5

David W. Brown
Notary Public.

My commission expires: Feb 24/06

Applications for Enrollment of Choctaw Newborn
Act of 1905 Volume III

AFFIDAVIT OF ATTENDING PHYSICIAN OR MIDWIFE

UNITED STATES OF AMERICA
INDIAN TERRITORY
Central   DISTRICT

I, Martha McGillbrey[sic]   a   Midwife on oath state that I attended on Mrs. Selina Luce   wife of   Tom Luce on the 20 day of July, 190 4, that there was born to her on said date a   Male   child, that said child is now living, and is said to have been named   Lester Luce

her
Martha M^c x Gillberry[sic]
mark

Subscribed and sworn to before me this, the   1   day of Feb   1905

David W. Brown   Notary Public.

WITNESSETH:
Must be two witnesses who are citizens { Dan Perry
David Scott

We hereby certify that we are well acquainted with   Martha McGillberry a   Midwife   and know   her   to be reputable and of good standing in the community.

_____   Jack Jackson

_____   Jackson Burns

United States of America }   Mary Leflore being
Ind Tery Central Dist   }   sworn state on oath that

I am 26 years of age. That I am a citizen by Blood of the Choctaw Nation That I have personal knowledge of the children of Thos and Selina Luce To Wit:
Herbert and Lester born on Nov the 21st of Nov 1902 and July the 20th 1904. That they are the children of Selina Luce who is a citizen by Blood of the Choctaw Nation and that said children are now liveing[sic].

Mary Leflore

Sworn to and subscribed before me this the 25th day of April 1905

M. W. Newman
Notary Public.

Applications for Enrollment of Choctaw Newborn
Act of 1905   Volume III

United States of America } Noel Leflore after
Ind Tery Central Dist } being duly sworn

State on oath that I am 23 years of age that I am a citizen by Blood of the Choctaw Nation That I have personal knowledge of the children of Thos and Selina Luce to wit: Herbert and Lester, born on Nov the 21st 1902, and July the 20th 1904, That they are the children of Selina Luce who is a citizen by blood of the Choctaw and that said children are now liveing[sic].

Noel Leflore

Sworn to and subscribed before me this the 25th day of April 1905.

M W Newman
Notary Public.

BIRTH AFFIDAVIT.

DEPARTMENT OF THE INTERIOR.
COMMISSION TO THE FIVE CIVILIZED TRIBES.

IN RE APPLICATION FOR ENROLLMENT, as a citizen of the   Choctaw   Nation, of Lester Luce   , born on the 20th day of July   , 1904

Name of Father: Thos Luce   a citizen of the   Choctaw   Nation.
Name of Mother: Selina Luce   a citizen of the   Choctaw   Nation.

Postoffice   Iron Bridge I.T.

AFFIDAVIT OF MOTHER.

UNITED STATES OF AMERICA, Indian Territory, }
Central   DISTRICT. }

    I,   Selina Luce   , on oath state that I am 29   years of age and a citizen by Blood   , of the   Choctaw   Nation; that I am the lawful wife of   Thos Luce   , who is a citizen, by Blood   of the   Choctaw   Nation; that a   Male   child was born to me on 20th day of   July   , 1904; that said child has been named   Lester Luce   , and was living March 4, 1905.

Selina Luce

Witnesses To Mark:
  { Mitchell Weston
    Sarah Weston

Applications for Enrollment of Choctaw Newborn
Act of 1905   Volume III

Subscribed and sworn to before me this 29" day of March , 1905

M. W. Newman
Notary Public.

AFFIDAVIT OF ATTENDING PHYSICIAN OR MID-WIFE.

UNITED STATES OF AMERICA, Indian Territory,
Central DISTRICT.

I, Thos Luce , a ...., on oath state that I attended on Mrs. Selina Luce   my , wife of .... on the 20" day of July, 1905[sic]; that there was born to her on said date a Male child; that said child was living March 4, 1905, and is said to have been named Lester Luce

his
Thos x Luce
mark

Witnesses To Mark:
{ Mitchell Weston
Sarah Weston

Subscribed and sworn to before me this 29" day of March , 1905

M. W. Newman
Notary Public.

BIRTH AFFIDAVIT.

DEPARTMENT OF THE INTERIOR.
COMMISSION TO THE FIVE CIVILIZED TRIBES.

IN RE APPLICATION FOR ENROLLMENT, as a citizen of the   Choctaw   Nation, of Lester Luce , born on the 20" day of July , 1904

Name of Father: Thomas Luce   a citizen of the   Choctaw   Nation.
Name of Mother: Selina Luce   a citizen of the   Choctaw   Nation.

Postoffice   Iron Bridge I.T.

Applications for Enrollment of Choctaw Newborn
Act of 1905   Volume III

AFFIDAVIT OF MOTHER.

UNITED STATES OF AMERICA, Indian Territory, ⎫
    Central   DISTRICT. ⎬

    I, Selina Luce, on oath state that I am 29 years of age and a citizen by blood, of the Choctaw Nation; that I am the lawful wife of Thomas Luce, who is a citizen, by blood of the Choctaw Nation; that a male child was born to me on 20" day of July, 1904; that said child has been named Lester Luce, and was living March 4, 1905.

                                      Selina Luce

Witnesses To Mark:
   { Nicodemus King
     Mitchell Weston

    Subscribed and sworn to before me this 15th day of April, 1905

                                      M. W. Newman
                                      Notary Public.

AFFIDAVIT OF ATTENDING PHYSICIAN OR MID-WIFE.

UNITED STATES OF AMERICA, Indian Territory, ⎫
    Central   DISTRICT. ⎬

    I, Thomas Luce, a ...., on oath state that I attended on Mrs. Selina Luce, wife of Thomas Luce on the 20" day of July, 1904; that there was born to her on said date a male child; that said child was living March 4, 1905, and is said to have been named Lester Luce

                                          his
                               Thomas x Luce
                                    mark

Witnesses To Mark:
   { Nicodemus King
     Mitchell Weston

    Subscribed and sworn to before me this 15th day of April, 1905

                                      M. W. Newman
                                      Notary Public.

My Com Expires Jan the 17" 1907

Applications for Enrollment of Choctaw Newborn
Act of 1905   Volume III

7-2489
7-2540

Muskogee, Indian Territory, December 29, 1902.

Thomas Luce,
    Ironbridge, Indian Territory.

Dear Sir:

    Receipt is hereby acknowledged of the application for enrollment as a citizen of the Choctaw Nation of Herbert Luce, infant son of Thomas and Salina Luce, born November 21, 1902.

    You are advised that the Commission is without authority to enroll the child as a citizen of the Choctaw Nation, it appearing that said child was born November 21, 1902, subsequent to the ratification by the citizens of the Choctaw and Chickasaw Nations September 25, 1902, of an act of Congress, approved July 1, 1902, approved July 1, 1902 (32 Stats., 641).

    Section twenty-eight thereof provides as follows:

    "The names of all persons living on the date of the final ratification of this agreement entitled to be enrolled as provided in section 27 hereof shall be placed upon the rolls made by said Commission; and no child born thereafter to a citizen or freedman and no person intermarried thereafter to a citizen shall be entitled to enrollment or to participate in the distribution of the tribal property of the Choctaws and Chickasaws."

Respectfully,

Acting Chairman.

7-2489
7-2540

Muskogee, Indian Territory, *(Date illegible)*.

M. W. Newman,
    Iron Bridge, Indian Territory.

Dear Sir:

    Receipt is hereby acknowledged of your letter of the 2nd instant, requesting to be advised whether the infant child of Tom and Selina Luce, born November 1[sic], 1902, has been enrolled as a citizen of the Choctaw Nation.

Applications for Enrollment of Choctaw Newborn
Act of 1905   Volume III

Your attention is invited to Section 28 of the Act of Congress approved July 1, 1902 (32 Stats. 641), which is as follows:

"The names of all persons living on the date of the final ratification of this agreement entitled to be enrolled as provided in section 27 hereof shall be placed upon the rolls made by said Commission; and no child born thereafter to a citizen or freedman and no person intermarried thereafter to a citizen shall be entitled to enrollment or to participate in the distribution of the tribal property of the Choctaws and Chickasaws."

Under the above legislation the Commission has no authority to enroll children born subsequent to the ratification of the above act of Congress by the citizens of the Choctaw and Chickasaw Nations September 25, 1902.

Respectfully,

Commissioner in Charge.

7-2540

Muskogee, Indian Territory, September 29, 1904.

Thomas Luce,
Ironbridge, Indian Territory.

Dear Sir:-

Receipt is hereby acknowledged of the affidavits of Salina Luce and Martha McGilbrey relative to the birth of your infant son Lester Luce July 20, 1904, which it is presumed have been forwarded to this office as an application for enrollment of said child as a citizen by blood of the Choctaw Nation.

The act of Congress approved July 1, 1902, which was ratified by the citizens of the Choctaw and Chickasaw Nations September 25, 1902, among other things provides that no child born to a citizen of the Choctaw or Chickasaw Nation subsequent to the date of said ratification shall be entitled to enrollment or to participate in the distribution of the tribal property of the Choctaws and Chickasaws.

Respectfully,

Chairman.

Applications for Enrollment of Choctaw Newborn
Act of 1905   Volume III

Choctaw 2540

Muskogee, Indian Territory, April 3, 1905.

Thomas Luce,
    Ironbridge, Indian Territory.

Dear Sir:

    Receipt is hereby acknowledged of the affidavits of Salina Luce and Thomas Luce to the birth of Herbert Luce and Lester Luce, children of Thomas and Salina Luce, November 21, 1902, and July 20, 1905, respectively.

    As there is an evident error in the date of the birth of Lester Luce there is enclosed herewith for your convenience another blank for the enrollment of said child, which you are requested to have executed showing the correct date of his birth, and have the same returned to this office within sixty days from March 3, 1905.

Respectfully,

B.C.   Chairman.

COPY   N. B. 148

Muskogee, Indian Territory, April 5, 1905.

Thos. Luce,
    Ironbridge, Indian Territory.

Dear Sir:

    There is inclosed you herewith for execution application for the enrollment of your infant children, Herbert Luce and Lester Luce, born November 21, 1902 and July 20, 1904, respectively.

    The affidavits heretofore filed with the Commission were of the mother only. You will notice from the inclosed application that the affidavit of the physician or midwife is also required. You will please insert the age of the mother in the space provided for the purpose.

    In having these affidavits executed care should be exercised to see that all names are written in full, as they appear in the body of the affidavit, and in the event that either of the persons signing the affidavit are unable to write, signatures by mark must be attested by two witnesses. Each affidavit must be executed before a Notary Public and the notarial seal and signature of the officer must be attached to each separate affidavit.

Applications for Enrollment of Choctaw Newborn
Act of 1905 Volume III

LM 5-4

Respectfully,
SIGNED
T. B. Needles.
Commissioner in Charge.

COPY Choctaw N.B. 148.

Muskogee, Indian Territory, April 21, 1905.

Thomas Luce,
    Ironbridge, Indian Territory.

Dear Sir:

    Receipt is hereby acknowledged of the affidavits of Selina Luce and Thomas Luce to the birth of Herbert Luce and Lester Luce, sons of Selina and Thomas Luce, November 21, 1902, and July 20, 1904, respectively.

    It appears you have filled out the affidavits of the physician or midwife in both applications, and you are advised that if there was no physician or midwife in attendance it will be necessary for you to forward the affidavits of two disinterested persons who know of the birth of these children, that they are the children of your wife, Selina Luce, and that they are still living.

    This matter should receive your immediate attention.

Respectfully,
SIGNED
Tams Bixby
Chairman.

COPY Choctaw N B 148.

Muskogee, Indian Territory, April 29, 1905.

Thomas Luce,
    Iron Bridge, Indian Territory.

Dear Sir:

    Receipt is hereby acknowledged of the affidavits of Mary Leflore and Noel Leflore to the birth of your children, Herbert an Lester Luce, November 22[sic], 1902, and July 20, 1904, respectively, and the same have been filed with the records in the matter of the enrollment of the above named children.

Applications for Enrollment of Choctaw Newborn
Act of 1905 Volume III

Respectfully,
SIGNED
Tams Bixby
Chairman.

Choc New Born 149
    Floy May Hill
    (Born Dec. 18, 1902)

BIRTH AFFIDAVIT.

DEPARTMENT OF THE INTERIOR,
COMMISSION TO THE FIVE CIVILIZED TRIBES.

In Re Application for Enrollment, as a citizen of the Choctaw Nation, of Floy May Hill, born on the 18 day of December, 1902

Name of Father: Jeff W Hill   a citizen of the Choctaw Nation.
Name of Mother: Jennie Hill   a citizen of the Choctaw Nation.

Post-Office :   Massey, Ind. Ter.

AFFIDAVIT OF MOTHER.

UNITED STATES OF AMERICA, }
  INDIAN TERRITORY,
  Western   District.

I, Jennie Hill, on oath state that I am twenty years of age and a citizen by blood, of the Choctaw Nation; that I am the lawful wife of Jeff W Hill, who is a citizen, by marriage of the Choctaw Nation; that a female child was born to me on the 18th day of Dec, 1902, that said child has been named Floy May Hill, and is now living.

                                          her
                                  Jennie x Hill

WITNESSES TO MARK: mark
{ SM Gold
  J H Bynum

Applications for Enrollment of Choctaw Newborn
Act of 1905 Volume III

Subscribed and sworn to before me this 9th day of May, 1903

H.T. Norman
NOTARY PUBLIC.

AFFIDAVIT OF ATTENDING PHYSICIAN OR MID-WIFE.

UNITED STATES OF AMERICA,
INDIAN TERRITORY,
....District.

I, Francis D Bush, a Physician, on oath state that I attended on Mrs. Jennie Hill, wife of Jeff W Hill on the 18 day of December, 190 2; that there was born to her on said date a Female child; that said child is now living and is said to have been named Floy May

Francis D Bush, M.D.

WITNESSES TO MARK:

Subscribed and sworn to before me this 27 day of April, 1903.

Aaron H. *(Illegible)*
NOTARY PUBLIC.

BIRTH AFFIDAVIT.

DEPARTMENT OF THE INTERIOR.
COMMISSION TO THE FIVE CIVILIZED TRIBES.

IN RE APPLICATION FOR ENROLLMENT, as a citizen of the Choctaw Nation, of Floy May Hill, born on the 18 day of Dec, 1902

Name of Father: Jefferson W Hill   a citizen of the Choctaw Nation.
Name of Mother: Jennie Hill   a citizen of the Choctaw Nation.

Postoffice   Grady, I.T.

AFFIDAVIT OF MOTHER.

UNITED STATES OF AMERICA, Indian Territory,
    Southern   DISTRICT.

I, Jennie Hill, on oath state that I am 22 years of age and a citizen by Blood, of the Choctaw Nation; that I am the lawful wife of Jefferson W Hill, who is a citizen, by Inter Marriage of the Choctaw Nation; that a Female

Applications for Enrollment of Choctaw Newborn
Act of 1905   Volume III

child was born to me on 18 day of Dec   , 1902; that said child has been named Floy May Hill , and was living March 4, 1905.

            her
          Jennie x Hill
Witnesses To Mark: mark
{ Geo. M. Eakin
 A. J. Wells

  Subscribed and sworn to before me this 10 day of April   , 1905

         J. G. *(Illegible)*
           Notary Public.
  My Commission expires Nov 7-1908

AFFIDAVIT OF ATTENDING PHYSICIAN OR MID-WIFE.

UNITED STATES OF AMERICA, Indian Territory,
....DISTRICT.

  I, Francis D Bush M.D. , a Doctor of Medicine , on oath state that I attended on Mrs. Jennie Hill , wife of Jefferson W Hill on the 18 day of Dec   , 1902; that there was born to her on said date a Female   child; that said child was living March 4, 1905, and is said to have been named Floy May Hill

         F.D. Bush M.D.
Witnesses To Mark:
{

  Subscribed and sworn to before me this 25 day of April   , 1905

         A. H. Crouthamel
          Notary Public.
My Com. Ex 2-3-1907

To the Commission of the Five Civilized Tribes.
Indian Territory, SS.
Southern District.

  In re Application for enrollment as a citizen of the Choctaw Nation of Floy May Hill, born on the 18 day of December 1902.

  G.C. Wilton, M.D.   of Ryan Indian Territory,
 and J.E. Reed   of Grady Indian Territory,

Applications for Enrollment of Choctaw Newborn
Act of 1905   Volume III

of lawful age being first duly sworn upon their oaths say, that they are well acquainted with the said Floy May Hill and her father Jefferson Hill and her mother Jennie Hill, that said child was living on March 4, 1905, and that she is still living, to the knowledge of the said affiants.

G.C. Wilton, M.D.

J E Reed

Subscribed and sworn to before me this 11" day of September 1905.

C A McBrian
Notary Public.

My Com Ex May 9" 1909.

7-NB-149

Muskogee, Indian Territory, March 9, 1906.

T. L. Wright,
    Attorney at Law,
        Ardmore, Indian Territory.

Dear Sir:

    Receipt is hereby acknowledged of your letter of March 6, 1906, relative to the application for the enrollment of Floy May Hill as a new born citizen of the Choctaw Nation.

    In reply to your letter you are advised that the name of Floy May Hill has been placed upon a schedule of new born citizens of the Choctaw Nation which has been forwarded the Secretary of the Interior for approval, but this office has not yet been notified of Departmental action thereon. Mr. Hill will be advised when the enrollment of his child is approved by the Secretary of the Interior.

Respectfully,

Acting Commissioner.

Applications for Enrollment of Choctaw Newborn
Act of 1905   Volume III

N. B. 149

Muskogee, Indian Territory, April 7, 1905.

Jefferson W. Hill,
    Massey, Indian Territory.

Dear Sir:

    There is inclosed you herewith for execution application for the enrollment of your infant child, Floy May Hill, born December 18, 1902.

    The affidavits heretofore filed with the Commission show the child was living on April 27, 1903. It is necessary, for the child to be enrolled, that she was living on March 4, 1905. You will please insert the age of the mother in the space left blank for that purpose.

    In having these affidavits executed care should be exercised to see that all names are written in full, as they appear in the body of the affidavit, and in the event that either of the persons signing the affidavit are unable to write, signatures by mark must be attested by two witnesses. Each affidavit must be executed before a Notary Public and the notarial seal and signature of the officer must be attached to each separate affidavit.

    Respectfully,

LM 7-3
    Commissioner in Charge.

---

7 NB 149

Muskogee, Indian Territory, August 30, 1905.

Jefferson W. Hill,
    Grady, Indian Territory.

Dear Sir:

    Receipt is hereby acknowledged of your letter of August 23rd with reference to procuring the affidavit of the attending physician at the birth of your child, Floy May Hill, to the effect that said child was living on March 4, 1905.

    In the absence of your ability to secure the affidavit of the attending physician to this effect, this office will accept the affidavits of two reliable persons living in your neighborhood who know that Floy May Hill is the child of your wife, Jennie Hill and that the said child is now living. These affidavits should be transmitted at the earliest possible date.

Applications for Enrollment of Choctaw Newborn
Act of 1905 Volume III

Respectfully,

Commissioner.

---

7 N.B. 149.

Muskogee, Indian Territory, May 15, 1905.

Jefferson W. Hill,
    Grady, Indian Territory.

Dear Sir:

    Receipt is hereby acknowledged of your letter of May 5, enclosing affidavits of Jennie Hill and F. D. Bush to the birth of Floy May Hill, daughter of Jefferson W. and Jennie Hill, December 18, 1902, and the same have been filed with our records in the matter of the application for the enrollment of said child.

Respectfully,

Chairman.

7-NB-149

Muskogee, Indian Territory, August 2, 1905.

Jefferson W. Hill,
    Massey, Indian Territory.

Dear Sir:

    There is inclosed you herewith for execution application for the enrollment of your infant child, Floy May Hill, born December 18, 1902.

    In the affidavit of the physician of April 25, 1905, heretofore filed in this office, it is alleged that "that said child was said to be living March 4, 1905."

    You are advised that the affidavit of the attending physician must show that said child <u>was</u> living March 4, 1905. You will therefore, have the affidavit executed as prepared and return to this office immediately, as no further action can be taken relative to the enrollment of your said child until the evidence requested is supplied.

Respectfully,

LM 1/2   Commissioner

Applications for Enrollment of Choctaw Newborn
Act of 1905   Volume III

W-O.B

REFER IN REPLY TO THE FOLLOWING:

7 NB 149

DEPARTMENT OF THE INTERIOR,
COMMISSIONER TO THE FIVE CIVILIZED TRIBES.

Muskogee, Indian Territory, August 30, 1905.

Jefferson W. Hill,
    Grady, Indian Territory.

Dear Sir:--

    Receipt is hereby acknowledged of your letter of August 23rd with reference to procuring the affidavit of the attending physician at the birth of your child, Floy May Hill, to the effect that said child was living on March 4, 1905.

    In the absence of your ability to secure the affidavit of the attending physician to this effect, this office will accept the affidavits of two reliable persons living in your neighborhood who know that Floy May Hill is the child of your wife, Jennie Hill and that the said child is now living. These affidavits should be transmitted at the earliest possible date.

                        Respectfully,

                                Tams Bixby
                                Commissioner.

7-NB-149.

Muskogee, Indian Territory, September 18, 1905.

Jefferson W. Hill,
    Grady, Indian Territory.

Dear Sir:

    Receipt is hereby acknowledged of your letter of the 11th instant transmitting the joint affidavit of G. C. Milton[sic] and J. E. Reid to the effect that your minor daughter Floy May Hill was living on March 4, 1905 and is still living. Said affidavit has been filed with the record in the matter of the application for the enrollment of said child as a citizen by blood of the Choctaw Nation.

    As soon as the enrollment of said child is approved by the Secretary of the Interior you will be notified.

Applications for Enrollment of Choctaw Newborn
Act of 1905 Volume III

Respectfully,

Acting Commissioner.

7-NB-149

Muskogee, Indian Territory, November 25, 1905.

Jefferson W. Hill,
    Grady, Indian Territory.

Dear Sir:

Receipt is hereby acknowledged of your letter of November 21, 1905, asking why your child Floy May Hill has not yet been approved.

In reply to your letter you are advised that the name of your child Floy May Hill has not yet been placed upon a schedule of new born citizens of the Choctaw Nation prepared for forwarding to the Secretary of the Interior, but you will be advised when his enrollment is approved by the Department.

Respectfully,

Acting Commissioner.

7-NB-149

Muskogee, Indian Territory, February 7, 1906.

Jeff W. Hill,
    Grady, Indian Territory.

Dear Sir:

Receipt is hereby acknowledged of your letter of January 31, 1906, asking why the enrollment of your child Floy May Hill has not been approved.

In reply to your letter you are advised that the name of your child Floy May Hill has been placed upon a schedule of new born citizens of the Choctaw Nation which has been forwarded the Secretary of the Interior and you will be notified when her enrollment is approved by the Department.

Respectfully,

Acting Commissioner.

Applications for Enrollment of Choctaw Newborn
Act of 1905   Volume III

Choc New Born 150
    Theodore Claton[sic] Allen
    (Born Aug 8, 1904)

BIRTH AFFIDAVIT.

DEPARTMENT OF THE INTERIOR.
COMMISSION TO THE FIVE CIVILIZED TRIBES.

IN RE APPLICATION FOR ENROLLMENT, as a citizen of the   Choctaw   Nation, of Theodore Claton   , born on the   8   day of   Aug   , 1902

Name of Father: Andy Allen   a citizen of the   Choctaw   Nation.
Name of Mother: Kate Allen   a citizen of the   Choctaw   Nation.

    Postoffice   Purdy, Ind. Ter.

AFFIDAVIT OF MOTHER.

UNITED STATES OF AMERICA, Indian Territory, ⎫
    Southern   DISTRICT. ⎭

    26

    I,   Kate Allen   , on oath state that I am   the mother   years of age and a citizen by   blood   , of the   Choctaw   Nation; that I am the lawful wife of   Andrew J. Allen   , who is a citizen, by   marriage   of the   Choctaw   Nation; that a male   child was born to me on   8   day of   Aug   , 1904, that said child has been named   Theodore Claton   , and is now living.

    Kate Allen

Witnesses To Mark:
{

    Subscribed and sworn to before me this   19   day of   Jan   , 1905.

    V Smith
    Notary Public.

AFFIDAVIT OF ATTENDING PHYSICIAN OR MID-WIFE.

UNITED STATES OF AMERICA, Indian Territory, ⎫
    Southern   DISTRICT. ⎭

    I,   Jas W. Tucker   , a   Physician   , on oath state that I attended on Mrs.   Katie Allen   , wife of   Andy Allen   on the   8   day of Aug , 1904; that

Applications for Enrollment of Choctaw Newborn
Act of 1905   Volume III

there was born to her on said date a male child; that said child is now living and is said to have been named Theodore Clayton[sic]

Jas. W. Tucker M.D.

Witnesses To Mark:
{

Subscribed and sworn to before me this 19 day of Jan , 1905.

V Smith
Notary Public.

BIRTH AFFIDAVIT.

DEPARTMENT OF THE INTERIOR.
COMMISSION TO THE FIVE CIVILIZED TRIBES.

IN RE APPLICATION FOR ENROLLMENT, as a citizen of the Choctaw Nation, of Therdore[sic] Claton Allen , born on the 8" day of August , 1904

Name of Father: Andrew J Allen   a citizen of the Choctaw Nation.
Name of Mother: Kate Allen   a citizen of the Choctaw Nation.

Postoffice   Purdy I.T.

AFFIDAVIT OF MOTHER.

UNITED STATES OF AMERICA, Indian Territory, }
    Southern   DISTRICT.

I, Kate Allen , on oath state that I am 26 years of age and a citizen by blood , of the Choctaw Nation; that I am the lawful wife of Andrew J Allen , who is a citizen, by intermarriage of the Choctaw Nation; that a male child was born to me on 8th day of August , 1904; that said child has been named Therdore Claton Allen , and was living March 4, 1905.

Kate Allen

Witnesses To Mark:
{

Subscribed and sworn to before me this 13 day of April , 1905

V. Smith
Notary Public.

Applications for Enrollment of Choctaw Newborn
Act of 1905 Volume III

AFFIDAVIT OF ATTENDING PHYSICIAN OR MID-WIFE.

UNITED STATES OF AMERICA, Indian Territory,
   Southern   DISTRICT.

    I,   J W Tucker , a Physician , on oath state that I attended on Mrs. Kate Allen, wife of Andrew J Allen on the 8" day of August, 1904; that there was born to her on said date a male child; that said child was living March 4, 1905, and is said to have been named Therdore Claton Allen

                                      J W Tucker M.D.

Witnesses To Mark:

    Subscribed and sworn to before me this 13 day of April , 1905

                                      V. Smith
                                              Notary Public.

                                                          7-2501

                    Muskogee, Indian Territory, January 25, 1905.

Andy Allen,
    Purdy, Indian Territory.

Dear Sir:

    Receipt is hereby acknowledged of the affidavits of Kate Allen and James W. Tucker to the birth of Theodore Claton Allen, child of Andy and Kate Allen, August 8, 1904, which it is presumed have been forwarded as an application for enrollment of said child.

    You are informed that under the provisions of the act of Congress approved July 1, 1902, no children born to citizens of the Choctaw and Chickasaw Nations subsequent to September 25, 1902, the date of the ratification of said act, are entitled to enrollment and allotment in the Choctaw and Chickasaw Nations.

                          Respectfully,

                                            Chairman.

Applications for Enrollment of Choctaw Newborn
Act of 1905 Volume III

COPY N. B. 150

Muskogee, Indian Territory, April 7, 1905.

Andrew J. Allen,
    Purdy, Indian Territory.

Dear Sir:

    There is inclosed you herewith for execution application for the enrollment of your infant child, Therdore[sic] Claton Allen, born August 8, 1904.

    The affidavits heretofore filed with the Commission show the child was living on January 19, 1905. It is necessary, for the child to be enrolled, that he was living on March 4, 1905. You will please insert the age of the mother in space provided for the purpose.

    In having these affidavits executed care should be exercised to see that all names are written in full, as they appear in the body of the affidavit, and in the event that either of the persons signing the affidavit are unable to write, signatures by mark must be attested by two witnesses. Each affidavit must be executed before a Notary Public and the notarial seal and signature of the officer must be attached to each separate affidavit.

                          Respectfully,
                            SIGNED
                          T. B. Needles.

LM 7-2   Commissioner in Charge.

COPY Choctaw N.B. 150.

Muskogee, Indian Territory, April 19, 1905.

Andrew J. Allen,
    Purdy, Indian Territory.

Dear Sir:

    Receipt is hereby acknowledged of the affidavits of Kate Allen and J. W. Tucker to the birth of Therdore[sic] Claton Allen, son of Andrew and Kate Allen, August 8, 1904, and the same have been filed with our records in the matter of the enrollment of said child.

                          Respectfully,
                          SIGNED
                            Tams Bixby
                            Chairman.

Applications for Enrollment of Choctaw Newborn
Act of 1905   Volume III

Choc New Born 151
    Ruel Finton Sexton
    (Born June 3, 1904)

NEW-BORN AFFIDAVIT.

Number..............

Choctaw Enrolling Commission.

IN THE MATTER OF THE APPLICATION FOR ENROLLMENT, as a citizen of the Choctaw   Nation, of   Rual[sic] Finton Sexton

born on the   3rd day of   June   1904

Name of father   Ben Sexton   a citizen of   Choctaw
Nation final enrollment No   7264
Name of mother   Lou Sexton   a citizen of   Choctaw
Nation final enrollment No   108

          Postoffice   Durant IT

AFFIDAVIT OF MOTHER.

UNITED STATES OF AMERICA,
   INDIAN TERRITORY,
  Central   DISTRICT

    I   Lou Sexton   , on oath state that I am   39   years of age and a citizen by   inter marriage   of the   Choctaw   Nation, and as such have been placed upon the final roll of the   Choctaw   Nation, by the Honorable Secretary of the Interior my final enrollment number being   108   ; that I am the lawful wife of   Ben Sexton   , who is a citizen of the   Choctaw Nation, and as such has been placed upon the final roll of said Nation by the Honorable Secretary of the Interior, his final enrollment number being   7264   and that a male   child was born to me on the   3rd day of   June   1904   ; that said child has been named   Rual Finton Sexton   , and is now living.

WITNESSETH: Lou Sexton
  Must be two   Thos J Sexton
  Witnesses who
  are Citizens.   E E Dyer

    Subscribed and sworn to before me this   16   day of   Jan   1905

                        W. A. Shoney
                              Notary Public.

My commission expires

Applications for Enrollment of Choctaw Newborn
Act of 1905 Volume III

AFFIDAVIT OF ATTENDING PHYSICIAN OR MIDWIFE

UNITED STATES OF AMERICA
INDIAN TERRITORY
Central DISTRICT

I, Dr. J. L. Shuler a Physician on oath state that I attended on Mrs. Lou Sexton wife of Ben Sexton on the 3rd day of June , 190 4 , that there was born to her on said date a male child, that said child is now living, and is said to have been named Rual Finton Sexton

Jas L Shuler M.D.

Subscribed and sworn to before me this, the 18 day of Jany 190 5

SH Kyle
Notary Public.

WITNESSETH:
Must be two witnesses who are citizens and know the child.
{ Thos J Sexton
E E Dyer

We hereby certify that we are well acquainted with Dr. Shuler a Physician and know him to be reputable and of good standing in the community.

Thos J Sexton
E E Dyer

BIRTH AFFIDAVIT.

DEPARTMENT OF THE INTERIOR.
COMMISSION TO THE FIVE CIVILIZED TRIBES.

IN RE APPLICATION FOR ENROLLMENT, as a citizen of the Choctaw Nation, of Ruel Finton Sexton , born on the 3 day of June , 1904

Name of Father: Benj. F. Sexton a citizen of the Choctaw Nation.
Name of Mother: Lou Sexton a citizen of the Choctaw Nation.

Postoffice Durant, I.T.

Applications for Enrollment of Choctaw Newborn
Act of 1905   Volume III

AFFIDAVIT OF MOTHER.

UNITED STATES OF AMERICA, Indian Territory, }
Central   DISTRICT.

    I,   Lou Sexton   , on oath state that I am   27   years of age and a citizen by marriage   , of the   Choctaw   Nation; that I am the lawful wife of   Benj. F. Sexton, who is a citizen, by blood   of the   Choctaw   Nation; that a   male   child was born to me on   3rd day of   June   , 1904; that said child has been named   Ruel Finton Sexton   , and was living March 4, 1905.

                                              Lou Sexton

Witnesses To Mark:
{

    Subscribed and sworn to before me this   20   day of   March   , 1905

                                            W T Sprowls
                                            Notary Public.

AFFIDAVIT OF ATTENDING PHYSICIAN OR MID-WIFE.

UNITED STATES OF AMERICA, Indian Territory, }
Central   DISTRICT.

    I,   Jas. L. Shuler   , a   Physician   , on oath state that I attended on Mrs.   Lou Sexton   , wife of   Benj. F. Sexton   on the   3 day of   June   , 1904; that there was born to her on said date a   male   child; that said child was living March 4, 1905, and is said to have been named Ruel Finton

                                            Jas. L. Shuler

Witnesses To Mark:
{

    Subscribed and sworn to before me this   20   day of   March   , 1905

                                            W T Sprowls
                                            Notary Public.

Applications for Enrollment of Choctaw Newborn
Act of 1905 Volume III

Choc New Born 151
    Jas. William A. Moore
    (Born Nov. 4, 1904)

BIRTH AFFIDAVIT.

DEPARTMENT OF THE INTERIOR,
COMMISSION TO THE FIVE CIVILIZED TRIBES.

In Re Application for Enrollment, as a citizen of the Choctaw Nation, of Jas William A. Moore, born on the 4th day of November, 1903

Name of Father: Jon[sic] Henry Moore   a citizen of the Choctaw Nation.
Name of Mother: Luvenay Moore   a citizen of the Choctaw Nation.

    Post-office   Cameron I.T.

AFFIDAVIT OF MOTHER.

UNITED STATES OF AMERICA,
   INDIAN TERRITORY,
   Central   District.

I, Luvenay Moore, on oath state that I am 23 years of age and a citizen by Blood, of the Choctaw Nation; that I am the lawful wife of John Henry Moore, who is a citizen, by Marriage of the Choctaw Nation; that a Male child was born to me on 4th day of November, 1903, that said child has been named Jas William A Moore, and is now living.

                Luvenay Moore

WITNESSES TO MARK:

Subscribed and sworn to before me this 6th day of July, 1904

                Stewart F. Green
                   NOTARY PUBLIC.

Applications for Enrollment of Choctaw Newborn
Act of 1905 Volume III

AFFIDAVIT OF ATTENDING PHYSICIAN OR MID-WIFE.

UNITED STATES OF AMERICA,
   INDIAN TERRITORY,
  Central   District.

I, Margrette[sic] T. Pounds, a Midwife, on oath state that I attended on Mrs. Luvenay Moore, wife of Jon[sic] Henry Moore on the 4th day of November, 1903; that there was born to her on said date a male child; that said child is now living and is said to have been named Jas William A Moore

Margret T. Pounds

WITNESSES TO MARK:

Subscribed and sworn to before me this 6th day of July, 1904

Stewart F. Green
My time expires Feb 19.1907   NOTARY PUBLIC.

BIRTH AFFIDAVIT.
DEPARTMENT OF THE INTERIOR.
COMMISSION TO THE FIVE CIVILIZED TRIBES.

IN RE APPLICATION FOR ENROLLMENT, as a citizen of the Choctaw Nation, of James William Arthur Moore, born on the 4th day of November, 1903

Name of Father: Henry Moore   a citizen of the United States Nation.
Name of Mother: Louvina E. Moore   a citizen of the Choctaw Nation.

Postoffice Cameron, Ind. Ter.

AFFIDAVIT OF MOTHER.

UNITED STATES OF AMERICA, Indian Territory,
  Central   DISTRICT.

I, Louvina E. Moore, on oath state that I am 23 years of age and a citizen by blood, of the Choctaw Nation; that I am the lawful wife of Henry Moore, who is a citizen, by .... of the United States Nation; that a male child was born to me on 4th day of November, 1903; that said child has been named James William Arthur Moore, and was living March 4, 1905.

Louvina E Moore

Applications for Enrollment of Choctaw Newborn
Act of 1905   Volume III

Witnesses To Mark:

{

Subscribed and sworn to before me this 30th   day of   March   , 1905

Wirt Franklin
Notary Public.

Department of the Interior.
Commission to the Five Civilized Tribes.

In the matter of the birth of a~~ Jas William A. Moore   a citizen of the   Choctaw Nation who was born on the   4   day of   Nov.   A.D. 190 3

United States of America,
Indian Territory,
Central District.

I,   J.B. Pilgreen   on oath state that I am   22   years of age; that my post office is   Cameron   Indian Territory; that I am am[sic] acquainted with   Jas William A. Moore   who was born on the   4   day of   Nov   A.D. 1903; that I know to my own knowledge that the said   Jas William A. Moore   is the son of   John Henry Moore   a citizen of the   U.S.   ~~Nation~~ and who resides at   Cameron   Indian Territory.

I am also acquainted with   Louvina E Moore   who is a citizen of the   Choctaw Nation, the wife of   John Henry Moore   and who is the mother of the said   Jas William A. Moore   and who resides at   Cameron   Indian Territory.

Signed   J.B. Pilgreen

Subscribed and sworn to before me this   29   day of April, 1905.

Hosea S. Pilgreen
Notary Public.

My Com. expires Dec. 9, 1907.

Applications for Enrollment of Choctaw Newborn
Act of 1905   Volume III

Department of the Interior.
Commission to the Five Civilized Tribes.

In the matter of the birth of   Jas William A. Moore   a citizen of the   Choctaw Nation who was born on the   4   day of   Nov.   A.D. 190 3

United States of America,
Indian Territory,
Central District.

I,   John F. Germon   on oath state that I am   27   years of age; that my postoffice is   Cameron   Indian Territory; that I am acquainted with   Jas William A. Moore   who was born on the   4   day of   Nov   A.D. 190 3 ; that I know of my own knowledge that the said   Jas William A. Moore   is the   son   of   John Henry Moore   a citizen of the   ~~Choctaw~~   U.S.   ~~Nation~~ and who resides at   Cameron   Indian Territory.

I am also acquainted with   Louvena[sic] E. Moore   who is a citizen of the Choctaw   Nation, the wife of   John Henry Moore   and who is the mother of the said Jas William A. Moore   and who resides at   Cameron   Indian Territory.

John F. Germon
before
Subscribed and sworn to ~~Deere~~ me this the   29   day of   Nov   A.D. 1905.

Hosea S. Pilgreen
Notary Public.

BIRTH AFFIDAVIT.

DEPARTMENT OF THE INTERIOR.
COMMISSION TO THE FIVE CIVILIZED TRIBES.

IN RE APPLICATION FOR ENROLLMENT, as a citizen of the   Choctaw   Nation, of Jas William A Moore   , born on the   4   day of   November   , 1903

Name of Father: John Henry Moore   a citizen of the   U. S.   Nation.
Name of Mother: Louvina E Moore (Nail)   a citizen of the   Choctaw   Nation.

Postoffice   Cameron, Ind. Ter.

Applications for Enrollment of Choctaw Newborn
Act of 1905 Volume III

AFFIDAVIT OF MOTHER.

UNITED STATES OF AMERICA, Indian Territory, }
Central   DISTRICT.

I, Louvina E Moore (Nail)   , on oath state that I am 23   years of age and a citizen by   Blood   , of the   Choctaw   Nation; that I am the lawful wife of John Henry Moore   , who is a citizen, by ———— of the   United States   Nation; that a   male   child was born to me on 4   day of   November   , 1903; that said child has been named Jas William A Moore   , and was living March 4, 1905.

                                              Louvina E Moore

Witnesses To Mark:
{

    Subscribed and sworn to before me this 10 day of   April   , 1905

                                           Hosea S Pilgreen
My Comm expires Dec 9-07   Notary Public.

AFFIDAVIT OF ATTENDING PHYSICIAN OR MID-WIFE.

UNITED STATES OF AMERICA, Indian Territory, }
Central   DISTRICT.

I, John Henry Moore Husband of Louvina E Moore , on oath state that I attended on Mrs.   Louvina E Moore (Nail)   , wife of   John Henry Moore   on the 4 day of   November   , 1903; That I was unable to have a physician attend her that there was born to her on said date a   male   child; that said child was living March 4, 1905, and is said to have been named Jas William A Moore

                                            his
                                     John x Henry Moore
Witnesses To Mark: mark
{ T. B. Lunsford
  Martin *(Illegible)*

    Subscribed and sworn to before me this 10 day of   April   , 1905

                                           Hosea S Pilgreen
My Comm expires Dec 9-07   Notary Public.

Applications for Enrollment of Choctaw Newborn
Act of 1905 Volume III

Muskogee, Indian Territory, December 5, 1904.

John Henry Moore,
(Ink smudge over city) Indian Territory.

Dear Sir:

On July 10, 1904, there was received at this office the affidavits of Louena[sic] Moore and Margaret T. Pounds relative to the birth of your infant son James William A. Moore November 4, 1903.

It is stated in the affidavit of the mother that her name is Louena Moore, that she is twenty-three years of age, a citizen by blood of the Choctaw Nation, and the lawful wife of John Henry Moore, a citizen by intermarriage of the Choctaw Nation.

You are kindly requested to state the full maiden name of Louena Moore, the time and place application was made for her enrollment, together with the names of the other members of the family to which she belongs for whom application was made at the same time.

You are further requested to state your age, the time and place application was made for your enrollment as an intermarried citizen of the Choctaw Nation, returning your reply in the enclosed envelope which requires no postage.

Respectfully,

Chairman.

COPY

7-2517

Muskogee, Indian Territory, January 7, 1905.

Louvina Nail,
Cameron, Indian Territory.

Dear Madam:

Receipt is hereby acknowledged of your letter of December 27, 1904, stating that your maiden name is Louvinia[sic] E. Nail; that your married name is Louvina E. Moore, and that on July 10, you forwarded your affidavit and the affidavit of Margret T. Pounds relative to the birth of your infant son James William A. Moore, and that your name was mispelled[sic] by the Notary.

Applications for Enrollment of Choctaw Newborn
Act of 1905   Volume III

In reply to your letter you are advised that the information contained therein has enabled the Commission to identify you as having been enrolled under the Act of Congress approved March 3, 1905, as number name of Louvina E. Nail.

Referring to your affidavit and the affidavit of Margret T. Pounds relative to the birth of James William A. Moore, infant son of John Henry and Louvina Moore November 4, 1903, You are advised that under the provisions of the act of Congress approved July 1, 1902, the provisions of the act of Congress approved July 1, 1902, no children born to citizens of the Choctaw and Chickasaw Nations subsequent to September 25, 1902, the date of the ratification of said act, are entitled to enrollment and allotment.

Respectfully,
SIGNED

Tams Bixby
Chairman.

Choctaw 2517

Muskogee, Indian Territory, March 20, 1905.

Louvinia E. Moore,
Cameron, Indian Territory.

Dear Madam:

Receipt is hereby acknowledged of your letter of March 7, stating that you have forwarded affidavits to the birth of your son, James William A. Moore, and requesting to be advised if further action is necessary in the matter of his enrollment.

In reply to your letter you are advised that the affidavits heretofore forwarded relative to the birth of James William A. Moore son of Louvina E. Nail, have been filed with our records as an application for the enrollment of said child.

Respectfully,

Chairman.

Applications for Enrollment of Choctaw Newborn
Act of 1905 Volume III

COPY N. B. 152

Muskogee, Indian Territory, April 4, 1905.

John Henry Moore,
    Cameron, Indian Territory.

Dear Sir:

    There is inclosed you herewith for execution application for the enrollment of your infant child, Jas. William A. Moore, born November 4, 1903.

    The affidavits heretofore filed with the Commission show the child was living on July 6, 1904. It is necessary, for the child to be enrolled, that he was living on March 4, 1905.

    In having these affidavits executed care should be exercised to see that all names are written in full, as they appear in the body of the affidavit, and in the event that either of the persons signing the affidavit are unable to write, signatures by mark must be attested by two witnesses. Each affidavit must be executed before a Notary Public and the notarial seal and signature of the officer must be attached to each separate affidavit.

    Respectfully,
    SIGNED
    T. B. Needles.

LM 4-21   Commissioner in Charge.

COPY Choctaw N.B. 152.

Muskogee, Indian Territory, April 14, 1905.

John Henry Moore,
    Cameron, Indian Territory.

Dear Sir:

    Receipt is hereby acknowledged of the affidavits of Louvina E. Moore and John Henry Moore to the birth of Jas. William A. Moore, son of John Henry and Louvina E. Moore, November 4, 1903.

    It appears from your affidavit that there was no physician or midwife in attendance on your wife at the birth of Jas. William A. Moore, and in that event it will be necessary for you to forward the affidavits of two disinterested persons who know of the birth of said child that it is the child of your wife, Louvina E. Moore and that it is still living.

Applications for Enrollment of Choctaw Newborn
Act of 1905   Volume III

This matter should receive immediate attention in order that proper disposition may be made of the application for the enrollment of your child.

Respectfully,
SIGNED
T. B. Needles.
Commissioner in Charge.

COPY

7-N.B. 152.

Muskogee, Indian Territory, May 3, 1905.

John Henry Moore,
  Cameron, Indian Territory.

Dear Sir:

Receipt is hereby acknowledged of the affidavits of J. B. Pilgreen and John F. Germon to the birth of Jas. William A. Moore, son of John Henry and Louvina E. Moore, November 4, 1903, and the same have been filed with our records in the matter of the enrollment of said child.

Respectfully,
SIGNED
Tams Bixby
Chairman.

7-NB-152

Muskogee, Indian Territory, July 10, 1905.

John Henry Moore,
  Cameron, Indian Territory.

Dear Sir:

Receipt is hereby acknowledged of your letter of July 8, 1905, asking if you can file for your son James William A. Moore.

In reply to your letter you are advised that on June 30, 1905, the Secretary of the Interior approved the enrollment of your son James William A. Moore as a citizen by blood of the Choctaw Nation and selection of allotment may now be made in his behalf in accordance with the rules and regulations governing the selection of allotments and the designation of homesteads in the Choctaw and Chickasaw Nations.

Applications for Enrollment of Choctaw Newborn
Act of 1905   Volume III

Respectfully,

Commissioner.

Choc New Born 153
   Ella Gertrude Smith
   (Born Feb. 20, 1904)

BIRTH AFFIDAVIT.

DEPARTMENT OF THE INTERIOR,
COMMISSION TO THE FIVE CIVILIZED TRIBES.

In Re Application for Enrollment, as a citizen of the   Choctaw   Nation, of   Ella Gertrude , born on the   20th day of   February   , 1904

Name of Father: C.D. Smith   a citizen of the   U. S.   Nation.
Name of Mother: Martha (Ainsworth) Smith   a citizen of the   Choctaw   Nation.

Post-office   Lindsay I.T.

AFFIDAVIT OF MOTHER.

UNITED STATES OF AMERICA, ⎱
   INDIAN TERRITORY,   ⎰
   Southern   District.

I, Martha (Ainsworth) Smith , on oath state that I am twenty six years of age and a citizen by   birth (blood) , of the   Choctaw   Nation; that I am the lawful wife of   C.D. Smith , who is a citizen, by U. S. of the ✓ Nation; that a   Female   child was born to me on   20th day of   Feburary[sic] , 1904, that said child has been named   Ella Gertrude , and is now living.

Martha (Ainsworth) Smith

WITNESSES TO MARK:
 ⎰ H.L. Wallace
 ⎱ C. M. McClain

Subscribed and sworn to before me this   26th day of   April   , 1904.

Robt. May
NOTARY PUBLIC.

135

Applications for Enrollment of Choctaw Newborn
Act of 1905 Volume III

___

AFFIDAVIT OF ATTENDING PHYSICIAN OR MID-WIFE.

___

UNITED STATES OF AMERICA, }
   INDIAN TERRITORY,
....District. }

    I, S W Wilson , a Physician , on oath state that I attended on Mrs. Martha Smith , wife of C. D. Smith on the 20th day of February , 1904; that there was born to her on said date a Female child; that said child is now living and is said to have been named Ella Gertrude Smith

                                  S W Wilson M.D.

WITNESSES TO MARK:
{ H.L. Wallace
{ C. M. McClain

    Subscribed and sworn to before me this 26th day of April , 1904.

                                  Robt. May
                                       NOTARY PUBLIC.

___

BIRTH AFFIDAVIT.

                       DEPARTMENT OF THE INTERIOR.
                COMMISSION TO THE FIVE CIVILIZED TRIBES.

___

      IN RE APPLICATION FOR ENROLLMENT, as a citizen of the   Choctaw   Nation, of Ella G. Smith , born on the 20th day of February , 1904

Name of Father: Charles D. Smith   a citizen of the ——— Nation.
                                 now Smith
Name of Mother: Martha E Ainsworth   a citizen of the Choctaw Nation.

                       Postoffice   Lindsay Ind Ter

___

                      AFFIDAVIT OF MOTHER.

UNITED STATES OF AMERICA, Indian Territory, }
    Southern   **DISTRICT.** }
                      now Smith
    I, Martha E Ainsworth , on oath state that I am 27 years of age and a citizen by ~~Choctaw~~ Blood , of the Choctaw Nation; that I am the lawful wife of Charles D. Smith , who is a citizen, by ——— of the ——— Nation; that a

Applications for Enrollment of Choctaw Newborn
Act of 1905   Volume III

female   child was born to me on   20th day of   February   , 1904; that said child has been named   Ella G Smith   , and was living March 4, 1905.

Martha E Ainsworth Smith

Witnesses To Mark:
{

Subscribed and sworn to before me this 25th day of   March   , 1905

Claire L McArthur
Notary Public.

AFFIDAVIT OF ATTENDING PHYSICIAN OR MID-WIFE.

UNITED STATES OF AMERICA, Indian Territory, }
   Southern   DISTRICT.

I,   S.W. Wilson   , a   Physician   , on oath state that I attended on Mrs.   Martha E Smith   , wife of   Chas Smith   on the 20 day of Feb   , 1904; that there was born to her on said date a   Female   child; that said child was living March 4, 1905, and is said to have been named   Ella G. Smith

S. W. Wilson M.D.

Witnesses To Mark:
{

Subscribed and sworn to before me this 25th day of   March   , 1905

Claire L McArthur
Notary Public.

7-2523

Muskogee, Indian Territory, May 2, 1904.

C. D. Smith,
   Lindsay, Indian Territory.

Dear Sir:

   Receipt is hereby acknowledged of the affidavits of Martha Ainsworth Smith and S. W. Wilson, relative to the birth of your infant daughter, Ella Gertrude Smith, February 20, 1904, which it is presumed have been forwarded as an application for enrollment of said child as a citizen by blood of the Choctaw Nation.

Applications for Enrollment of Choctaw Newborn
Act of 1905   Volume III

You are informed that under the provisions of the Act of Congress, approved July 1, 1902, the Commission is now without authority to receive or consider the original application for enrollment of any person whomsoever as a citizen of the Choctaw or Chickasaw Nation.

Respectfully,

Chairman.

Choctaw 2523.

Muskogee, Indian Territory, April 4, 1905.

C. L. McArthur, Attorney,
Lindsey, Indian Territory.

Dear Sir:

Receipt is hereby acknowledged of the affidavits of Martha E. Ainsworth Smith and E[sic]. W. Wilson to the birth of Ella G. Smith, daughter of Charles D. and Martha E. Ainsworth Smith, February 20, 1904, and the same have been filed with our records as an application for the enrollment of said child.

Respectfully,

Commissioner in Charge.

Applications for Enrollment of Choctaw Newborn
Act of 1905   Volume III

Choc New Born 154
Ivery Elen D. Fitzer
(Born Sep. 28, 1902)
Raymon W. Fitzer
(Born Feb. 28, 1904)

NEW-BORN AFFIDAVIT.

Number............

...Choctaw Enrolling Commission...

IN THE MATTER OF THE APPLICATION FOR ENROLLMENT, as a citizen of the Choctaw Nation, of Raymon Wesley Fitzer

born on the 28th day of February 1904

Name of father   James Fitzer   a citizen of   white
Nation final enrollment No.
Name of mother   Frances Fitzer   a citizen of   Choctaw
Nation final enrollment No.   xx 7362

Postoffice   Golconda IT

AFFIDAVIT OF MOTHER.

UNITED STATES OF AMERICA
INDIAN TERRITORY
   Western   DISTRICT

I   Frances Fitzer   , on oath state that I am 34 years of age and a citizen by blood of the Choctaw Nation, and as such have been placed upon the final roll of the Choctaw Nation, by the Honorable Secretary of the Interior my final enrollment number being xx 7362 ; that I am the lawful wife of   James Fitzer   , who is a citizen of the white Nation, and as such has been placed upon the final roll of said Nation by the Honorable Secretary of the Interior, his final enrollment number being ——— and that a male child was born to me on the 28th day of February 1904 ; that said child has been named Raymon Wesley Fitzer , and is now living.

Witnesseth.   Frances Fitzer

Must be two
Witnesses who   Tobias Brashears
are Citizens.   Jess Walls

Applications for Enrollment of Choctaw Newborn
Act of 1905 Volume III

Subscribed and sworn to before me this 5 day of June 190 4

John M Linz

Notary Public.

My commission expires: Nov 27 1907

AFFIDAVIT OF ATTENDING PHYSICIAN OR MIDWIFE

UNITED STATES OF AMERICA
INDIAN TERRITORY
Western   DISTRICT

Who has been a practicing
I,   J.N. Ritter   a   Physician
on oath state that I attended on Mrs. Francis Fitzer   wife of   James Fitzer
on the 28th day of February , 190 4 , that there was born to her on said date a male child, that said child is now living, and is said to have been named Raymon Wesley Fitzer

J. N. Ritter M.D.

Subscribed and sworn to before me this, the 5 day of January 190 5

John M Luntz   Notary Public.

WITNESSETH:
Must be two witnesses who are citizens { Martha Collier
T. J. Walls

We hereby certify that we are well acquainted with Dr J N Ritter a who has been a practicing physician and know him to be reputable and of good standing in the community.

T. J. Walls   _____

Thomas J Walls, Jr   _____

BIRTH AFFIDAVIT.

Department of the Interior,
COMMISSION TO THE FIVE CIVILIZED TRIBES.

IN RE APPLICATION FOR ENROLLMENT, as a citizen of the Choctaw Nation, of Ivrey[sic] Elen D. Fitzer , born on the 28 day of September , 190 2

Name of Father: Jim H Fitzer   a citizen of the United StatesNation.
Name of Mother: Frances Fitzer   a citizen of the Choctaw Nation.

Applications for Enrollment of Choctaw Newborn
Act of 1905   Volume III

Post-Office: Enterprise Ind Ter

AFFIDAVIT OF MOTHER.

UNITED STATES OF AMERICA,
    INDIAN TERRITORY,
Western   District.

I, Frances Fitzer, on oath state that I am 31 years of age and a citizen by Blood, of the Choctaw Nation; that I am the lawful wife of James H Fitzer, who is a citizen, ~~by~~ .... of the U.S. Nation; that a Female child was born to me on 28 day of September, 190 2, that said child has been named Ivery Elen D Fitzer, and is now living.

Frances Fitzer

WITNESSES TO MARK:
{

Subscribed and sworn to before me this 22 day of December, 190 2

A. J. Rodden N.P.
Notary Public.

AFFIDAVIT OF ATTENDING PHYSICIAN OR MID-WIFE.

UNITED STATES OF AMERICA,
    INDIAN TERRITORY,
Western   District.

I, B.E. Dunman, a Physician, on oath state that I attended on Mrs. Frances Fitzer, wife of James H Fitzer on the 28 day of September, 190 2; that there was born to her on said date a Female child; that said child is now living and is said to have been named Ivery Elen D. Fitzer

B. E. Dunman M.D.

WITNESSES TO MARK:
{

Subscribed and sworn to before me this 22 day of December, 190 2

A. J. Rodden N.P.
Notary Public.

Applications for Enrollment of Choctaw Newborn
Act of 1905 Volume III

NEW-BORN AFFIDAVIT.

Number ....

...Choctaw Enrolling Commission...

IN THE MATTER OF THE APPLICATION FOR ENROLLMENT, as a citizen of the Choctaw Nation, of Ellen D Fitzer

born on the 28th day of September 190 2

Name of father   James Fitzer   a citizen of   white
Nation final enrollment No.   ———
Name of mother   Frances Fitzer   a citizen of   Choctaw
Nation final enrollment No.   xx 7362

Postoffice   Golconda IT

AFFIDAVIT OF MOTHER.

UNITED STATES OF AMERICA }
INDIAN TERRITORY
   Western   DISTRICT

I   Frances Fitzer   , on oath state that I am 34 years of age and a citizen by blood of the _____ Nation, and as such have been placed upon the final roll of the Choctaw Nation, by the Honorable Secretary of the Interior my final enrollment number being xx 7362 ; that I am the lawful wife of James Fitzer , who is a citizen of the white Nation, and as such has been placed upon the final roll of said Nation by the Honorable Secretary of the Interior, his final enrollment number being ———— and that a female child was born to me on the 28th day of September 190 2 ; that said child has been named Ellen D Fitzer , and is now living.

Witnesseth.   Frances Fitzer

Must be two }   T. J. Walls
Witnesses who
are Citizens.   Loucinda Fitzer

Subscribed and sworn to before me this 5 day of Jan 190 5

                                           John M Linz
                                                Notary Public.
My commission expires: Nov 27 1907

Applications for Enrollment of Choctaw Newborn
Act of 1905 Volume III

AFFIDAVIT OF ATTENDING PHYSICIAN OR MIDWIFE

UNITED STATES OF AMERICA
INDIAN TERRITORY
Western DISTRICT

I, Mary Lytle   a   Midwife on oath state that I attended on Mrs. Frances Fitzer   wife of   James Fitzer on the 28   day of September , 190 2 , that there was born to her on said date a   female child, that said child is now living, and is said to have been named   Ellen D. Fitzer

Mary Lytle
Subscribed and sworn to before me this, the   4   day of January   190 5

WITNESSETH: John M Linz   Notary Public.

Must be two witnesses who are citizens { Martha Collier
T. J. Walls

We hereby certify that we are well acquainted with   Mary Lytle a   midwife   and know   her   to be reputable and of good standing in the community.

T. J. Walls   _____

J. D. Bench   _____

BIRTH AFFIDAVIT.

DEPARTMENT OF THE INTERIOR.
COMMISSION TO THE FIVE CIVILIZED TRIBES.

IN RE APPLICATION FOR ENROLLMENT, as a citizen of the   Choctaw   Nation, of Iverey[sic] Elen D Fitzer   , born on the 28   day of September , 1902

Name of Father: James H Fitzer Intermarriage   a citizen of the   Choct[sic]   Nation.
Name of Mother: Frances Fitzer   a citizen of the   Choct   Nation.

Postoffice   Golconda, Ind. Ter

Applications for Enrollment of Choctaw Newborn
Act of 1905   Volume III

AFFIDAVIT OF MOTHER.

UNITED STATES OF AMERICA, Indian Territory, }
Western DISTRICT.

I, Frances Fitzer, on oath state that I am 33 years of age and a citizen by Blood, of the Choctaw Nation; that I am the lawful wife of James H Fitzer, who is a citizen, by marriage of the Choctaw Nation; that a Female child was born to me on 28 day of September, 1902; that said child has been named Iverey Elen D Fitzer, and was living March 4, 1905.

Frances Fitzer

Witnesses To Mark:
{ Thomas J Walls
  B F Grace

Subscribed and sworn to before me this 1st day of April, 1905
My Commission
Expires Nov 27 1907   John M Linz
                            Notary Public.

AFFIDAVIT OF ATTENDING PHYSICIAN OR MID-WIFE.

UNITED STATES OF AMERICA, Indian Territory, }
Western DISTRICT.

I, Mary Lytle, a Midwife, on oath state that I attended on Mrs. Frances Fitzer, wife of James H Fitzer on the 28 day of September, 1902; that there was born to her on said date a Female child; that said child was living March 4, 1905, and is said to have been named Ivery Elen D Fitzer

Witnesses To Mark:
{ Thomas J Walls
  B F Grace

Subscribed and sworn to before me this 1st day of April, 1905
My Commission
Expires Nov 27 1907   John M Linz
                            Notary Public.

Applications for Enrollment of Choctaw Newborn
Act of 1905 Volume III

BIRTH AFFIDAVIT.

DEPARTMENT OF THE INTERIOR.
COMMISSION TO THE FIVE CIVILIZED TRIBES.

IN RE APPLICATION FOR ENROLLMENT, as a citizen of the Choctaw Nation, of Raymon W Fitzer, born on the 28 day of Feb, 1904

Name of Father: James H Fitzer Intermarriage a citizen of the Choctaw Nation.
Name of Mother: Frances Fitzer a citizen of the Choctaw Nation.

Postoffice Golconda, Ind. Ter

AFFIDAVIT OF MOTHER.

UNITED STATES OF AMERICA, Indian Territory, Western DISTRICT.

I, Frances Fitzer, on oath state that I am 33 years of age and a citizen by Blood, of the Choctaw Nation; that I am the lawful wife of James H Fitzer, who is a citizen, by intermarriage of the Choctaw Nation; that a Boy child was born to me on 28 day of Feb, 1904; that said child has been named Raymon W Fitzer, and was living March 4, 1905.

Frances Fitzer

Witnesses To Mark:
{

Subscribed and sworn to before me this 3 day of April, 1905

S P Davis
Notary Public.

AFFIDAVIT OF ATTENDING PHYSICIAN OR MID-WIFE.

UNITED STATES OF AMERICA, Indian Territory, Western DISTRICT.

I, J N Ritter, a Doct[sic], on oath state that I attended on Mrs. Frances Fitzer, wife of James H Fitzer on the 28 day of Feb, 1904; that there was born to her on said date a Boy child; that said child was living March 4, 1905, and is said to have been named Raymon W Fitzer

J N Ritter M.D.

Witnesses To Mark:
{

Applications for Enrollment of Choctaw Newborn
Act of 1905 Volume III

Subscribed and sworn to before me this 3 day of April , 1905

S P Davis

My Comm Expires Feb 9- 1907　　　　　　　　Notary Public.

7-2537

Muskogee, Indian Territory, December 3, 1904.

James H. Fitzer,
　　Enterprise, Indian Territory.

Dear Sir:

On December 24, 1902, there was received at the postoffice, Muskogee, Indian Territory, the affidavits of Frances Fitzer and B. E Dunman relative to the birth of your infant daughter Ivery Ellen D. Fitzer, September 28, 1902, which it is presumed was forwarded to this office as an application for enrollment of said child as a citizen by blood of the Choctaw Nation.

The Act of Congress approved July 1, 1902, which was ratified by the citizens of the Choctaw and Chickasaw Nations September 25, 1902, among other things provides that no child born to a citizen of the Choctaw or Chickasaw Nation subsequent to the date of said ratification shall be entitled to enrollment or to participate in the distribution of the tribal property of the Choctaw and Chickasaws.

　　　　　　　　　　　　　　　　　Respectfully,

　　　　　　　　　　　　　　　　　　　Chairman.

N. B. 154

Muskogee, Indian Territory, April 4, 1905.

James Fitzer,
　　Enterprise, Indian Territory.

Dear Sir:

There is inclosed you herewith for execution application for the enrollment of your infant child, Ivery Elen D. Fitzer, born September 28, 1902.

The affidavits heretofore filed with the Commission show the child was living on December 22, 1902. It is necessary, for the child to be enrolled, that she was living on March 4, 1905.

Applications for Enrollment of Choctaw Newborn
Act of 1905   Volume III

In having these affidavits executed care should be exercised to see that all names are written in full, as they appear in the body of the affidavit, and in the event that either of the persons signing the affidavit are unable to write, signatures by mark must be attested by two witnesses. Each affidavit must be executed before a Notary Public and the notarial seal and signature of the officer must be attached to each separate affidavit.

Respectfully,

LM 4-20.   Commissioner in Charge.

Choctaw 2537.

Muskogee, Indian Territory, April 10, 1905.

Frances Fitzer,
    Golconda, Indian Territory.

Dear Madam:

Receipt is hereby acknowledged of the affidavits of Frances Fitzer and Mary Lytle to the birth of Ivery Elen D. Fitzer, daughter of James H. and Frances Fitzer, September 28, 1902; also the affidavits of Frances Fitzer and J. N. Ritter to the birth of Raymon W. Fitzer, son of James H. and Frances Fitzer, February 28, 1904, and the same have been filed with our records as an applications for the enrollment of said children.

Respectfully,

Commissioner in Charge.

Applications for Enrollment of Choctaw Newborn
Act of 1905   Volume III

Choc New Born 155
    Edith Sims
    (Born March 27, 1903)

BIRTH AFFIDAVIT.

DEPARTMENT OF THE INTERIOR,
COMMISSION TO THE FIVE CIVILIZED TRIBES.

In Re Application for Enrollment, as a citizen of the Choctaw Nation, of Edith Sims, born on the 27 day of March, 1903 Inter marriage

Name of Father: Thomas J Sims   a citizen of the Choctaw Nation.
Name of Mother: Lula Sims   a citizen of the Choctaw Nation.

Post-office   Wister Ind Ter

AFFIDAVIT OF MOTHER.

UNITED STATES OF AMERICA, }
    INDIAN TERRITORY,
    Central   District.

    I, Lula Sims, on oath state that I am 22 years of age and a citizen by Blood, of the Choctaw Nation; that I am the lawful wife of Thomas J Sims, who is a citizen, by Inter marriage of the Choctaw Nation; that a female child was born to me on 27 day of March, 1903, that said child has been named Edith Sims, and is now living.

                        Lula Sims

WITNESSES TO MARK:
{

    Subscribed and sworn to before me this 6 day of August, 1904

                        J. J. Biggs
                            NOTARY PUBLIC.

Applications for Enrollment of Choctaw Newborn
Act of 1905   Volume III

AFFIDAVIT OF ATTENDING PHYSICIAN OR MID-WIFE.

UNITED STATES OF AMERICA,
 INDIAN TERRITORY,
  Central   District.

I,   E E Shiffey   , a   M D , on oath state that I attended on Mrs. Lula Sims , wife of Thomas J Sims on the 27 day of March , 1903 ; that there was born to her on said date a   female   child; that said child is now living and is said to have been named Edith Sims

Dr E. E. Shiffey

WITNESSES TO MARK:

Subscribed and sworn to before me this 6 day of August , 1904

J. J. Biggs
NOTARY PUBLIC.

NEW BORN AFFIDAVIT

No ....

CHOCTAW ENROLLING COMMISSION

IN THE MATTER OF THE APPLICATION FOR ENROLLMENT as a citizen of the Choctaw Nation, of   Edith Sims   born on the 27 day of March   190 3

Name of father   T. J. Sims   a citizen of   non   Nation, final enrollment No. ——

Name of mother   Lula Sims   a citizen of   Choctaw   Nation, final enrollment No.   6817

Wister I.T.   Postoffice.

AFFIDAVIT OF MOTHER

UNITED STATES OF AMERICA
 INDIAN TERRITORY
DISTRICT   Central

I   Lula Sims   , on oath state that I am   23   years of age and a citizen by   blood   of the   Choctaw   Nation, and as such

Applications for Enrollment of Choctaw Newborn
Act of 1905   Volume III

have been placed upon the final roll of the   Choctaw   Nation, by the Honorable Secretary of the Interior my final enrollment number being   6817 ; that I am the lawful wife of   T. J. Sims   , who is a citizen of the   non   Nation, and as such has been placed upon the final roll of said Nation by the Honorable Secretary of the Interior, his final enrollment number being —— and that a   Female   child was born to me on the   27   day of   March   190 3; that said child has been named   Edith Sims   , and is now living.

WITNESSETH: Lula Sims

Must be two witnesses { Charley Jones
who are citizens   { Barnabas Peter

Subscribed and sworn to before me this, the   18   day of   February   190 5

James Bower
Notary Public.

My Commission Expires:
Sept 23-1907

Affidavit of Attending Physician or Midwife

UNITED STATES OF AMERICA, }
   INDIAN TERRITORY,   }
   Central   DISTRICT   }

I,   E E Shiffey   a   Practicing Physician on oath state that I attended on Mrs.   Lula Sims   wife of   T. J. Sims   on the   27   day of   March   , 190 3 , that there was born to her on said date a   female   child, that said child is now living, and is said to have been named   Edith Sims

E. E. Shiffey   M. D.

Subscribed and sworn to before me this the   18   day of   February   1905

James Bower
Notary Public.

WITNESSETH:
Must be two witnesses { Charley Jones
who are citizens and   {
know the child.   { Barnabas Peter

We hereby certify that we are well acquainted with   E. E. Shiffey   a **Practicing Physician**   and know   him   to be reputable and of good standing in the community.

Must be two citizen { Charley Jones
witnesses.   { Barnabas Peter

150

Applications for Enrollment of Choctaw Newborn
Act of 1905 Volume III

BIRTH AFFIDAVIT.

DEPARTMENT OF THE INTERIOR.
COMMISSION TO THE FIVE CIVILIZED TRIBES.

IN RE APPLICATION FOR ENROLLMENT, as a citizen of the Choctaw Nation, of Edith Sims , born on the 27th day of March , 1903

Name of Father: Thomas J Sims a citizen of the United States Nation.
Name of Mother: Lula Sims a citizen of the Choctaw Nation.

Postoffice Wister, Ind Ter

AFFIDAVIT OF MOTHER.

UNITED STATES OF AMERICA, Indian Territory,
Central DISTRICT.

I, Lula Sims , on oath state that I am 23 years of age and a citizen by blood , of the Choctaw Nation; that I am the lawful wife of Thomas J Sims , who is a citizen, by .... of the United States Nation; that a female child was born to me on 27th day of March , 1903; that said child has been named Edith Sims , and was living March 4, 1905.

Lula Sims

Witnesses To Mark:
{

Subscribed and sworn to before me this 27th day of March , 1905

Wirt Franklin
Notary Public.

AFFIDAVIT OF ATTENDING PHYSICIAN OR MID-WIFE.

UNITED STATES OF AMERICA, Indian Territory,
Central DISTRICT.

I, E. E. Shiffey , a M.D. , on oath state that I attended on Mrs. Lula Sims , wife of Thomas Sims on the 27 day of March , 1903; that there was born to her on said date a female child; that said child was living March 4, 1905, and is said to have been named Edith Sims

E. E. Shiffey M.D.

Witnesses To Mark:
{

Applications for Enrollment of Choctaw Newborn
Act of 1905 Volume III

Subscribed and sworn to before me this 1 day of Apr, 1905

J. J. Biggs
Notary Public.

7-6817
BIRTH AFFIDAVIT.

DEPARTMENT OF THE INTERIOR,
COMMISSION TO THE FIVE CIVILIZED TRIBES.

IN RE APPLICATION FOR ENROLLMENT, as a citizen of the Choctaw Nation, of Edith Sims, born on the 27 day of March, 1903

Name of Father: Thomas J Sims   a citizen of the U. S. Nation.
Name of Mother: Lula Sims   a citizen of the Choctaw Nation.

Postoffice Wister Ind. Ter.

AFFIDAVIT OF MOTHER.

UNITED STATES OF AMERICA, Indian Territory, }
Central District. }

I, Lula Sims, on oath state that I am 22 years of age and a citizen by Blood, of the Choctaw Nation; that I am the lawful wife of Thomas J Sims, who is a citizen, by ———— of the United States Nation; that a female child was born to me on 27 day of March, 1903, that said child has been named Edith Sims, and was living March 4, 1905.

Lula Sims

Witness to Mark:
{

Subscribed and sworn to before me this 19 day of April, 1905.

O L Johnson
Notary Public.

Applications for Enrollment of Choctaw Newborn
Act of 1905   Volume III

AFFIDAVIT OF ATTENDING PHYSICIAN OR MID-WIFE.

UNITED STATES OF AMERICA, Indian Territory,
Central District.

I, Dr E. E. Shiffey , a   M.D. , on oath state that I attended on Mrs. Lula Sims , wife of Thomas J Sims   on the 27 day of March , 1903 ; that there was born to her on said date a Female child; that said child was living March 4, 1905, and is said to have been named Edith Sims

Dr. E. E. Shiffey

Witness to Mark:
{

Subscribed and sworn to before me this 14 day of Apr , 1905.

J. J. Biggs
Notary Public.

COPY   N. B. 155

Muskogee, Indian Territory, April 4, 1905.

Thomas J. Sims,
   Wister, Indian Territory.

Dear Sir:

There is inclosed you herewith for execution application for the enrollment of your infant child, Edith Sims, born March 27, 1903.

The affidavits heretofore filed with the Commission show the child was living on August 6, 1904. It is necessary, for the child to be enrolled, that she was living on March 4, 1905.

In having these affidavits executed care should be exercised to see that all names are written in full, as they appear in the body of the affidavit, and in the event that either of the persons signing the affidavit are unable to write, signatures by mark must be attested by two witnesses. Each affidavit must be executed before a Notary Public and the notarial seal and signature of the officer must be attached to each separate affidavit.

Respectfully,
SIGNED
T. B. Needles.
Commissioner in Charge.

LM 4-23

Applications for Enrollment of Choctaw Newborn
Act of 1905 Volume III

Choctaw 2355.

Muskogee, Indian Territory, April 5, 1905.

Thomas J. Sims,
    Wister, Indian Territory.

Dear Sir:

    Receipt is hereby acknowledged of the affidavits of Lula Sims and E. E. Shiffey to the birth of Edith Sims, daughter of Thomas J. and Lula Sims, March 27, 1903, and the same have been filed with our records as an application for the enrollment of said child.

    Respectfully,

    Commissioner in Charge.

Choc New Born 156
    Charles James Harris
    (Born Nov. 12, 1903)

BIRTH AFFIDAVIT.

DEPARTMENT OF THE INTERIOR.
COMMISSION TO THE FIVE CIVILIZED TRIBES.

IN RE APPLICATION FOR ENROLLMENT, as a citizen of the Choctaw Nation, of Charles James Harris, born on the 12th day of November, 1903

Name of Father: Aaron Harris   a citizen of the Choctaw Nation.
Name of Mother: Sillin Harris   a citizen of the Choctaw Nation.

    Postoffice   Wister, Indian Territory.

AFFIDAVIT OF MOTHER.

UNITED STATES OF AMERICA, Indian Territory,
Central DISTRICT.

    I, Sillin Harris, on oath state that I am 27 years of age and a citizen by blood, of the Choctaw Nation; that I am the lawful wife of Aaron Harris, who is a citizen, by blood of the Choctaw Nation; that a male child

Applications for Enrollment of Choctaw Newborn
Act of 1905   Volume III

was born to me on   12th   day of   November   , 1903; that said child has been named Charles James Harris   , and was living March 4, 1905.

her
Sillin x Harris
mark

Witnesses To Mark:
  { Victor M Locks Jr
    Lee P Calfee

    Subscribed and sworn to before me this   25th   day of   March   , 1905

Wirt Franklin
Notary Public.

AFFIDAVIT OF ATTENDING PHYSICIAN OR MID-WIFE.

UNITED STATES OF AMERICA, Indian Territory, }
  Central   DISTRICT.

    I,   Malinda[sic] Collin   , a   midwife   , on oath state that I attended on Mrs.   Sillin Harris   , wife of   Aaron Harris   on the 12th day of November   , 1903; that there was born to her on said date a   male   child; that said child was living March 4, 1905, and is said to have been named   Charles James Harris

Melinda Collin

Witnesses To Mark:
  {

    Subscribed and sworn to before me this   25th   day of   March   , 1905

Wirt Franklin
Notary Public.

Applications for Enrollment of Choctaw Newborn
Act of 1905   Volume III

Choc New Born 157
    Duel Joe Casey
    (Born Nov. 27, 1903)

BIRTH AFFIDAVIT.

DEPARTMENT OF THE INTERIOR,
COMMISSION TO THE FIVE CIVILIZED TRIBES.

IN RE Application for Enrollment, as a citizen of the Choctaw Nation, of ...., born on the 27 day of November, 1903

Name of Father: John F. Casey   a citizen of the U.S. Nation.
Name of Mother: Eliza Casey   a citizen of the Choctaw Nation.

        Post-office   Oak Lodge, Ind. Ty.

AFFIDAVIT OF MOTHER.

UNITED STATES OF AMERICA, }
   INDIAN TERRITORY,
   Central   District.

    I, Eliza Casey, on oath state that I am 25 years of age and a citizen by Blood, of the Choctaw Nation; that I am the lawful wife of John F Casey, who is a citizen, by .... of the U. S. Nation; that a Male child was born to me on 27 day of November, 1903, that said child has been named Duel Joe Casey, and is now living.

                  Eliza Casey

WITNESSES TO MARK:

    Subscribed and sworn to before me this 28 day of November, 1903.

                  J. F. Casey
                      NOTARY PUBLIC.

Applications for Enrollment of Choctaw Newborn
Act of 1905 Volume III

AFFIDAVIT OF ATTENDING PHYSICIAN OR MID-WIFE.

UNITED STATES OF AMERICA, }
INDIAN TERRITORY,
Central District.

I, Mrs N. J. Willkett , a Midwife , on oath state that I attended on Mrs. Eliza Casey , wife of John F. Casey on the 27 day of November , 1903 ; that there was born to her on said date a male child; that said child is now living and is said to have been named Duel Joe Casey

Mrs. N. J. Willkett

WITNESSES TO MARK:

{

Subscribed and sworn to before me this 28 day of November , 1903.

J. F. Casey
NOTARY PUBLIC.

NEW-BORN AFFIDAVIT.

Number..................

...Choctaw Enrolling Commission...

IN THE MATTER OF THE APPLICATION FOR ENROLLMENT, as a citizen of the Choctaw Nation, of Duel Joe Casey

born on the 27 day of __November__ 190 3

Name of father John F. Casey	a citizen of	U. S.
Nation final enrollment No. _____		
Name of mother Eliza Casey	a citizen of	Choctaw
Nation final enrollment No. 7029		
	Postoffice	Oak Lodge I.T.

Applications for Enrollment of Choctaw Newborn
Act of 1905   Volume III

AFFIDAVIT OF MOTHER.

UNITED STATES OF AMERICA
INDIAN TERRITORY
Central   DISTRICT

I   Eliza Casey   , on oath state that I am 26   years of age and a citizen by   Blood   of the   Choctaw Nation, and as such have been placed upon the final roll of the   Choctaw Nation, by the Honorable Secretary of the Interior my final enrollment number being 7036[sic] ; that I am the lawful wife of   John F. Casey   , who is a citizen of the   U. S.   Nation, and as such has been placed upon the final roll of said Nation by the Honorable Secretary of the Interior, his final enrollment number being _____ and that a   Male   child was born to me on the   27   day of   November   190 3 ; that said child has been named   Duel Joe Casey   , and is now living.

Witnesseth.   Eliza Casey
Must be two ⎫   Edward *(Illegible)*
Witnesses who⎬
are Citizens. ⎭   Felix Leflore

Subscribed and sworn to before me this   4   day of   Mar   190 5

James Bower
Notary Public.

My commission expires:
Sept 23 1907

AFFIDAVIT OF ATTENDING PHYSICIAN OR MIDWIFE

UNITED STATES OF AMERICA
INDIAN TERRITORY
Central   DISTRICT

I,   Nancy J Willkett   a   Midwife on oath state that I attended on Mrs.   Eliza Casey   wife of   John F Casey on the   27   day of   November   , 190 3 , that there was born to her on said date a   Male child, that said child is now living, and is said to have been named   Duel Joe Casey
                                                                her
                                                Nancy J. x Willkett   M.D.
                                                        mark

Subscribed and sworn to before me this, the   4   day of   March   190 5

WITNESSETH: James Bower   Notary Public.
Must be two witnesses ⎧   L R Moore
who are citizens   ⎨
                       ⎩   Joe *(Illegible)*

Applications for Enrollment of Choctaw Newborn
Act of 1905 Volume III

We hereby certify that we are well acquainted with   Nancy J Willkett
a   midwife   and know   her   to be reputable and of good standing in the community.

Edward *(Illegible)*   _____

Felix Leflore   _____

_____

BIRTH AFFIDAVIT.

DEPARTMENT OF THE INTERIOR.
COMMISSION TO THE FIVE CIVILIZED TRIBES.

_____

IN RE APPLICATION FOR ENROLLMENT, as a citizen of the   Choctaw   Nation, of Duel Joe Casey   , born on the   27th   day of   November   , 1903

Name of Father: John F. Casey   a citizen of the U. States   Nation.
Name of Mother: Eliza Casey   a citizen of the   Choctaw   Nation.

Postoffice   Oak Lodge Ind Ty

_____

AFFIDAVIT OF MOTHER.

UNITED STATES OF AMERICA, Indian Territory, ⎫
Central   DISTRICT.   ⎭

I,   Eliza Casey   , on oath state that I am   25   years of age and a citizen by blood   , of the   Choctaw   Nation; that I am the lawful wife of   John F. Casey   , who is a citizen, by – —— –of the —— —— ——Nation; that a   male   child was born to me on 27th   day of   November   , 1903; that said child has been named Duel Joe Casey   , and was living March 4, 1905.

Eliza Casey

Witnesses To Mark:
{

Subscribed and sworn to before me this   24th day of   April   , 1905

Jas H Bowman
Notary Public.

Applications for Enrollment of Choctaw Newborn
Act of 1905 Volume III

AFFIDAVIT OF ATTENDING PHYSICIAN OR MID-WIFE.

UNITED STATES OF AMERICA, Indian Territory,
Central   DISTRICT.

I, N. J. Willkett , a Mid wife , on oath state that I attended on Mrs. Eliza Casey , wife of John F Casey on the 27th day of November , 1903; that there was born to her on said date a male child; that said child was living March 4, 1905, and is said to have been named Duel Joe Casey

Mrs N. J. Willkett

Witnesses To Mark:

Subscribed and sworn to before me this 24th day of April , 1905

Jas H Bowman
My Commission expires March 8th 1906   Notary Public.

7-2431

Muskogee, Indian Territory, March 25, 1905.

Eliza Casey,
   Oaklodge, Indian Territory.

Dear Madam:

Receipt is hereby acknowledged of your letter of March 18, 1905, asking if you can now file for your child Duel Joe Casey for whom you have heretofore forwarded birth certificate.

In reply to your letter you are informed that the affidavits heretofore forwarded to the birth of your son Duel Joe Casey have been filed with our records as an application for the enrollment of said child.

You are advised, however, that no selection of allotment can be made for said child until his enrollment has been approved by the Secretary of the Interior.

Respectfully,

Chairman.

Applications for Enrollment of Choctaw Newborn
Act of 1905 Volume III

COPY N. B. 157

Muskogee, Indian Territory, April 4, 1905.

John F. Casey,
    Oaklodge, Indian Territory.

Dear Sir:

    There is inclosed you herewith for execution application for the enrollment of your infant child, Duel Joe Casey, born November 27, 1903,

    The affidavits heretofore filed with the Commission show the child was living on November 28, 1903. It is necessary, for the child to be enrolled, that he was living on March 4, 1905.

    In having these affidavits executed care should be exercised to see that all names are written in full, as they appear in the body of the affidavit, and in the event that either of the persons signing the affidavit are unable to write, signatures by mark must be attested by two witnesses. Each affidavit must be executed before a Notary Public and the notarial seal and signature of the officer must be attached to each separate affidavit.

                        Respectfully,
                          SIGNED
                        T. B. Needles.

LM 4-19.   Commissioner in Charge.

7-NB-157.

Muskogee, Indian Territory, April 28, 1905.

John F. Casey,
    Oak Lodge, Indian Territory.

Dear Sir:

    Receipt is hereby acknowledged of your letter of April 24, 1905, enclosing the affidavits of Eliza Casey and N. J. Willkett, to the birth of Duel Joe Casey, child of John F. and Eliza Casey, November 27, 1903, and the same have been filed with our records as an application for the enrollment of said child.

    You are advised that no selection of allotment can be permitted for children for whom application is made, under the provisions of the Act of Congress approved March 3, 1905, until their enrollment has been approved by the Secretary of the Interior.

Applications for Enrollment of Choctaw Newborn
Act of 1905   Volume III

You are further advised that it does not appear from our records that application has been made to this Commission by you or in your behalf, for enrollment as an intermarried citizen of the Choctaw Nation, and under the provisions of the Act of Congress approved July 1, 1902, the Commission is now without authority to receive or consider such an application in your behalf.

Replying to that portion of your letter in which you ask relative to removal of restrictions, you are advised that this is a matter which is within the jurisdiction of the United States Indian Agent, and for information relative thereto, you should address him at Muskogee, Indian Territory.

Respectfully,
SIGNED

Tams Bixby
Chairman.

Choc New Born 158
    Mary Weston
    (Born Aug. 18, 1904)

BIRTH AFFIDAVIT.

DEPARTMENT OF THE INTERIOR.
COMMISSION TO THE FIVE CIVILIZED TRIBES.

IN RE APPLICATION FOR ENROLLMENT, as a citizen of the   Choctaw   Nation, of Mary Weston   , born on the   18th   day of   Aug   , 1904

Name of Father: Mitchel Weston   a citizen of the   Choctaw   Nation.
Name of Mother: Sarah Weston   a citizen of the   Choctaw   Nation.

Postoffice   Stigler I.T.

Applications for Enrollment of Choctaw Newborn
Act of 1905   Volume III

AFFIDAVIT OF MOTHER.

UNITED STATES OF AMERICA, Indian Territory, }
    Central   DISTRICT.

    I, Sarah Weston, on oath state that I am 20 years of age and a citizen by Blood, of the Choctaw Nation; that I am the lawful wife of Mitchel Weston, who is a citizen, by Blood of the Choctaw Nation; that a Female child was born to me on 18th day of August, 1904, that said child has been named Mary Weston, and is now living.

                                  Sarah Weston

Witnesses To Mark:
{

    Subscribed and sworn to before me this 17th day of Sept, 1904

                                  M. W. Newman
                                  Notary Public.

AFFIDAVIT OF ATTENDING PHYSICIAN OR MID-WIFE.

UNITED STATES OF AMERICA, Indian Territory, }
    Central   DISTRICT.

    I, Sarah Jones, a Midwife, on oath state that I attended on Mrs. Sarah Weston, wife of Mitchel Weston on the 18th day of Aug, 1904; that there was born to her on said date a Female child; that said child is now living and is said to have been named Mary Weston

                              her
                        Sarah x Jones
Witnesses To Mark: mark
  { John Jones
    (Name Illegible)

    Subscribed and sworn to before me this 17th day of Sept, 1904

                                  M. W. Newman
                                  Notary Public.

My Com Expires Jan 14th 1905

Applications for Enrollment of Choctaw Newborn
Act of 1905   Volume III

BIRTH AFFIDAVIT.

DEPARTMENT OF THE INTERIOR.
COMMISSION TO THE FIVE CIVILIZED TRIBES.

IN RE APPLICATION FOR ENROLLMENT, as a citizen of the Choctaw Nation, of Mary Weston, born on the 18" day of August, 1904

Name of Father: Mitchell Weston   a citizen of the Choctaw Nation.
Name of Mother: Sarah Weston   a citizen of the Choctaw Nation.

Postoffice Stigler, I. T.

AFFIDAVIT OF MOTHER.

UNITED STATES OF AMERICA, Indian Territory,
Central DISTRICT.

I, Sarah Weston, on oath state that I am 23 years of age and a citizen by blood, of the Choctaw Nation; that I am the lawful wife of Mitchell Weston, who is a citizen, by blood of the Choctaw Nation; that a female child was born to me on 18" day of August, 1904; that said child has been named Mary Weston, and was living March 4, 1905.

Sarah Weston

Witnesses To Mark:

Subscribed and sworn to before me this 16 day of May, 1905.

Martin Switzer
Notary Public.

AFFIDAVIT OF ATTENDING PHYSICIAN OR MID-WIFE.

UNITED STATES OF AMERICA, Indian Territory,
Central DISTRICT.

I, Sarah Jones, a Mid-Wife, on oath state that I attended on Mrs. Sarah Weston, wife of Mitchell Weston on the 18" day of August, 1904; that there was born to her on said date a female child; that said child was living March 4, 1905, and is said to have been named Mary Weston

Sarah X Jones

Applications for Enrollment of Choctaw Newborn
Act of 1905 Volume III

Witnesses To Mark:
- John Jones
- Elvira Nale

Subscribed and sworn to before me this 16 day of May , 1905

Martin Switzer
Notary Public.

LETTERS OF ADMINISTRATION.

UNITED STATES OF AMERICA,
INDIAN TERRITORY,
CENTRAL DISTRICT.
Poteau Division. } ss.

The President of the United States of America.

To All Persons to Whom These Presents Shall Come – Greeting:

Know ye, that whereas Mary Weston of the Central District of the Indian Territory, died intestate, as it is said, on or about the 21st day of March A.D., 1905 having at the time of ~~his~~ her death personal property in the Indian Territory which may be lost, destroyed, or diminished in value, if speedy care be not taken of the same; to the end, therefore, that the said property may be collected, preserved, and disposed of according to law, we do hereby appoint R. H. Gardner of said Central District of the Indian Territory, administrator of all and singular the goods and chattels, rights and credits which were of the said Mary Watson at the time of ~~his~~ her death, with full power and authority to dispose of the said property, according to law, and to collect all moneys due the said deceased, and in general to do and perform all other acts and things which are or hereafter may be required of him by law.

Witness, the Honorable Wm H. H. Clayton Judge of the United States Court in the Central District of the Indian Territory, and the seal thereof, at Poteau in the Indian Territory, this 26th day of September A. D. 190 5.

E. J. Fannin Clerk

By S.G. Brink Deputy

Applications for Enrollment of Choctaw Newborn
Act of 1905   Volume III

N. B. 158

Muskogee, Indian Territory, April 7, 1905.

Mitchell Weston,
    Stigler, Indian Territory.

Dear Sir:

    There is inclosed you herewith for execution application for the enrollment of your infant child, Mary Weston, born August 18, 1904.

    The affidavits heretofore filed with the Commission show the child was living on September 17, 1904. It is necessary, for the child to be enrolled, that she was living on March 4, 1905. You will please insert the age and maiden name of the mother in the space provided for the purpose.

    Referring to the affidavits heretofore forwarded to the birth of Mary Weston it is stated in the affidavit of the mother, Sarah Weston, that she is a citizen by blood of the Choctaw Nation.

    If this is correct you are requested to state when, where and under what name she was listed for enrollment, the names of her parents and other members of her family for whom application was made at the same time.

    In having these affidavits executed care should be exercised to see that all names are written in full, as they appear in the body of the affidavit, and in the event that either of the persons signing the affidavit are unable to write, signatures by mark must be attested by two witnesses. Each affidavit must be executed before a Notary Public and the notarial seal and signature of the officer must be attached to each separate affidavit.

    Respectfully,

LM 7-7
    Commissioner in Charge.

7-N.B. 158.

Muskogee, Indian Territory, May 10, 1905.

Mitchell Weston,
    Stigler, Indian Territory.

Dear Sir:

    There is enclosed you herewith for execution application for the enrollment of your infant child, Mary Weston, born August 18, 1904.

Applications for Enrollment of Choctaw Newborn
Act of 1905   Volume III

Your attention is called to the Commission's letter of the 7th ultimo, which contained an application similar to the one above mentioned and in which you were asked to furnish information by which your wife might be identified.

Before this matter can be finally disposed of it will be necessary to have the enclosed application executed and filed with the Commission. The affidavits heretofore filed with the Commission show the child was living on September 17, 1904. It is necessary, for the child to be enrolled, that she was living on March 4, 1905. If your wife, Sarah Weston, is a Choctaw by blood, as she states in the original application, you are requested to state when, where and under what name she was listed for enrollment, the names of her parents and other members of her family for whom application was made at the same time, and if she has selected an allotment to give her roll number as the same appears on her allotment certificate.

In having these affidavits executed care should be exercised to see that all names are written in full, as they appear in the body of the affidavit, and in the event that either of the persons signing the affidavit are unable to write, signatures by mark must be attested by two witnesses. Each affidavit must be executed before a Notary Public and the notarial seal and signature of the officer must be attached to each separate affidavit.

Respectfully,

Chairman.

V. 10/9.

Chairman.

7 NB 158

Muskogee, Indian Territory, May 19, 1905.

Mitchell Weston,
    Stigler, Indian Territory.

Dear Sir:

Receipt is hereby acknowledged of the affidavits of Sarah Weston and Sarah Jones to the birth of Mary Weston, daughter of Mitchell and Sarah Weston, August 18, 1904.

It is stated in the affidavit of the mother that she is a citizen by blood of the Choctaw Nation. If this is correct you are requested to state the name under which she was enrolled, the names of her parents, and if she has selected an allotment of the lands of the Choctaw or Chickasaw Nations please give her roll number as it appears upon her allotment certificate.

Applications for Enrollment of Choctaw Newborn
Act of 1905   Volume III

Respectfully,

Chairman.

7-NB-158

Muskogee, Indian Territory, August 2, 1905.

Mitchell Weston,
Stigler, Indian Territory.

Dear Sir:

Referring to the application for the enrollment of your infant child, Mary Weston, born August 18, 1904, it is stated in the affidavit of the mother that she is a citizen by blood of the Choctaw Nation.

If this is correct you are requested to state where, when and under what name she was listed for enrollment, the names of her parents, and other members of her family for whom application was made at the same time, and if she has selected an allotment give her roll number as it appears upon her allotment certificate.

If not a citizen by blood of the Choctaw Nation you are requested to furnish this office with either the original or a certified copy of the license and certificate of your marriage to her.

This matter should receive your immediate attention as no further action can be taken relative to the enrollment of said child until the evidence requested is supplied.

Respectfully,

Commissioner in Charge.

7-NB-158

Muskogee, Indian Territory, August 4, 1905.

C. T. Mitchell,
    Attorney at Law,
        McCurtain, Indian Territory.

Dear Sir:

Receipt is hereby acknowledged of your letter of July 29, 1905, asking if Mary Weston, daughter of Mitchell and Sarah Weston has been approved.

In reply to your letter you are advised that the name of Mary Weston has not yet been placed upon a schedule of citizens by blood of the Choctaw Nation prepared for forwarding to the Secretary of the Interior.

Applications for Enrollment of Choctaw Newborn
Act of 1905   Volume III

It appears from the affidavits heretofore forwarded to the birth of this child that Sarah Weston is a citizen by blood of the Choctaw Nation, but this office has not been able to identify her upon its records. A letter has been addressed to Mitchell Weston requesting him to state when, where and under what name Sarah Weston was listed for enrollment, the names of her parents, and if she has selected an allotment to give her roll number as it appears upon her allotment certificate. If she is not a citizen of the Choctaw Nation it will be necessary for him to furnish the original or a certified copy of the marriage license and certificate between himself and Sarah Weston, the mother of this child.

Respectfully,

Commissioner.

(The letter below typed as given.)

Keota, I. T. Aug. 8, 1905.

Commission to the Five Civilized Tribes
Muskogee, Ind. Ter.

In reply to your request in relative to Sarah Weston as affidavit of the mother of Infant Born (Mary Weston) who was a citizen by blood of the Choctaw Nation and her father's name is Lyman Perry and her mother's name Elizabeth Perry. And said Sarah Weston has listed for enrollment at Spiro Indian Territory under the name of Sarah Jackson which is now Sarah Weston (nee Jackson) and that her roll number obtain in Land Certificate is No. 7628 Choc. B. B.

Yours Truly-
(Signed) Mitchell Weston

7-NB-158

Muskogee, Indian Territory, August 14, 1905.

Mitchell Weston,
    Keota, Indian Territory.

Dear Sir:

Receipt is hereby acknowledged of your letter of August 8, 1904, stating that your wife Sarah Weston was enrolled as Sarah Jackson, and that she is a daughter of Lyman and Elizabeth Perry and that her roll number is 7628.

In reply to your letter you are advised that this information has enabled this office to identify your wife as an enrolled citizen by blood of the Choctaw Nation and has been made a matter of record in the application for the enrollment of your infant child Mary Weston.

Applications for Enrollment of Choctaw Newborn
Act of 1905   Volume III

Respectfully,

Acting Commissioner.

Choc New Born 159
    Edward George McClaim[sic]
    (Born May 15, 1903)

BIRTH AFFIDAVIT.

DEPARTMENT OF THE INTERIOR,
COMMISSION TO THE FIVE CIVILIZED TRIBES.

IN RE Application for Enrollment, as a citizen of the   Choctaw   Nation, of   Edward George McClain   , born on the   15"   day of   May   , 1903

Name of Father: James T McClain   a citizen of the   Choctaw   Nation.
Name of Mother: Susan McClain   a citizen of the   Choctaw   Nation.

Post-office   Oak Lodge Ind T.

AFFIDAVIT OF MOTHER.

UNITED STATES OF AMERICA,
    INDIAN TERRITORY,
Central   District.

    I, Susan McClain , on oath state that I am   23   years of age and a citizen by blood , of the   Choctaw   Nation; that I am the lawful wife of   James T McClain   , who is a citizen, by blood of the   Choctaw   Nation; that a   male   child was born to me on   15th day of   May   , 1903 , that said child has been named   Edward George McClain   , and is now living.

                                      Susan McClain

WITNESSES TO MARK:

Subscribed and sworn to before me this   26th day of   December   , 1903

                                  J. Wesley Smith
                                      NOTARY PUBLIC.

Applications for Enrollment of Choctaw Newborn
Act of 1905 Volume III

AFFIDAVIT OF ATTENDING PHYSICIAN OR MID-WIFE.

UNITED STATES OF AMERICA,
INDIAN TERRITORY,
Central District.

I, Charles H Mahar, a physician, on oath state that I attended on Mrs. Susan McClain, wife of James T McClain on the 15 day of May, 1903; that there was born to her on said date a male child; that said child is now living and is said to have been named Edward George McClain

Charles H Mahar, M.D.

WITNESSES TO MARK:

Subscribed and sworn to before me this 30th day of December, 1903.

J Wesley Smith
NOTARY PUBLIC.

BIRTH AFFIDAVIT.

DEPARTMENT OF THE INTERIOR.
COMMISSION TO THE FIVE CIVILIZED TRIBES.

IN RE APPLICATION FOR ENROLLMENT, as a citizen of the Choctaw Nation, of Edward George McClain, born on the 15th day of May, 1903

Name of Father: James Thomas McClain   a citizen of the Choctaw Nation.
Name of Mother: Susan McClain   a citizen of the Choctaw Nation.

Postoffice   Oaklodge, Ind. Ter.

AFFIDAVIT OF MOTHER.

UNITED STATES OF AMERICA, Indian Territory,
Central DISTRICT.

I, Susan McClain, on oath state that I am 24 years of age and a citizen by blood, of the Choctaw Nation; that I am the lawful wife of James Thomas McClain, who is a citizen, by blood of the Choctaw Nation; that a male child was born to me on 15th day of May, 1903; that said child has been named Edward George McClain, and was living March 4, 1905.

Susan McClain

Applications for Enrollment of Choctaw Newborn
Act of 1905   Volume III

Witnesses To Mark:
{

Subscribed and sworn to before me this 30th day of   March   , 1905

Wirt Franklin
Notary Public.

AFFIDAVIT OF ATTENDING PHYSICIAN OR MID-WIFE.

UNITED STATES OF AMERICA, Indian Territory, ⎫
Central   DISTRICT.   ⎬

I, Charles H Mahar , a physician , on oath state that I attended on Mrs. Susan McClain , wife of James Thomas McClain on the 15th day of May , 1903; that there was born to her on said date a male child; that said child was living March 4, 1905, and is said to have been named Edward George McClain

Charles H. Mahar

Witnesses To Mark:
{

Subscribed and sworn to before me this 30th day of   March   , 1905

Wirt Franklin
Notary Public.

7-2548

Muskogee, Indian Territory, January 2, 1904.

James T. McClain,
   Oak Lodge, Indian Territory.

Dear Sir:

   Receipt is hereby acknowledged of the affidavits of Susan McClain and Charles H. Mahar relative to the birth of Edward George McClain, infant son of James T. and Susan McClain, May 15, 1903, which it is presumed have been forwarded to this office as an application for enrollment of the above named child as a citizen of the Choctaw Nation.

   You are informed that under the provisions of the Act of Congress approved July 1, 1902 (32 Stats., 641), the Commission is now without authority to receive or

Applications for Enrollment of Choctaw Newborn
Act of 1905 Volume III

consider the original application for enrollment of any person whomsoever as a citizen of the Choctaw or Chickasaw Nation.

                Respectfully,

                                  Chairman.

(The letter below does not belong with the current applicant. It belongs to N.B. 146, page 79 of this book.)

                                  7-2475

                Muskogee, Indian Territory, April 10, 1905.

Nichodemus M. King,
    Ironbridge, Indian Territory.

Dear Sir:

        Receipt is hereby acknowledged of the affidavits of Anne King and Hanah Sockey to the birth of Betsy King, daughter of Nichodemus M. and Anne King, February 15, 1904.

        It is stated in the affidavit of the mother that she is a citizen by blood of the Choctaw Nation and is this is correct you are requested to state the name under which she was enrolled, the names of her parents, and if she has selected an allotment of the lands of the Choctaw or Chickasaw Nation, please give her allotment number as it appears upon her allotment certificate.

        This matter should have your immediate attention in order that proper disposition may be made of the application for the enrollment of this child.

                Respectfully,

                          Commissioner in Charge.

                COPY   N. B. 159

                Muskogee, Indian Territory, April 4, 1905.

James R. McClain,
    Oaklodge, Indian Territory.

Dear Sir:

        There is inclosed you herewith for execution application for the enrollment of your infant child, Edward George McClain, born May 15, 1903.

Applications for Enrollment of Choctaw Newborn
Act of 1905   Volume III

The affidavits heretofore filed with the Commission show the child was living on December 30, 1903. It is necessary, for the child to be enrolled, that he was living on March 4, 1905.

In having these affidavits executed care should be exercised to see that all names are written in full, as they appear in the body of the affidavit, and in the event that either of the persons signing the affidavit are unable to write, signatures by mark must be attested by two witnesses. Each affidavit must be executed before a Notary Public and the notarial seal and signature of the officer must be attached to each separate affidavit.

                Respectfully,
                SIGNED
                T. B. Needles.
LM 4-18   Commissioner in Charge.

Choc New Born 160
    Gracie Baker
    (Born March 10, 1903)
    Willie Alma Baker
    (Born Jan. 14, 1905)

BIRTH AFFIDAVIT.

DEPARTMENT OF THE INTERIOR.
COMMISSION TO THE FIVE CIVILIZED TRIBES.

IN RE APPLICATION FOR ENROLLMENT, as a citizen of the   Choctaw   Nation, of Gracie Baker , born on the 10 day of March , 1903

Name of Father: W. L. Baker   a citizen of the United States Nation.
Name of Mother: Rosa Baker   a citizen of the   Choctaw   Nation.

                Postoffice   Ego, I.T.

Applications for Enrollment of Choctaw Newborn
Act of 1905 Volume III

AFFIDAVIT OF MOTHER.

UNITED STATES OF AMERICA, Indian Territory, }
Central   DISTRICT.

I,   Rosa Baker   , on oath state that I am 21 years of age and a citizen by Blood , of the   Choctaw   Nation; that I am the lawful wife of   W. L. Baker , who is a citizen, by .... of the   United States ~~Nation~~; that a   Female   child was born to me on   10 day of   March , 1903, that said child has been named Gracie Baker , and is now living.

                                      Rosa Baker

Witnesses To Mark:
{

Subscribed and sworn to before me this   14 day of   March   , 1905.

                                      J. T. Hoover
                                      Notary Public.

AFFIDAVIT OF ATTENDING PHYSICIAN OR MID-WIFE.

UNITED STATES OF AMERICA, Indian Territory, }
....DISTRICT.

I,   Thomas M. Morgan   , a   Physician   , on oath state that I attended on Mrs. Mrs[sic] Rosa Baker , wife of   W. L. Baker   on the 10 day of March , 1903; that there was born to her on said date a   Female   child; that said child is now living and is said to have been named Gracie Baker

                                    Thos M. Morgan M.D.

Witnesses To Mark:
{

Subscribed and sworn to before me this 16 day of   March   , 1905.

                                      J. T. Hoover
                                      Notary Public.

Applications for Enrollment of Choctaw Newborn
Act of 1905 Volume III

BIRTH AFFIDAVIT.

DEPARTMENT OF THE INTERIOR.
COMMISSION TO THE FIVE CIVILIZED TRIBES.

IN RE APPLICATION FOR ENROLLMENT, as a citizen of the Choctaw Nation, of Willie Alma Baker, born on the 14 day of Jan, 1905

Name of Father: W. L. Baker   a citizen of the U. S. Nation.
Name of Mother: Rosa Baker   a citizen of the Choctaw Nation.

Postoffice Ego I.T.

AFFIDAVIT OF MOTHER.

UNITED STATES OF AMERICA, Indian Territory, }
Central   DISTRICT.

I, Rosa Baker, on oath state that I am 22 years of age and a citizen by Blood, of the Choctaw Nation; that I am the lawful wife of W. L. Baker, who is a citizen, by .... of the U. S. Nation; that a Female child was born to me on 14th day of January, 1905; that said child has been named Willie Alma Baker, and was living March 4, 1905.

                                       Rosa Baker

Witnesses To Mark:
{

Subscribed and sworn to before me this 30 th day of March, 1905

                                       J. T. Hoover
                                       Notary Public.

AFFIDAVIT OF ATTENDING PHYSICIAN OR MID-WIFE.

UNITED STATES OF AMERICA, Indian Territory, }
Central   DISTRICT.

I, Thos. M. Morgan, a Physician, on oath state that I attended on Mrs. Rosa Baker, wife of W. L. Baker on the 14 day of January, 1905; that there was born to her on said date a Female child; that said child was living March 4, 1905, and is said to have been named Willie Alma Baker

                                       Thos. M. Morgan M.D.

Witnesses To Mark:
{

Applications for Enrollment of Choctaw Newborn
Act of 1905 Volume III

Subscribed and sworn to before me this 30 th day of March , 1905

J. T. Hoover
Notary Public.

7-2556

Muskogee, Indian Territory, March 22, 1905.

Mrs. Rosa Baker,
Ego, Indian Territory.

Dear Madam:

Receipt is hereby acknowledged of your letter of March 15, 1905, enclosing your affidavit and the affidavit of Thomas M. Morgan to the birth of Gracie Baker, daughter of W. L. and Rosa Baker, March 10, 1903, and the same have been filed with the records of the Commission as an application for the enrollment of said child.

In compliance with your request there is inclosed herewith another blank for the enrollment of infant children.

Respectfully,

Chairman.

B. C.

7-2556

Muskogee, Indian Territory, April 5, 1905.

W. L. Baker,
Ego, Indian Territory.

Dear Sir:

Receipt is hereby acknowledged of the affidavits of Rosa Baker and Thomas M. Morgan to the birth of Willie Alma Baker, daughter of W. L. and Rosa Baker, January 14, 1905, and the same have been filed with our records as an application for the enrollment of said child.

Respectfully,

Commissioner in Charge.

Applications for Enrollment of Choctaw Newborn
Act of 1905 Volume III

7 NB 160

Muskogee, Indian Territory, April 26, 1905.

W. L. Baker,
    Hugo, Indian Territory. Ego I.T. June 2 1905

Dear Sir:

    Receipt is hereby acknowledged of your letter of April 18, 1905, asking when you will be allowed to file for you two children for whom application has recently been made.

    In reply to your letter you are informed that the affidavits heretofore forwarded to the birth of your children, Gracie and Willie Alma Baker have been filed with our records as an applications for the enrollment of said children, but no selection of land can be permitted to be made for children for whom application has been made under the provisions of the act of Congress approved March 3, 1905, until their enrollment has been approved by the Secretary of the Interior.

                  Respectfully,

                          Chairman.

Choc New Born 161
    Elnora Holder
    (Born Jan. 3, 1903)
    Idris Imogen Holder
    (Born Nov. 25, 1904)

BIRTH AFFIDAVIT.

DEPARTMENT OF THE INTERIOR,
COMMISSION TO THE FIVE CIVILIZED TRIBES.

    In Re Application for Enrollment, as a citizen of the Choctaw Nation, of Wilmoth Elnorah , born on the 3 day of January , 1903

Name of Father: Ed Holder   a citizen of the United States Nation.
Name of Mother: Katie Holder   a citizen of the Choctaw Nation.

                  Post-office   Hoyt I T

Applications for Enrollment of Choctaw Newborn
Act of 1905   Volume III

AFFIDAVIT OF MOTHER.

UNITED STATES OF AMERICA,
   INDIAN TERRITORY,
Western   District.

    I,   Katie Holder   , on oath state that I am   29   years of age and a citizen by   Blood   , of the   Choctaw   Nation; that I am the lawful wife of   Ed Holder   , who is a citizen, by ~~Blood~~ Marriage of the ~~United States~~ Choctaw   Nation; that a a Female   child was born to me on   3   day of   January   , 1903 , that said child has been named   Wilmoth Elnorah   , and is now living.

                                         Katie Holder

WITNESSES TO MARK:
{ Mrs Annie Martin
  Mrs John Hammons

    Subscribed and sworn to before me this   26   day of   March   , 1903.

                                    L. D. Allen
My Commission Expires Feb 28-1907   NOTARY PUBLIC.

AFFIDAVIT OF ATTENDING PHYSICIAN OR MID-WIFE.

UNITED STATES OF AMERICA,
   INDIAN TERRITORY,
Western   District.

    I,   T. B. Turner   , a   Physician   , on oath state that I attended on Mrs.   Katie Holder   , wife of   Ed Holder   on the   3rd   day of   January   , 1903 ; that there was born to her on said date a   Female   child; that said child is now living and is said to have been named   Wilmoth Elnorah

                                    T. B. Turner M.D.

WITNESSES TO MARK:
{ Mrs Annie Martin
  Mrs John Hammons

    Subscribed and sworn to before me this   9th   day of   June , 1903

                                    J. F. Griffin
                                    NOTARY PUBLIC.
              My Commission expires June 27th 1907

Applications for Enrollment of Choctaw Newborn
Act of 1905 Volume III

NEW-BORN AFFIDAVIT.

Number..........

...Choctaw Enrolling Commission...

IN THE MATTER OF THE APPLICATION FOR ENROLLMENT, as a citizen of the Choctaw Nation, of Edris Emma Jane Holder

born on the 25 day of November 190 4

Name of father G. E. Holder   a citizen of white
Nation final enrollment No. ———
Name of mother Catherine Holder   a citizen of Choctaw
Nation final enrollment No. x x x x 7431

Postoffice Whitefield

AFFIDAVIT OF MOTHER.

UNITED STATES OF AMERICA
INDIAN TERRITORY
Central DISTRICT

I Catherine Holder , on oath state that I am 31 years of age and a citizen by blood of the Choctaw Nation, and as such have been placed upon the final roll of the Choctaw Nation, by the Honorable Secretary of the Interior my final enrollment number being x x x 7431 ; that I am the lawful wife of G. E. Holder , who is a citizen of the white Nation, and as such has been placed upon the final roll of said Nation by the Honorable Secretary of the Interior, his final enrollment number being ——— and that a female child was born to me on the 25 day of November 190 4 ; that said child has been named Edris Emma Jane Holder , and is now living.

Witnesseth.   Catherine Holder

Must be two ⎤ Alice Forrest
Witnesses who ⎰
are Citizens.   James Cooper

Subscribed and sworn to before me this 3 day of Jan 190 5

James Bower
Notary Public.

My commission expires:
Sept 23 1907

Applications for Enrollment of Choctaw Newborn
Act of 1905 Volume III

NEW-BORN AFFIDAVIT.

Number..................

...Choctaw Enrolling Commission...

IN THE MATTER OF THE APPLICATION FOR ENROLLMENT, as a citizen of the Choctaw Nation, of Wilmoth L Holder

born on the 3rd day of __January__ 190 3

Name of father G. E. Holder   a citizen of   white Nation final enrollment No. ~~1431~~
Name of mother Catherine Holder   a citizen of   Choctaw Nation final enrollment No. 7431

Postoffice   Whitefield

AFFIDAVIT OF MOTHER.

UNITED STATES OF AMERICA
INDIAN TERRITORY
~~Northern~~ DISTRICT
Central

I   Catherine Holder   , on oath state that I am 31 years of age and a citizen by blood of the Choctaw Nation, and as such have been placed upon the final roll of the Choctaw Nation, by the Honorable Secretary of the Interior my final enrollment number being 7431 ; that I am the lawful wife of G. E. Holder , who is a citizen of the white Nation, and as such has been placed upon the final roll of said Nation by the Honorable Secretary of the Interior, his final enrollment number being ——— and that a Male[sic] child was born to me on the 3rd day of January 190 3 ; that said child has been named Wilmoth L Holder , and is now living.

Witnesseth.   Catherine Holder

Must be two Witnesses who are Citizens.
Minnie Farris
James Cooper

Subscribed and sworn to before me this 3 day of Jan 190 5

James Bower
Notary Public.

My commission expires:
Sept 23 - 1907

Applications for Enrollment of Choctaw Newborn
Act of 1905   Volume III

AFFIDAVIT OF ATTENDING PHYSICIAN OR MIDWIFE

UNITED STATES OF AMERICA
INDIAN TERRITORY
Northern   DISTRICT

I,   T. B. Turner   a   Physician on oath state that I attended on Mrs. Catherine Holder   wife of   G. E. Holder on the   25th day of   November   , 190 4 , that there was born to her on said date a   female   child, that said child is now living, and is said to have been named   Edris Emma Jane Holder

T B Turner

Subscribed and sworn to before me this, the   3   day of Jan   190 5

WITNESSETH: James Bower   Notary Public.
Must be two witnesses   { Alice Forrest
who are citizens   { James Cooper

We hereby certify that we are well acquainted with _____
_____ a _____ and know _____
to be reputable and of good standing in the community.

Alice Forrest   _____

James Cooper   _____

AFFIDAVIT OF ATTENDING PHYSICIAN OR MIDWIFE

UNITED STATES OF AMERICA
INDIAN TERRITORY
Northern   DISTRICT

I,   T. B. Turner   a   Physician on oath state that I attended on Mrs. Catherine Holder   wife of   G. E. Holder on the 3rd day of   January   , 190 3 , that there was born to her on said date a   fe male[sic] child, that said child is now living, and is said to have been named   Wilmoth L Holder

T B Turner

Subscribed and sworn to before me this, the _____ day of
_____ 190 5

WITNESSETH: James Bower   Notary Public.
Must be two witnesses   { Alice Forrest
who are citizens   { James Cooper

Applications for Enrollment of Choctaw Newborn
Act of 1905   Volume III

We hereby certify that we are well acquainted with _____
_____ a _____ and know _____
to be reputable and of good standing in the community.

    Alice Forrest   _____

    James Cooper   _____

BIRTH AFFIDAVIT.

DEPARTMENT OF THE INTERIOR.
COMMISSION TO THE FIVE CIVILIZED TRIBES.

IN RE APPLICATION FOR ENROLLMENT, as a citizen of the Choctaw Nation, of Wilmot Elnora Holder , born on the 3rd day of January , 1903

Name of Father: Edward Holder   a citizen of the United States Nation.
Name of Mother: Catherine Holder   a citizen of the Choctaw Nation.

                   Postoffice   Whitefield, Indian Territory

AFFIDAVIT OF MOTHER.

UNITED STATES OF AMERICA, Indian Territory, ⎫
    Central   DISTRICT. ⎭

     I, Catherine Holder , on oath state that I am 30 years of age and a citizen by blood , of the Choctaw Nation; that I am the lawful wife of Edward Holder , who is a citizen, by .... of the United States Nation; that a female child was born to me on 3rd day of January , 1903; that said child has been named Wilmot Elnora Holder , and was living March 4, 1905.

                         Catherine Holder
Witnesses To Mark:

Subscribed and sworn to before me this twenty-fifth day of March , 1905

                     Edwin O. Clark
                       Notary Public.

Applications for Enrollment of Choctaw Newborn
Act of 1905 Volume III

AFFIDAVIT OF ATTENDING PHYSICIAN OR MID-WIFE.

UNITED STATES OF AMERICA, Indian Territory,
Central DISTRICT.

I, T. B. Turner, a physician, on oath state that I attended on Mrs. Catherine Holder, wife of Edward Holder on the 3rd day of January, 1903; that there was born to her on said date a female child; that said child was living March 4, 1905, and is said to have been named Wilmot Elnora Holder

T B Turner M.D.

Witnesses To Mark:

Subscribed and sworn to before me this twenty-fifth day of March, 1905

Edwin O. Clark
Notary Public.

BIRTH AFFIDAVIT.

DEPARTMENT OF THE INTERIOR.
COMMISSION TO THE FIVE CIVILIZED TRIBES.

IN RE APPLICATION FOR ENROLLMENT, as a citizen of the Choctaw Nation, of Edris Imogen Holder, born on the 25th day of November, 1904

Name of Father: Edward Holder — a citizen of the United States Nation.
Name of Mother: Catherine Holder — a citizen of the Choctaw Nation.

Postoffice Whitefield, Indian Territory

AFFIDAVIT OF MOTHER.

UNITED STATES OF AMERICA, Indian Territory,
Central DISTRICT.

I, Catherine Holder, on oath state that I am 30 years of age and a citizen by blood, of the Choctaw Nation; that I am the lawful wife of Edward Holder, who is a citizen, by .... of the United States Nation; that a female child was born to me on 25th day of November, 1904; that said child has been named Edris Imogen Holder, and was living March 4, 1905.

Catherine Holder

Witnesses To Mark:

Applications for Enrollment of Choctaw Newborn
Act of 1905   Volume III

Subscribed and sworn to before me this twenty-fifth day of March , 1905

Edwin O. Clark
Notary Public.

AFFIDAVIT OF ATTENDING PHYSICIAN OR MID-WIFE.

UNITED STATES OF AMERICA, Indian Territory,
Central DISTRICT.

I, T. B. Turner , a physician , on oath state that I attended on Mrs. Catherine Holder , wife of Edward Holder on the 25th day of November , 1904; that there was born to her on said date a female child; that said child was living March 4, 1905, and is said to have been named Edris Imogen Holder

T B Turner M.D.

Witnesses To Mark:
{

Subscribed and sworn to before me this twenty-fifth day of March , 1905

Edwin O. Clark
Notary Public.

COPY   N. B. 161

Muskogee, Indian Territory, April 4, 1905.

Ed Holder,
    Hoyt, Indian Territory.

Dear Sir:

There is inclosed you herewith for execution application for the enrollment of your infant child, Wilmoth Elnorah Holder, born January 3, 1903.

The affidavits heretofore filed with the Commission show the child was living on June 9, 1903. It is necessary, for the child to be enrolled, that she was living on March 4, 1905.

In having these affidavits executed care should be exercised to see that all names are written in full, as they appear in the body of the affidavit, and in the event that either of the persons signing the affidavit are unable to write, signatures by mark must be attested by two witnesses. Each affidavit must be executed before a Notary Public and the notarial seal and signature of the officer must be attached to each separate affidavit.

Applications for Enrollment of Choctaw Newborn
Act of 1905   Volume III

LM 4-17.

Respectfully,
SIGNED
T. B. Needles.
Commissioner in Charge.

COPY

Muskogee, Indian Territory, April 6, 1905.

Edwin O. Clark,
Stigler, Indian Territory.

Dear Sir:

Receipt is hereby acknowledged of your letter of March 25, 1905, enclosing the affidavits of Catherine Holder and T. B. Turner to the birth of Edris Imogene and Wilmot Elnora Holder, children of Edward and Catherine Holder, January 3, 1903, and November 25, 1904.

It is stated in the affidavit of the mother that she is a citizen by blood of the Choctaw Nation. If this is correct you are requested to state when, where and under what name she was listed for enrollment, the names of her parents and such other information as will enable us to identify her upon our records.

Please give this matter your immediate attention in order that proper disposition may be made of the application for the enrollment of the above named children.

Respectfully,
SIGNED
T. B. Needles.
Commissioner in Charge.

Choctaw 2558.

Muskogee, Indian Territory, April 11, 1905.

Edwin O. Clark,
Stigler, Indian Territory.

Dear Sir:

Referring to our letter of April 6, 1905, requesting information as to the identification of Catherine Holder, mother of Edris Imogene and Wilmot Elnora Holder, in the matter of their enrollment as citizens by blood of the Choctaw Nation, you are advised that we have been able to identify Catherine Holder upon our records as an

Applications for Enrollment of Choctaw Newborn
Act of 1905 Volume III

enrolled citizen by blood of the Choctaw Nation and it will not, therefore, be necessary to reply to our letter of that date.

Respectfully,

Commissioner in Charge.

COPY   7 N. B. 161

Muskogee, Indian Territory, April 12, 1905.

Edward Holder,
    Whitefield, Indian Territory.

Dear Sir:

    There is inclosed you herewith for execution application for the enrollment of your infant child, Edris Imogene Holder, born November 25, 1904.

    In having these affidavits executed care should be exercised to see that all names are written in full, as they appear in the body of the affidavit, and in the event that either of the persons signing the affidavit are unable to write, signatures by mark must be attested by two witnesses. Each affidavit must be executed before a Notary Public and the notarial seal and signature of the officer must be attached to each separate affidavit.

Respectfully,
SIGNED
T. B. Needles.
LM 12-3   Commissioner in Charge.

7-N.B. 161

Muskogee, Indian Territory, May 10, 1905.

Edward Holder,
    Whitefield, Indian Territory.

Dear Sir:

    There is enclosed herewith affidavit of Catherine Holder and T. B. Turner, M.D/,[sic] which were filed with the Commission in the matter of the application for the enrollment of Wilmot Elnora Holder, and Edris Imogen Holder, born January 3, 1903, and November 25, 1904.

Applications for Enrollment of Choctaw Newborn
Act of 1905   Volume III

    It will be noted that the seal of the notary public, Edwin O. Clark, before whom the affidavits were made, has been omitted. The seal of the above mentioned notary must be attached to each separate affidavit.

    Please have the seal attached to the affidavits and return the same to this office promptly.

Respectfully,

Chairman.

V. 10/10.

Choctaw N B 161

Muskogee, Indian Territory, May 17, 1905.

Ed Holder,
    Whitefield, Indian Territory.

Dear Sir:

    Receipt is hereby acknowledged of affidavits of Catherine Holder and T. B. Turner, to the birth of Wilmot Elnora and Edris Imogen Holder, January 3, 1903 and November 25, 1904, respectively, *(illegible)*eted by affixing the seal of the notary public before whom the same were acknowledged, and the affidavits have been filed with our records in the matter of the enrollment of the above named child. the matter of the enrollment of said children.

Respectfully,

Chairman.

Applications for Enrollment of Choctaw Newborn
Act of 1905   Volume III

Choc New Born 162
  J. Crosby Hazel
  (Born Oct. 21, 1904)

THIS IS TO CERTIFY THAT

Mr. Arthur O. Hazel

of Ind. Ty.

and Miss Lydia Ane Crosby

of Mason, Tex.

Were united by me in

HOLY MATRIMONY

according to the Ordinance of God and the Laws of the

State of Texas

at Mason on the sixt[sic] day of January in the Year of OUR LORD,

One Thousand Nine Hundred and four.

  J. P. Lyle,

  Mason,

  Texas.

Witnesses

  Bernice A. Doole.

  Emma Lindsay.

"Those whom God hath joined together, let no man put asunder"

I, Kate DeBord, Stenographer to the Commission to the Five Civilized Tribes, being first duly affirmed, state that the above is a full, true and correct copy of the certificate of marriage between Mr. Arthur O. Hazel and Miss Lydia Ane Crosby January 6, 1904.

Kate D^{e}Bord

Applications for Enrollment of Choctaw Newborn
Act of 1905   Volume III

Subscribed and affirmed to before me this 13 day of April 1905.

(Name Illegible)
Notary Public.

BIRTH AFFIDAVIT.

DEPARTMENT OF THE INTERIOR.
COMMISSION TO THE FIVE CIVILIZED TRIBES.

IN RE APPLICATION FOR ENROLLMENT, as a citizen of the   Choctaw   Nation, of J. Crosby Hazel   , born on the   21"   day of   October   , 1904

Name of Father: Arthur O Hazel   a citizen of the   Choctaw   Nation.
Name of Mother: Ane Crosby Hazel   a citizen of the   ———   Nation.

Postoffice ....

AFFIDAVIT OF MOTHER.

UNITED STATES OF AMERICA, Indian Territory,
Southern   DISTRICT.

I, Ane Crosby Hazel   , on oath state that I am   26   years of age and a citizen ~~by~~ ——, of the —— Nation; that I am the lawful wife of   Arthur O Hazel   , who is a citizen, by   blood   of the   Choctaw   Nation; that a   male   child was born to me on   21"   day of   October   , 1904, that said child has been named   J Crosby Hazel   , and is now living.

Ane Crosby Hazel

Witnesses To Mark:
{

Subscribed and sworn to before me this   28"   day of   Feby   , 1905.

Joseph P Smith
Notary Public.

AFFIDAVIT OF ATTENDING PHYSICIAN OR MID-WIFE.

UNITED STATES OF AMERICA, Indian Territory,
Southern   DISTRICT.

I, Benj. W. Ralston   , a physician   , on oath state that I attended on Mrs. Ane Crosby Hazel   , wife of   Arthur O Hazel   on the   21"   day of October , 1904; that there was born to her on said date a   male   child; that said child is now living and is said to have been named   J Crosby Hazel

Applications for Enrollment of Choctaw Newborn
Act of 1905   Volume III

Benj. W. Ralston M.D.

Witnesses To Mark:
{

Subscribed and sworn to before me this   2nd   day of   March   , 1905.

Joseph P Smith
Notary Public.

BIRTH AFFIDAVIT.

DEPARTMENT OF THE INTERIOR.
COMMISSION TO THE FIVE CIVILIZED TRIBES.

IN RE APPLICATION FOR ENROLLMENT, as a citizen of the   Choctaw   Nation, of J Crosby Hazel   , born on the   21   day of   October , 1904

Name of Father: Arthur O Hazel   a citizen of the   Choctaw   Nation.
Name of Mother: Ane Crosby Hazel   a citizen of the   U S   Nation.

Postoffice   Erin Springs, Ind Ter

AFFIDAVIT OF MOTHER.

UNITED STATES OF AMERICA, Indian Territory, }
....DISTRICT. }

I,   Ane Crosby Hazel   , on oath state that I am   26   years of age and a citizen ~~by~~ ...., of the   United States   Nation; that I am the lawful wife of Arthur O Hazel   , who is a citizen, by   Blood   of the   Choctaw   Nation; that a   Male   child was born to me on   21   day of   October   , 1904; that said child has been named   J Crosby Hazel   , and was living March 4, 1905.

Ane Crosby Hazel

Witnesses To Mark:
{

Subscribed and sworn to before me this   7th   day of   April   , 1905

Claire L. McArthur
Notary Public.

Applications for Enrollment of Choctaw Newborn
Act of 1905   Volume III

AFFIDAVIT OF ATTENDING PHYSICIAN OR MID-WIFE.

UNITED STATES OF AMERICA, Indian Territory, }
....DISTRICT.

    I, Benj. W. Ralston   , a physician   , on oath state that I attended on Mrs. Ane Crosby Hazel   , wife of   Arthur O Hazel   on the 21 day of October   , 1904; that there was born to her on said date a   Male   child; that said child was living March 4, 1905, and is said to have been named J Crosby Hazel

                                          Benj. W. Ralston M.D.

Witnesses To Mark:
{

    Subscribed and sworn to before me this 7th day of April , 1905

                                        Claire L. McArthur
                                          Notary Public.

COPY

                                                                  N.B. 162

                Muskogee, Indian Territory, April 3, 1905.

Arthur O. Hazel,
    Erin Springs, Indian Territory.

Dear Sir:

    There is inclosed you herewith for execution application for the enrollment of your infant child, J. Crosby Hazel, born October 21, 1904.

    The affidavits heretofore filed with the Commission show the child was living on March 2, 1905. It is necessary, for the child to be enrolled, that he was living on March 4, 1905.

    The affidavit also shows that the applicant claims through you. It is, therefore, necessary that the license and the certificate of your marriage to the applicant's mother be forwarded with the return of the inclosed affidavit.

    In having these affidavits executed care should be exercised to see that all names are written in full, as they appear in the body of the affidavit, and in the event that either of the persons signing the affidavit are unable to write, signatures by mark must be attested by two witnesses. Each affidavit must be executed before a Notary Public and the notarial seal and signature of the officer must be attached to each separate affidavit.

Applications for Enrollment of Choctaw Newborn
Act of 1905   Volume III

LM 1-31

Respectfully,
SIGNED
Tams Bixby
Chairman.

COPY Choctaw N.B. 162

Muskogee, Indian Territory, April 13, 1905.

C. L. McArthur,
    Attorney at Law,
        Lindsey, Indian Territory.

Dear Sir:

    Receipt is hereby acknowledged of your letter of April 7, transmitting the affidavits of Ane Crosby Hazel and Benj. W. Ralston to the birth of J. Crosby Hazel, Indian Territory son of Arthur O. and Ane Crosby Hazel, Indian Territory October 21, 1904, and the same have been filed with our records in the matter of the application for the enrollment of said child.

    Receipt is also acknowledged of the marriage certificate between Arthur O. Hazel and Miss Lydia Ane Crosby, January 6, 1904, and a certified copy has been made and filed with our records and the original is returned herewith for delivery to Mr. Hazel.

Respectfully,
SIGNED
T. B. Needles.
Commissioner in Charge.

DeB--2/13.

Applications for Enrollment of Choctaw Newborn
Act of 1905   Volume III

Choc New Born 163
    Joanna Brady
    (Born Dec. 28, 1903)

BIRTH AFFIDAVIT.

DEPARTMENT OF THE INTERIOR.
COMMISSION TO THE FIVE CIVILIZED TRIBES.

IN RE APPLICATION FOR ENROLLMENT, as a citizen of the   Choctaw   Nation, of Female ———— , born on the   28   day of   Dec.   , 1903

Name of Father: R. G. Brady   a citizen of the   U.S.   Nation.
Name of Mother: Selina C. Ross (nee Brady)   a citizen of the   Choctaw   Nation.

Postoffice   Jesse I.T.

AFFIDAVIT OF MOTHER.

UNITED STATES OF AMERICA, Indian Territory, ⎫
    Southern   DISTRICT. ⎬

    I,   Selina C. Ross (nee Brady)   , on oath state that I am   31   years of age and a citizen by   Birth   , of the   Choctaw   Nation; that I ~~am~~ was the lawful wife of   R. G. Brady   , who ~~is~~ was a citizen, by Marriage   of the   Choctaw Nation; that a   Female   child was born to me on   28th day of   December   , 1903; that said child has been named   Joanna Brady   , and was living March 4, 1905.

                                   Selina C Ross nee Brady
Witnesses To Mark:
{

    Subscribed and sworn to before me this   22   day of   March   , 1905

                                  Price Statler
                                  Notary Public.

AFFIDAVIT OF ATTENDING PHYSICIAN OR MID-WIFE.

UNITED STATES OF AMERICA, Indian Territory, ⎫
    Southern   DISTRICT. ⎬

              & Nora Kelley   we know We,   Allice Thompson   , a ...., on oath state that ~~I attended on~~ Mrs.   Selina C Ross (nee Brady)   , wife of   R. G. Brady   on the   28th day of   Dec

Applications for Enrollment of Choctaw Newborn
Act of 1905   Volume III

, 1904[sic]; that there was born to her on said date a   Female   child; that said child was living March 4, 1905, and is said to have been named Joanna Brady

Witnesses To Mark:
{

Allice Thompson
Nora Kelley

Subscribed and sworn to before me this 22   day of   March   , 1905

Price Statler
Notary Public.

BIRTH AFFIDAVIT.
DEPARTMENT OF THE INTERIOR.
COMMISSION TO THE FIVE CIVILIZED TRIBES.

IN RE APPLICATION FOR ENROLLMENT, as a citizen of the   Choctaw   Nation, of Joanna Brady , born on the   28   day of   Dec.   , 1902[sic]

Name of Father: Robert G. Brady   a citizen of the   Choctaw   Nation.
Name of Mother: Selina Brady   a citizen of the   Choctaw   Nation.

Postoffice   Jesse Ind. Ter.

AFFIDAVIT OF MOTHER.

UNITED STATES OF AMERICA, Indian Territory,
Southern   DISTRICT.

I,   Selina Brady   , on oath state that I am   31   years of age and a citizen by blood , of the   Choctaw   Nation; that I ~~am~~ was the lawful wife of   Robert G. Brady , who is a citizen, by   intermarriage   of the   Choctaw   Nation; that a   female   child was born to me on 28th day of December   , 1902; that said child has been named Joanna Brady , and was living March 4, 1905.

Selina Ross nee Brady

Witnesses To Mark:
{

Subscribed and sworn to before me this 25th day of   May   , 1905

Price Statler
Notary Public.

Applications for Enrollment of Choctaw Newborn
Act of 1905 Volume III

AFFIDAVIT OF ATTENDING PHYSICIAN OR MID-WIFE.

UNITED STATES OF AMERICA, Indian Territory, }
Southern DISTRICT.

We, Geo. B Thompson & S.A. Thompson, on oath state that ~~I~~ we attended on Mrs. Selina Brady, wife of Robert G. Brady on the 28th day of December, 1902; that there was born to her on said date a female child; that said child was living March 4, 1905, and is said to have been named Joanna Brady

                                      Geo. B. Thompson
Witnesses To Mark: SA Thompson
{

    Subscribed and sworn to before me this 25th day of May, 1905

                                      Price Statler
                                        Notary Public.

BIRTH AFFIDAVIT.

DEPARTMENT OF THE INTERIOR.
COMMISSION TO THE FIVE CIVILIZED TRIBES.

    IN RE APPLICATION FOR ENROLLMENT, as a citizen of the Choctaw Nation, of Joanna Brady, born on the 28 day of Dec., 1902[sic]
                                Roll IW1058
Name of Father: Robert G. Brady   a citizen of the Choctaw Nation.
Name of Mother: Selina Brady Roll 15159   a citizen of the Choctaw Nation.

                         Postoffice   Jesse Ind. Ter.

AFFIDAVIT OF MOTHER.

UNITED STATES OF AMERICA, Indian Territory, }
Southern DISTRICT.

    I, Selina Brady, on oath state that I am 31 years of age and a citizen by blood, of the Choctaw Nation; that I am the lawful wife of Robert G. Brady, who is a citizen, by marriage of the Choctaw Nation; that a female child was born to me on 28th day of December, 1902; that said child has been named Joanna Brady, and was living March 4, 1905.

                                Selina Ross nee Brady
Witnesses To Mark:
{

Applications for Enrollment of Choctaw Newborn
Act of 1905 Volume III

Subscribed and sworn to before me this 11th day of Aug, 1905

Price Statler
Notary Public.

AFFIDAVIT OF ATTENDING PHYSICIAN OR MID-WIFE.

UNITED STATES OF AMERICA, Indian Territory,
Southern DISTRICT.

we are acquainted with We, GB & S.A. Thompson and[sic], a ...., on oath state that ~~I attended on~~ Mrs. Selina Brady, wife of Robert G. Brady on the 28th day of Dec ,1902; that there was born to her on said date a female child; that said child was living March 4, 1905, and is said to have been named Joanna Brady

Witnesses To Mark:
{

G. B. Thompson
S. A. Thompson

Subscribed and sworn to before me this 11th day of Aug, 1905

Price Statler
Notary Public.

Muskogee, Indian Territory, March 28, 1905.

Price Statler,
Jesse, Indian Territory.

Dear Sir:

Receipt is hereby acknowledged of your letter of March 22, 1905, transmitting affidavits of Selina C. Ross (Brady) and joint affidavit of Alice Thompson and Nora Kelly[sic] to the birth of Joanna Brady, daughter of R. J[sic]. Brady and Selina C. Ross, December 28, 1903, and the same have been filed with our records as an application for the enrollment of said child.

Respectfully,

Chairman.

Applications for Enrollment of Choctaw Newborn
Act of 1905 Volume III

COPY.

7-N.B. 163.

Muskogee, Indian Territory, May 11, 1905.

Robert G. Brady,
Jesse, Indian Territory.

Dear Sir:

There is enclosed you herewith for execution application for the enrollment of your infant child, Joanna Brady, born December 28, 1903.

In the affidavit heretofore filed with the Commission the mother gives the date of birth of the applicant as December 28, 1903, while in the affidavits of the other parties, attached thereto, it is given as December 28, 1904. In the enclosed application you will please insert the correct date before having the affidavit executed.

In having these affidavits executed care should be exercised to see that all names are written in full, as they appear in the body of the affidavit, and in the event that either of the persons signing the affidavit are unable to write, signatures by mark must be attested by two witnesses. Each affidavit must be executed before a Notary Public and the notarial seal and signature of the officer must be attached to each separate affidavit.

Respectfully,
SIGNED

Tams Bixby
Chairman.

7-N.B. 163.

Muskogee, Indian Territory, May 31, 1905.

Robert G. Brady,
Jesse, Indian Territory.

Dear Sir:

Receipt is hereby acknowledged of the affidavits of Selina Ross Brady and Geo?[sic] B. and S. A. Thompson to the birth of Joanna Brady, daughter of Robert G. and Selina Brady, December 20[sic], 1902, and the same have been filed with our records in the matter of the enrollment of said child.

Respectfully,

Chairman.

Applications for Enrollment of Choctaw Newborn
Act of 1905   Volume III

7-NB-163

Muskogee, Indian Territory, August 4, 1905.

Robert G. Brady,
    Jesse, Indian Territory.

Dear Sir:

    There is inclosed you herewith for execution application for the enrollment of your infant child, Joanna Brady.

    In the affidavit of the mother, executed March 25, 1905, the date of birth of said child is given as December 28, 1903; in the joint affidavit of Alice Thompson and Nora Kelly, executed on the same date, the date of birth is given as December 28, 1904; in the affidavit of the mother and the joint affidavit of George B. Thompson and S. A. Thompson, executed May 25, 1905, the date of birth is given as December 28, 1902.

    In the inclosed application the date of birth is left blank. You will please insert the correct date and have the affidavits properly executed and return to this office immediately, as no further action can be taken relative to the enrollment of your said child, until the evidence requested is supplied.

                              Respectfully,

LM 1/4   Commissioner.

7-NB-163

Muskogee, Indian Territory, August 15, 1905.

Mrs. S. E. Ross,
    Jesse, Indian Territory.

Dear Madam:

    Receipt is hereby acknowledged of the affidavits of Selina Ross, nee Brady, and G. B. Thompson and S. A. Thompson to the birth of Joanna Brady, daughter of Robert G. and Selina Brady, December 28, 1902, and the same have been filed in the matter of the enrollment of the said child.

                              Respectfully,

                              Acting Commissioner.

Applications for Enrollment of Choctaw Newborn
Act of 1905 Volume III

Choc New Born 164
    Milton Elias Boatwright
    (Born Apr. 20, 1904)

BIRTH AFFIDAVIT.

DEPARTMENT OF THE INTERIOR,
COMMISSION TO THE FIVE CIVILIZED TRIBES.

In Re Application for Enrollment, as a citizen of the Choctaw Nation, of Milton Elias Boatwright, born on the 20 day of April, 1904

Name of Father: Joseph Boatwright   a citizen of the Choctaw Nation.
Name of Mother: Lu[sic] E Boatwright   a citizen of the Choctaw Nation.

        Post-office   Cowlington, I.T.

AFFIDAVIT OF MOTHER.

UNITED STATES OF AMERICA,
    INDIAN TERRITORY,
    Central   District.

    I, Lu E Boatwright, on oath state that I am 29 years of age and a citizen by marriage, of the Choctaw Nation; that I am the lawful wife of Joseph Boatwright, who is a citizen, by blood of the Choctaw Nation; that a male child was born to me on 20 day of April, 1904, that said child has been named Milton Elias Boatwright, and is now living.

        Lou E Boatwright

WITNESSES TO MARK:

    Subscribed and sworn to before me this 13 day of July, 1904

        A.H. Crouthamel
            NOTARY PUBLIC.

Applications for Enrollment of Choctaw Newborn
Act of 1905 Volume III

AFFIDAVIT OF ATTENDING PHYSICIAN OR MID-WIFE.

UNITED STATES OF AMERICA, }
INDIAN TERRITORY,
Central   District.

I, Martha J Moseby , a midwife , on oath state that I attended on Mrs. Lu E Boatwright , wife of Joseph Boatwright on the 20 day of April , 1904; that there was born to her on said date a male child; that said child is now living and is said to have been named Milton Elias Boatwright

Martha J Moseby

WITNESSES TO MARK:
{

Subscribed and sworn to before me this 13 day of July , 1904

My commission expires Feb. 3 1907

A.H. Crouthamel
NOTARY PUBLIC.

BIRTH AFFIDAVIT.

DEPARTMENT OF THE INTERIOR.
COMMISSION TO THE FIVE CIVILIZED TRIBES.

IN RE APPLICATION FOR ENROLLMENT, as a citizen of the Choctaw Nation, of Milton Elias Boatright , born on the 20 day of April , 1904

Name of Father: Joseph Boatright   a citizen of the Choctaw Nation.
Name of Mother: Lou E Boatright   a citizen of the Choctaw Nation.

Postoffice   Cowlington, Ind. Ter.

AFFIDAVIT OF MOTHER.

UNITED STATES OF AMERICA, Indian Territory, }
Central   DISTRICT.

I, Lou E Boatright , on oath state that I am 28 years of age and a citizen by intermarriage , of the Choctaw Nation; that I am the lawful wife of Joseph Boatright , who is a citizen, by blood of the Choctaw Nation; that a male child was born to me on 20" day of April , 1904; that said child has been named Milton Elias Boatright , and was living March 4, 1905.

Lou E Boatright

Applications for Enrollment of Choctaw Newborn
Act of 1905 Volume III

Witnesses To Mark:
{

Subscribed and sworn to before me this 14 day of April , 1905

A. H. Crouthamel
Notary Public.

My Com. Ex Feb. 3-1907

AFFIDAVIT OF ATTENDING PHYSICIAN OR MID-WIFE.

UNITED STATES OF AMERICA, Indian Territory,
Central DISTRICT. }

I, Martha J Mosby[sic] , a midwife , on oath state that I attended on Mrs. Lou E Boatright , wife of Joseph Boatright on the 20 day of April , 1904; that there was born to her on said date a male child; that said child was living March 4, 1905, and is said to have been named Milton Elias Boatright

Martha J Mosby

Witnesses To Mark:
{

Subscribed and sworn to before me this 14 day of April , 1905

A. H. Crouthamel
Notary Public.

My Com. Ex Feb. 3-1907

7-2763

Muskogee, Indian Territory, July 19, 1904.

Joseph Boatwright,
 Cowlington, Indian Territory.

Dear Sir :-

Receipt is hereby acknowledged of the affidavits of Lou E. Boatwright and Martha I. Mosely[sic], relative to the birth of your infant son, Milton Elias Boatwright, April 20, 1904, which it is presumed have been forwarded as an application for enrollment of said child as a citizen by blood of the Choctaw Nation.

The Act of Congress approved July 1, 1902, which was ratified by the citizens of the Choctaw and Chickasaw Nations September 25, 1902, among other things provides

Applications for Enrollment of Choctaw Newborn
Act of 1905   Volume III

that no child born to a citizen subsequent to the date of said ratification shall be entitled to enrollment or to participate in the distribution of the tribal property of the Choctaw and Chickasaws.

        Respectfully,

        Commissioner in Charge.

COPY.

N. B. 164

Muskogee, Indian Territory, April 6, 1905.

Joseph Boatright,
    Cowlington, Indian Territory.

Dear Sir:

    There is inclosed you herewith for execution application for the enrollment of your infant child, Milton Elias Boatright, born April 20, 1904.

    The affidavits heretofore filed with the Commission show the child was living on July 13, 1904. It is necessary, for the child to be enrolled, that he was living on March 4, 1905. You will please insert the mother's age in the place left blank for that purpose.

    In having these affidavits executed care should be exercised to see that all names are written in full, as they appear in the body of the affidavit, and in the event that either of the persons signing the affidavit are unable to write, signatures by mark must be attested by two witnesses. Each affidavit must be executed before a Notary Public and the notarial seal and signature of the officer must be attached to each separate affidavit.

        Respectfully,
        SIGNED
        T. B. Needles.
SEV 7-6.   Commissioner in Charge.

Applications for Enrollment of Choctaw Newborn
Act of 1905   Volume III

COPY.

Choctaw N.B. 164.

Muskogee, Indian Territory, April 22, 1905.

Joseph Boatwright,
    Cowlington, Indian Territory.

Dear Sir:

    Receipt is hereby acknowledged of the affidavits of Lou E. Boatwright and Martha I. Moseley to the birth of Milton Elias Boatwright, April 20, 1904, son of Joseph and Susie[sic] E. Boatwright, and the same have been filed with our records in the matter of the enrollment of said child.

                Respectfully,
                SIGNED

                Tams Bixby
                Chairman.

<u>Choc New Born 165</u>
    Campbell Russell
    (Born Dec. 9, 1904)

    Dismissed June 15, 1905

            DEPARTMENT OF THE INTERIOR,
      COMMISSION TO THE FIVE CIVILIZED TRIBES.

    Record in the matter of the application for enrollment as a citizen by blood of the Choctaw Nation of:

        CAMPBELL RUSSELL, JR.   7-NB-165.

Applications for Enrollment of Choctaw Newborn
Act of 1905   Volume III

NEW-BORN AFFIDAVIT.

Number..............

...Choctaw Enrolling Commission...

IN THE MATTER OF THE APPLICATION FOR ENROLLMENT, as a citizen of the Choctaw Nation, of Campbell Russell

born on the 9th day of December 190 4

Name of father   Campbell Russell   a citizen of   Choctaw Nation final enrollment No. 124
Name of mother   Mary A. Russell   a citizen of   Choctaw Nation final enrollment No. 8101

Postoffice   Hereford Ind. Ter.

AFFIDAVIT OF MOTHER.

UNITED STATES OF AMERICA
INDIAN TERRITORY
Western   DISTRICT

I   Mary A. Russell   , on oath state that I am 31 years of age and a citizen by Blood of the Choctaw Nation, and as such have been placed upon the final roll of the Choctaw Nation, by the Honorable Secretary of the Interior my final enrollment number being 8101 ; that I am the lawful wife of   Campbell Russell   , who is a citizen of the Choctaw   Nation, and as such has been placed upon the final roll of said Nation by the Honorable Secretary of the Interior, his final enrollment number being   124   and that a   male   child was born to me on the   9th   day of   December   190 4 ; that said child has been named   Campbell Russell   , and is now living.

Witnesseth.   Mary A. Russell

Must be two
Witnesses who   Alex *(Illegible)*
are Citizens.   L E Howland

Subscribed and sworn to before me this   13   day of   Feb   190 5

A. L. Beckett
Notary Public.

My commission expires: May 21" 1907

Applications for Enrollment of Choctaw Newborn
Act of 1905   Volume III

AFFIDAVIT OF ATTENDING PHYSICIAN OR MIDWIFE

UNITED STATES OF AMERICA
INDIAN TERRITORY
 Western   DISTRICT

I, F. B. Fite a Physician on oath state that I attended on Mrs. Mary A Russell wife of Campbell Russell on the 9th day of December , 190 4 , that there was born to her on said date a male child, that said child is now living, and is said to have been named Campbell Russell

 F. B. Fite   M.D.

WITNESSETH:
Must be two witnesses who are citizens and know the child.
 { Alex *(Illegible)*
   L.E. Howland

Subscribed and sworn to before me this, the 13' day of Feb 190 5

My Comm. Expires
  May 21" 1907   A.L. Beckett
    Notary Public.

We hereby certify that we are well acquainted with F B Fite of Muskogee I.T. a Physician and know him to be reputable and of good standing in the community.

 { Alex *(Illegible)*
   L.E. Howland

COPY

N. B. 165

Muskogee, Indian Territory, April 2, 1905.

Campbell Russell,
 Hereford, Indian Territory.

Dear Sir:

 There is inclosed you herewith for execution application for the enrollment of your infant child, Campbell Russell, Jr., born December 9, 1904.

 The affidavits heretofore filed with the Commission show the child was living on February 13, 1905. It is necessary, for the child to be enrolled, that he was living on March 4, 1905.

 In having these affidavits executed care should be exercised to see that all names are written in full, as they appear in the body of the affidavit, and in the event that either

Applications for Enrollment of Choctaw Newborn
Act of 1905 Volume III

of the persons signing the affidavit are unable to write, signatures by mark must be attested by two witnesses. Each affidavit must be executed before a Notary Public and the notarial seal and signature of the officer must be attached to each separate affidavit.

Respectfully,
SIGNED

LM 8-38.

T. B. Needles.
Commissioner in Charge.

Just throw aside the application. She lost *(illegible)* babe before March 4th. I had not yet seen coppy[sic] of Bill as passed, when I filed the application.

The Choctaw Enroling[sic] Commission were listing all children born since the closing of the Rolls whether they were still living or not.

BIRTH AFFIDAVIT.

DEPARTMENT OF THE INTERIOR.
COMMISSION TO THE FIVE CIVILIZED TRIBES.

IN RE APPLICATION FOR ENROLLMENT, as a citizen of the Choctaw Nation, of Campbell Russell Jr. , born on the 9" day of December , 1904

Name of Father: Campbell Russell   a citizen of the Choctaw Nation.
Name of Mother: Mary A. Russell   a citizen of the Choctaw Nation.

Postoffice   Hereford, Ind. Ter.

AFFIDAVIT OF MOTHER.

UNITED STATES OF AMERICA, Indian Territory,
....DISTRICT.

I, Mary A Russell , on oath state that I am .... years of age and a citizen by Blood , of the Choctaw Nation; that I am the lawful wife of Campbell Russell , who is a citizen, by Blood of the Choctaw Nation; that a Male child was born to me on 9" day of December , 1904; that said child has been named Campbell Russell Jr , and was living March 4, 1905.

Witnesses To Mark:
{

Applications for Enrollment of Choctaw Newborn
Act of 1905   Volume III

Subscribed and sworn to before me this .... day of ...., 190....

....
Notary Public.

AFFIDAVIT OF ATTENDING PHYSICIAN OR MID-WIFE.

UNITED STATES OF AMERICA, Indian Territory, }
.....................................DISTRICT.

I,.., a........................., on oath state that I attended on Mrs.   Mary A Russell   , wife of   Campbell Russell   on the 9" day of December   , 1904; that there was born to her on said date a   Male   child; that said child was living March 4, 1905, and is said to have been named Campbell Russell Jr.

....

Witnesses To Mark:
{

Subscribed and sworn to before me this .... day of ...., 190....

....
Notary Public.

COPY

Choctaw N.B.165.

Muskogee, Indian Territory, April 19, 1905.

Campbell Russell,
 Hereford, Indian Territory.

Dear Sir:

Receipt is hereby acknowledged of your letter without date, stating that your child, Campbell Russell, Jr., died before March 4, 1905.

This information has been made a matter of record.

Respectfully,
SIGNED

Tams Bixby
Chairman.

Applications for Enrollment of Choctaw Newborn
Act of 1905 Volume III

7-N.B. 165.

Muskogee, Indian Territory, May 10, 1905.

Campbell Russell,
    Hereford, Indian Territory.

Dear Sir:

    In your letter without date you state that your infant child, Campbell Russell, Jr., died before March 4, 1905. In order that this may be made a matter of record there is enclosed herewith a blank proof of death, which you will kindly have executed and return to this office.

    In having these affidavits executed care should be exercised to see that all names are written in full, as they appear in the body of the affidavit, and in the event that either of the persons signing the affidavit are unable to write, signatures by mark must be attested by two witnesses. Each affidavit must be executed before a Notary Public and the notarial seal and signature of the officer must be attached to each separate affidavit.

    Respectfully,

    SIGNED *Tams Bixby*
    Chairman.

V. 10/11.

DEPARTMENT OF THE INTERIOR.
COMMISSION TO THE FIVE CIVILIZED TRIBES.

In the matter of the death of Campbell Russell, Jr. a citizen of the Choctaw Nation, who formerly resided at or near Hereford, Ind. Ter., and died on the 14 day of Feb., 1905

AFFIDAVIT OF RELATIVE.

UNITED STATES OF AMERICA, Indian Territory, }
    Western DISTRICT.

    I, Campbell Russell, on oath state that I am 41 years of age and a citizen by marriage, of the Choctaw Nation; that my postoffice address is Hereford, Ind. Ter.; that I am the father of Campbell Russell, Jr who was a citizen, by Blood, of the Choctaw Nation and that said Campbell Russell, Jr died on the 14 day of Feb., 1905

    Campbell Russell

Applications for Enrollment of Choctaw Newborn
Act of 1905 Volume III

Witnesses To Mark:
{

Subscribed and sworn to before me this 31st day of May, 1905.

Com Expires May 29-1907

W.H. Bateman
Notary Public.

AFFIDAVIT OF ACQUAINTANCE.

UNITED STATES OF AMERICA, Indian Territory, }
Western DISTRICT.

I, F. B. Fite, on oath state that I am 43 years of age, and a citizen by marriage of the Choctaw Nation; that my postoffice address is Muskogee, Ind. Ter.; that I was personally acquainted with Campbell Russell Jr. who was a citizen, by Blood, of the Choctaw Nation; and that said Campbell Russell, Jr. died on the 14 day of Feb., 1905

F. B. Fite

Witnesses To Mark:
{

Subscribed and sworn to before me this 31st day of May, 1905.

Com Expires May 29-1907

W.H. Bateman
Notary Public.

W.F.
7-NB-165.

DEPARTMENT OF THE INTERIOR,
COMMISSION TO THE FIVE CIVILIZED TRIBES.

In the matter of the application for the enrollment of Campbell Russell, Jr., as a citizen by blood of the Choctaw Nation.

---oOo---

It appears from the record herein that on March 9, 1905 there was filed with the Commission application for the enrollment of Campbell Russell, Jr., as a citizen by blood of the Choctaw Nation.

It further appears from the record in this case and the records of the Commission that the applicant was born on December 9, 1904; that he is a son of Mary A. Russell, a recognized and enrolled citizen by blood of the Choctaw Nation whose name appears as number 8101 upon the final roll of citizens by blood of the Choctaw Nation, approved by the Secretary of the Interior January 17, 1903, and Campbell Russell, a recognized and

Applications for Enrollment of Choctaw Newborn
Act of 1905 Volume III

enrolled citizen by intermarriage of the Choctaw Nation whose name appears number 124 upon the final roll of citizens by intermarriage of the Choctaw Nation, approved by the Secretary of the Interior June 13, 1903; and that said applicant died on February 14, 1905. The Act of Congress approved March 3, 1905 (Public No. 212) among other things provides:

"That the Commission to the Five Civilized Tribes is authorized for sixty days after the date of the approval of this act to receive and consider applications for enrollment of children born subsequent to September twenty-fifth, nineteen hundred and two, and prior to March fourth, nineteen hundred and five, and who were living on said latter date, to citizens by blood of the Choctaw and Chickasaw tribes of Indians whose enrollment has been approved by the Secretary of the Interior prior to the date of the approval of this act; and to enroll and make allotments to such children."

It is, therefore, hereby ordered that the application for the enrollment of Campbell Russell, Jr., as a citizen by blood of the Choctaw Nation be dismissed in accordance with the order of the Commission of March 31, 1905.

COMMISSION TO THE FIVE CIVILIZED TRIBES,

Tams Bixby
Chairman.

Muskogee, Indian Territory.
JUN 15 1905

7-NB-165

Muskogee, Indian Territory, June 15, 1905.

Campbell Russell,   **COPY**
    Hereford, Indian Territory.

Dear Sir:

    Inclosed herewith you will find a copy of the order of this Commission, dated June 15, 1905, dismissing the application for the enrollment of your infant child, Campbell Russell, Jr., as a citizen by blood of the Choctaw Nation.

Respectfully,

Tams Bixby
SIGNED
Chairman.

Registered.
Incl. 7-NB-165.

Applications for Enrollment of Choctaw Newborn
Act of 1905   Volume III

7 NB 165

Muskogee, Indian Territory, June 15, 1905.

Mansfield, McMurray & Cornish,
    Attorneys for Choctaw and Chickasaw Nations,
        South McAlester, Indian Territory.

COPY

Gentlemen:

    Inclosed herewith you will find a copy of the order of this Commission, dated June 15, 1905, dismissing the application for the enrollment of Campbell Russell Jr, as a citizen by blood of the Choctaw Nation.

Respectfully,

Tams Bixby
SIGNED

Incl. 7-NB-165.   Chairman.

---

7 NB 165

Muskogee, Indian Territory, June 6, 1905.

Campbell Russell,
    Hereford, Indian Territory.

    Receipt is hereby acknowledged of your affidavit and the affidavit of F. B. Fite to the death of your child Campbell Russell, Jr., which occurred February 14, 1905.

    You are advised that under the provisions of the act of Congress approved March 3, 1905, the Commission was authorized for a period of sixty days from that date to receive applications for the enrollment of children born to enrolled citizens by blood of the Choctaw and Chickasaw Nations between September 25, 1902 and March 4, 1905, and living on the latter date. You will therefore see that the Commission is without authority to enroll your child.

Respectfully,

Chairman.

Applications for Enrollment of Choctaw Newborn
Act of 1905   Volume III

Choc New Born 166
    Dorris Gray
    (Born Aug. 25, 1904)

BIRTH AFFIDAVIT.

DEPARTMENT OF THE INTERIOR.
COMMISSION TO THE FIVE CIVILIZED TRIBES.

IN RE APPLICATION FOR ENROLLMENT, as a citizen of the Choctaw Nation, of Dorris Gray, born on the 25 day of August, 1904

                                non
Name of Father: Oscar Gray   a^citizen of the .... Nation.
                        nee Lowery
Name of Mother: Josephine Gray   a citizen of the Choctaw Nation.

                Postoffice   Haxbar[sic], Ind. Ter.

AFFIDAVIT OF MOTHER.

UNITED STATES OF AMERICA, Indian Territory, }
    Southern   DISTRICT.

    I, Josephine Gray nee Lowery, on oath state that I am 17 years of age and a citizen by Blood, of the Choctaw Nation; that I am the lawful wife of Oscar Gray, who is a non citizen, by ——— of the ——— Nation; that a Female child was born to me on 25 day of August, 1904; that said child has been named Dorris Gray, and was living March 4, 1905.

                                Josephine Gray
Witnesses To Mark:
  { J T Young
    (Name Illegible)

    Subscribed and sworn to before me this 21 day of March, 1905

                                U.T. Rexroat
                                  Notary Public.

Applications for Enrollment of Choctaw Newborn
Act of 1905 Volume III

AFFIDAVIT OF ATTENDING PHYSICIAN OR MID-WIFE.

UNITED STATES OF AMERICA, Indian Territory,　}
　　Southern　　　　　DISTRICT.

　　I, A B Davis , a Physician , on oath state that I attended on Mrs. Josephine Gray , wife of Oscar Gray on the 25 day of August , 1904; that there was born to her on said date a Female child; that said child was living March 4, 1905, and is said to have been named Dorris Gray

　　　　　　　　　　　　　　Dr AB Davis

Witnesses To Mark:
{ Jim Wilkins
　B.C. Rickts[sic]

　　Subscribed and sworn to before me this 20 day of March , 1905.

　　　　　　　　　　　U.T. Rexroat
　　　　　　　　　　　　　Notary Public.

BIRTH AFFIDAVIT.

DEPARTMENT OF THE INTERIOR.
COMMISSION TO THE FIVE CIVILIZED TRIBES.

　　IN RE APPLICATION FOR ENROLLMENT, as a citizen of the Choctaw Nation, of Dorris Gray , born on the 25 day of August , 1904

Name of Father: Oscar Gray　　　　a citizen of the　U S　Nation.
Name of Mother: Josephine Gray nee Lowery　a citizen of the　Choctaw　Nation.

　　　　　　　　　Postoffice　Haxbar[sic], Ind. Ter.

AFFIDAVIT OF MOTHER.

UNITED STATES OF AMERICA, Indian Territory,　}
　　Southern　　　　　DISTRICT.

　　I, Josephine Gray nee Lowery , on oath state that I am 17 years of age and a citizen by Blood , of the Choctaw Nation; that I am the lawful wife of Oscar Gray , who is a citizen, by .... of the U S Nation; that a Female child was born to me on 25 day of August , 1904; that said child has been named Dorris Gray , and was living March 4, 1905.

　　　　　　　　　　　　Josephine Gray

Applications for Enrollment of Choctaw Newborn
Act of 1905   Volume III

Witnesses To Mark:

{

      Subscribed and sworn to before me this 28 day of   April   , 1905

                                     U.T. Rexroat
                                       Notary Public.

AFFIDAVIT OF ATTENDING PHYSICIAN OR MID-WIFE.

UNITED STATES OF AMERICA, Indian Territory, }
    Southern   DISTRICT.

    I,   A B Davis   , a   Physician   , on oath state that I attended on Mrs. Josephine Gray   , wife of   Oscar Gray   on the 25 day of August   , 1904; that there was born to her on said date a   Female   child; that said child was living March 4, 1905, and is said to have been named   Dorris Gray

                                       A.B. Davis

Witnesses To Mark:

{

      Subscribed and sworn to before me this 29 day of   April   , 1905

                                     J.L. Wiggins
                                       Notary Public.

COPY.

                                        Choctaw N.B. 166.

                      Muskogee, Indian Territory, April 28, 1905.

Oscar Gray,
    Hoxbar, Indian Territory.

Dear Sir:

    Receipt is hereby acknowledged of your letter of April 24, asking if the application for the enrollment of Dorris Gray has been received.

    In reply to your letter you are advised that the affidavits heretofore forwarded to the birth of Dorris Gray have been filed with our records as an application for the enrollment of said child.

Applications for Enrollment of Choctaw Newborn
Act of 1905   Volume III

Respectfully,
SIGNED
Tams Bixby
Chairman.

7-235

Muskogee, Indian Territory, May 8, 1905.

Oscar Gray,
   Hoxbar, Indian Territory.

Dear Sir:

Receipt is hereby acknowledged of the affidavits of Josephine Gray and A. B. Davis to the birth of Dorris Gray, daughter of Oscar and Josephine Gray, August 25, 1904, and the same have been filed with our records as an application for the enrollment of said child.

Respectfully,

Commissioner in Charge.

Choc New Born 167
   Opal Delana Rexroat
   (Born Oct. 21 1903)

BIRTH AFFIDAVIT.
DEPARTMENT OF THE INTERIOR.
COMMISSION TO THE FIVE CIVILIZED TRIBES.

IN RE APPLICATION FOR ENROLLMENT, as a citizen of the   Choctaw Nation   Nation, of   Opal Delana Rexroat   , born on the 21st   day of   October   , 1903

Name of Father: U. T. Rexroat   a non- citizen of the ....Nation.
Name of Mother: Estella Belle Rexroat   a citizen of the   Choctaw   Nation.

Postoffice   Ardmore, I. T.

Applications for Enrollment of Choctaw Newborn
Act of 1905   Volume III

AFFIDAVIT OF MOTHER.

UNITED STATES OF AMERICA, Indian Territory, }
Southern DISTRICT.

I, Estella Belle Rexroat, on oath state that I am 23 years of age and a citizen by blood, of the Choctaw Nation; that I am the lawful wife of U.T. Rexroat, who is a non citizen, by .... of the .... Nation; that a female child was born to me on 21st day of October, 1903; that said child has been named Opal Delana Rexroat, and was living March 4, 1905.

Estella B. Rexroat

Witnesses To Mark:
{

Subscribed and sworn to before me this 17th day of March, 1905

JE Williams
Notary Public.

AFFIDAVIT OF ATTENDING PHYSICIAN OR MID-WIFE.

UNITED STATES OF AMERICA, Indian Territory, }
Southern DISTRICT.

I, F. P. von Keller, a physician, on oath state that I attended on Mrs. Estella Belle Rexroat, wife of U. T. Rexroat on the 21 day of October, 1903; that there was born to her on said date a female child; that said child was living March 4, 1905, and is said to have been named Opal Delana Rexroat

F. P. von Keller an M.D.

Witnesses To Mark:
{

Subscribed and sworn to before me this 17 day of March, 1905

Sam H Butler
Notary Public.

Applications for Enrollment of Choctaw Newborn
Act of 1905 Volume III

BIRTH AFFIDAVIT.

DEPARTMENT OF THE INTERIOR.
COMMISSION TO THE FIVE CIVILIZED TRIBES.

IN RE APPLICATION FOR ENROLLMENT, as a citizen of the Choctaw Nation, of Opal Delana Rexroat, born on the 21 day of October, 1903

Name of Father: U. T. Rexroat   a citizen of the U S Nation.
Name of Mother: Estella Belle Rexroat   a citizen of the Choctaw Nation.

Postoffice   Ardmore, Ind. Ter.

AFFIDAVIT OF MOTHER.

UNITED STATES OF AMERICA, Indian Territory, ⎫
     Southern   DISTRICT. ⎭

I, Estella Belle Rexroat, on oath state that I am 23 years of age and a citizen by Blood, of the Choctaw Nation; that I am the lawful wife of U.T. Rexroat, who is a citizen, by ———— of the United States Nation; that a female child was born to me on 21 day of October, 1903; that said child has been named Opal Delana Rexroat, and was living March 4, 1905.

                         Estella Belle Rexroat

Witnesses To Mark:
{

Subscribed and sworn to before me this 7th day of April, 1905

                         Harold Wallace
                         Notary Public.

AFFIDAVIT OF ATTENDING PHYSICIAN OR MID-WIFE.

UNITED STATES OF AMERICA, Indian Territory, ⎫
     Southern   DISTRICT. ⎭

I, Frederick P. von Keller M.D., a Physician, on oath state that I attended on Mrs. Estella Belle Rexroat, wife of U. T. Rexroat on the 21 day of October, 1903; that there was born to her on said date a female child; that said child was living March 4, 1905, and is said to have been named Opal Delana Rexroat

                         Frederick P. von Keller an M.D.

Witnesses To Mark:
{

Applications for Enrollment of Choctaw Newborn
Act of 1905 Volume III

Subscribed and sworn to before me this 10th day of April , 1905

F. S. Hyden
Notary Public.

7-235

Muskogee, Indian Territory, March 22, 1905.

U. T. Rexroat,
Ardmore, Indian Territory.

Dear Sir:

Receipt is hereby acknowledged of the affidavits of Estelle B. Rexroat and F. P. von Keller to the birth of Opal Delana Rexroat, daughter of U. T. and Estelle B. Rexroat, October 21, 1903, and the same have been filed with our records as an application for the enrollment of said child.

Replying to your letter of March 16, 1905, relative to the enrollment of your child in which you ask if it will be entitled to the $40 townsite payment, you are informed that the payment of moneys due the citizens of the Choctaw and Chickasaw Nations is a matter which is within the jurisdiction of the United States Indian Agent and for information relative thereto you should address him at Muskogee, Indian Territory.

Respectfully,

Chairman.

COPY.

N.B. 167

Muskogee, Indian Territory, April 3, 1905.

U. T. Rexroat,
Ardmore, Indian Territory.

Dear Sir:

There is inclosed you herewith for execution application for the enrollment of your infant child, Opal Delana Rexroat, born October 21, 1903.

Applications for Enrollment of Choctaw Newborn
Act of 1905   Volume III

    In having these affidavits executed care should be exercised to see that all names are written in full, as they appear in the body of the affidavit, and in the event that either of the persons signing the affidavit are unable to write, signatures by mark must be attested by two witnesses. Each affidavit must be executed before a Notary Public and the notarial seal and signature of the officer must be attached to each separate affidavit.

                          Respectfully,
                          SIGNED

LM 1-33   *Tams Bixby*
                            Chairman.

Choc New Born 168
    Paulina T. Coker
    (Born Nov. 11, 1902)

BIRTH AFFIDAVIT.

DEPARTMENT OF THE INTERIOR,
COMMISSION TO THE FIVE CIVILIZED TRIBES.

    IN RE Application for Enrollment, as a citizen of the   Choctaw   Nation, of Paulina T. Coker , born on the   11   day of   November , 1902

Name of Father: George C. Coker   a citizen of the   U. S.   ~~Nation~~.
Name of Mother: Lula Coker   a citizen of the   Choctaw   Nation.

                    Post-office   Ashland, I.T.

AFFIDAVIT OF MOTHER.

UNITED STATES OF AMERICA, }
   INDIAN TERRITORY,
   Central   District.

    I, Lula Coker , on oath state that I am   19   years of age and a citizen by blood , of the   Choctaw   Nation; that I am the lawful wife of   George C Coker , who is a citizen, ~~by~~ —— of the   U.S.   ~~Nation~~; that a   female   child was born to me on   11   day of   November , 1902 , that said child has been named   Paulina T. Coker , and is now living.
                                    Lula Coker

Applications for Enrollment of Choctaw Newborn
Act of 1905 Volume III

WITNESSES TO MARK:
{

Subscribed and sworn to before me this 22 day of December, 1902

(Name Illegible)
NOTARY PUBLIC.

(The affidavit below handwritten and typed as given.)

Legal I.T.   Dec 13 1902

    This is to certify that I attended at the birth of a femal child at G. C. Coker on the 11th of Nov. 1902

Signed

S Hawkins M.D.

Legal, I.T. 12/13/1902

Subscribe and sworn to before me this the 13 day of Dec 1902

J B Lee Notary Public
(seal)

NEW BORN AFFIDAVIT

No ....

CHOCTAW ENROLLING COMMISSION

IN THE MATTER OF THE APPLICATION FOR ENROLLMENT as a citizen of the Choctaw Nation, of   Palina[sic] T. Coker   born on the 11th day of November 190 2

Name of father   G.C. Coker   a citizen of   United States Nation,
final enrollment No. ———
Name of mother   Lula Coker (ne Herron)   a citizen of   Choctaw   Nation,
final enrollment No.   7449

Celestine Ind. Ter.   Postoffice.

Applications for Enrollment of Choctaw Newborn
Act of 1905 Volume III

AFFIDAVIT OF MOTHER

UNITED STATES OF AMERICA
INDIAN TERRITORY
DISTRICT Central
 (Ne Herron)

I Lula Coker , on oath state that I am 21 years of age and a citizen by Blood of the Choctaw Nation, and as such have been placed upon the final roll of the Choctaw Nation, by the Honorable Secretary of the Interior my final enrollment number being 7449 ; that I am the lawful wife of G.C. Coker , who is a citizen of the United States Nation, and as such has been placed upon the final roll of said Nation by the Honorable Secretary of the Interior, his final enrollment number being —— and that a Female child was born to me on the 11th day of November 190 2 ; that said child has been named Palina T Coker , and is now living.

WITNESSETH: Lula Coker

Must be two witnesses (Name Illegible)
who are citizens L.W. McMorriet

Subscribed and sworn to before me this, the 25th day of Feby 190 5

(Name Illegible)
Notary Public.

My Commission Expires: Dec 2nd 1905

Affidavit of Attending Physician or Midwife

UNITED STATES OF AMERICA,
INDIAN TERRITORY,
Central DISTRICT

I, Kity McClelon[sic] a Midwife on oath state that I attended on Mrs. Lula Coker wife of T[sic]. C. Coker on the 11th day of November , 190 2 , that there was born to her on said date a Female child, that said child is now living, and is said to have been named Palina T. Coker

Kittie McClellan ~~M.D.~~

Subscribed and sworn to before me this the 25th day of Feby 1905

(Name Illegible)
Notary Public.

Applications for Enrollment of Choctaw Newborn
Act of 1905   Volume III

WITNESSETH:

Must be two witnesses who are citizens and know the child. { *(Name Illegible)*
L. W. McMorriet

We hereby certify that we are well acquainted with Kittie McClellon a Midwife and know her to be reputable and of good standing in the community.

Must be two citizen witnesses. { *(Name Illegible)*
L. W. McMorriet

BIRTH AFFIDAVIT.

DEPARTMENT OF THE INTERIOR.
COMMISSION TO THE FIVE CIVILIZED TRIBES.

IN RE APPLICATION FOR ENROLLMENT, as a citizen of the Choctaw Nation, of Paulina T. Coker, born on the 11th day of November, 1902

Name of Father: George C. Coker   a citizen of the United States Nation.
Name of Mother: Lula Coker (Herron)   a citizen of the Choctaw Nation.

Postoffice   Ashland, Ind. Ter.

AFFIDAVIT OF MOTHER.

UNITED STATES OF AMERICA, Indian Territory, }
....DISTRICT. }

I, Lula Coker (Herron), on oath state that I am 21 years of age and a citizen by blood, of the Choctaw Nation; that I am the lawful wife of George C. Coker, who is a citizen, by ——of the United States Nation; that a female child was born to me on 11th day of November, 1902; that said child has been named Paulina T. Coker, and was living March 4, 1905.

Lula Coker

Witnesses To Mark:
{

Subscribed and sworn to before me this 15 day of April, 1905

H.G. Rowley
Notary Public.

My Commission expires Mch 9-1909.

Applications for Enrollment of Choctaw Newborn
Act of 1905 Volume III

AFFIDAVIT OF ATTENDING PHYSICIAN OR MID-WIFE.

UNITED STATES OF AMERICA, Indian Territory,
....DISTRICT.

I, Mrs H. M. Phillips, a Midwife, on oath state that I attended on Mrs. Lula Coker (Herron), wife of George C Coker on the 11th day of November, 1902; that there was born to her on said date a female child; that said child was living March 4, 1905, and is said to have been named Paulina T. Coker

H. M. Phillips

Witnesses To Mark:

Subscribed and sworn to before me this 15 day of April, 1905

H.G. Rowley
Notary Public.

My Commission expires Mch 9-1909.

COPY

N. B. 168

Muskogee, Indian Territory, April 5, 1905.

George C. Coker,
Ashland, Indian Territory.

Dear Sir:

There is inclosed you herewith for execution application for the enrollment of your infant child, Paulina T. Coker, born November 11, 1902.

The affidavit heretofore filed with the Commission show the child was living on December 22, 1902. It is necessary, for the child to be enrolled, that she was living on March 4, 1905.

In having these affidavits executed care should be exercised to see that all names are written in full, as they appear in the body of the affidavit, and in the event that either of the persons signing the affidavit are unable to write, signatures by mark must be attested by two witnesses. Each affidavit must be executed before a Notary Public and the notarial seal and signature of the officer must be attached to each separate affidavit.

Applications for Enrollment of Choctaw Newborn
Act of 1905   Volume III

LM 5-1

Respectfully,
SIGNED
T. B. Needles.
Commissioner in Charge.

7-2563

Muskogee, Indian Territory, April 8, 1905.

Lula Coker,
    Celestine, Indian Territory.

Dear Madam:

    Receipt is hereby acknowledged of your letter of March 29, 1905, in which you state that you have filed applications for your two little children Paulina Coker and Willie V. E. Coker, and you ask if their enrollment has been approved.

    In reply to your letter you are informed that the affidavits have heretofore been forwarded to the birth of Paulina T. Coker child of George Coker and Lula Coker, November 11, 1902, but it does not appear from our records that affidavits have been forwarded to the birth of your child Willie V. E. Coker and for your convenience there is inclosed herewith blank for the enrollment of an infant child which you should have executed and returned to this office within sixty days from March 3, 1905[sic].

Respectfully,

Commissioner in Charge.

B.C.

COPY.   7 NB 168

Muskogee, Indian Territory, April 20, 1905.

George C. Coker,
    Ashland, Indian Territory.

Dear Sir:

    Receipt is hereby acknowledged of the affidavits of Lula Coker and H. M. Phillips to the birth of Paulina T. Coker, daughter of George C. and Lula Coker (Herron) November 11, 1902, and the same have been filed with our records as an application for the enrollment of said child.

Respectfully,
SIGNED
Tams Bixby
Chairman.

Applications for Enrollment of Choctaw Newborn
Act of 1905   Volume III

Choctaw NB 168

Muskogee, Indian Territory, May 19, 1905.

G. C. Coker,
    Ashland, Indian Territory.

Dear Sir:

    Receipt is hereby acknowledged of your letter of May 11, giving information relative to the enrollment of your wife and you are advised that she has been identified upon our records as an enrolled citizen by blood of the Choctaw Nation and the affidavits to the birth of your daughter, Paulina T. Coker, have been filed with our records as an application for her enrollment, and her name has been placed upon a schedule of citizens by blood of the Choctaw Nation prepared for forwarding to the Secretary of the Interior.

        Respectfully,

        Chairman.

Choc New Born 169
    Verna T. Cromwell
    (Born Aug. 14, 1904)

BIRTH AFFIDAVIT.

DEPARTMENT OF THE INTERIOR,
COMMISSION TO THE FIVE CIVILIZED TRIBES.

In Re Application for Enrollment, as a citizen of the   Choctaw   Nation, of   Verner[sic] T. Cromwell , born on the   14   day of   August   , 1904

Name of Father: James D Cromwell   a citizen of the   Choctaw   Nation.
Name of Mother: Corrie[sic] O Cromwell   a citizen of the   ' '' ''   Nation.

        Post-office   Bokoshe IT

Applications for Enrollment of Choctaw Newborn
Act of 1905   Volume III

AFFIDAVIT OF MOTHER.

UNITED STATES OF AMERICA,
   INDIAN TERRITORY,
   Central   District.

    I, Corrie O Cromwell , on oath state that I am 28 years of age and a citizen by Blood , of the Choctaw Nation; that I am the lawful wife of James D Cromwell , who is a citizen, by Intermarage[sic] of the Choctaw Nation; that a Girl child was born to me on 14 day of August , 1904 , that said child has been named Vernie[sic] T Cromwell , and is now living.

                                        Carrie O. Cromwell

WITNESSES TO MARK:
{ Ida J Howard
{ J D. Shaw

    Subscribed and sworn to before me this 1 day of Nov , 1904

                                        J D Shaw
My Com Exp Feb 7 1906   NOTARY PUBLIC.

AFFIDAVIT OF ATTENDING PHYSICIAN OR MID-WIFE.

UNITED STATES OF AMERICA,
   INDIAN TERRITORY,
   Central   District.

    I,   F C Parrott   , a   Physician , on oath state that I attended on Mrs. Corrie O Cromwell , wife of James D Cromwell on the 14 day of August , 1904 ; that there was born to her on said date a   Girl   child; that said child is now living and is said to have been named Verner[sic] T. Cromwell

                                        F C Parrott M.D.

WITNESSES TO MARK:
{ *(Name Illegible)*
{ *(Name Illegible)*

    Subscribed and sworn to before me this 1 day of November , 1904

                                        J D Shaw
My Com Exp Feb 7 1906   NOTARY PUBLIC.

Applications for Enrollment of Choctaw Newborn
Act of 1905 Volume III

7-247
7-7473
BIRTH AFFIDAVIT.

DEPARTMENT OF THE INTERIOR.
COMMISSION TO THE FIVE CIVILIZED TRIBES.

IN RE APPLICATION FOR ENROLLMENT, as a citizen of the Choctaw Nation, of Verna T Cromwell, born on the 14th day of August, 1904 by intermarriage
Name of Father: James D Cromwell   a citizen of the Choctaw Nation.
Name of Mother: Carrie Cromwell   a citizen of the Choctaw Nation.

Postoffice   Milton, Ind Ter

AFFIDAVIT OF MOTHER.

UNITED STATES OF AMERICA, Indian Territory,
Central   DISTRICT.

I, Carrie Cromwell, on oath state that I am 28 years of age and a citizen by blood, of the Choctaw Nation; that I am the lawful wife of James D Cromwell, who is a citizen, by intermarriage of the Choctaw Nation; that a female child was born to me on 14th day of August, 1904; that said child has been named Verna T Cromwell, and was living March 4, 1905.

Carrie Cromwell

Witnesses To Mark:
{

Subscribed and sworn to before me this 3rd day of April, 1905

OL Johnson
Notary Public.

AFFIDAVIT OF ATTENDING PHYSICIAN OR MID-WIFE.

UNITED STATES OF AMERICA, Indian Territory,
Central   DISTRICT.

I, F C Parrott, a physician, on oath state that I attended on Mrs. Carrie Cromwell, wife of James D Cromwell on the 14th day of August, 1904; that there was born to her on said date a female child; that said child was living March 4, 1905, and is said to have been named Verna T Cromwell

F C Parrott

Applications for Enrollment of Choctaw Newborn
Act of 1905   Volume III

Witnesses To Mark:

{

  Subscribed and sworn to before me this 3rd day of   April   , 1905

            OL Johnson
             Notary Public.

              7-2575

       Muskogee, Indian Territory, November 4, 1904.

James D. Cromwell,
  Bokoshe, Indian Territory.

Dear Sir:-

  Receipt is hereby acknowledged of the affidavits of Carrie O. Cromwell and F. C. Parrott, relative to the birth of Verne T. Cromwell, daughter of James D. and Carrie O. Cromwell August 14, 1904, which it is presumed have been forwarded to this office as an application for enrollment of said child.

  In reply to your letter you are informed that under the provisions of the Act of Congress approved July 1, 1902, the Commission is now without authority to receive or consider the original application for enrollment of any person whomsoever as a citizen of the Choctaw or Chickasaw Nation.

        Respectfully,

              Chairman.

COPY

              N. B. 169

      Muskogee, Indian Territory, April 4, 1905.

James D. Cromwell,
  Bokoshe, Indian Territory.

Dear Sir:

  There is inclosed you herewith for execution application for the enrollment of your infant child, Vernie T. Cromwell, born August 14, 1904.

Applications for Enrollment of Choctaw Newborn
Act of 1905   Volume III

      The affidavits heretofore filed with the Commission show the child was living on November 1, 1904. It is necessary, for the child to be enrolled, that she was living on March 4, 1905.

      In having these affidavits executed care should be exercised to see that all names are written in full, as they appear in the body of the affidavit, and in the event that either of the persons signing the affidavit are unable to write, signatures by mark must be attested by two witnesses. Each affidavit must be executed before a Notary Public and the notarial seal and signature of the officer must be attached to each separate affidavit.

                                Respectfully,
                                SIGNED

                                T. B. Needles.
LM 4-15   Commissioner in Charge.

                    COPY   Choctaw N.B. 169.

                Muskogee, Indian Territory, April 19, 1905.

James H[sic]. Cromwell,
    Milton, Indian Territory.

Dear Sir:

      Receipt is hereby acknowledged of your letter of April 12, in which you refer to our communication of April 4 and state that on April 3 you made out application before the Choctaw enrolling commission for the enrollment of your child, Verna T. Cromwell, and you ask if this application has been received.

      In reply to your letter you are informed that the affidavits of Carrie Cromwell and F. C. Parrott which were executed before one of the enrolling parties on April 3, 1905, have been received and filed with our records in the matter of the application for the enrollment of your child, and it will not be necessary for you to execute the blank forwarded you with our letter of April 4.

                                Respectfully,
                                SIGNED

                                      Tams Bixby
                                       Chairman.

Applications for Enrollment of Choctaw Newborn
Act of 1905 Volume III

COPY

7 NB 169

Muskogee, Indian Territory, April 19, 1905.

James H[sic]. Cromwell,
   Milton, Indian Territory.

Dear Sir:

   Receipt is hereby acknowledged of the affidavits of Carrie Cromwell and F. C. Parrott to the birth of Verna T. Cromwell, daughter of James D. and Carrie Cromwell, August 14, 1904, and the same have been filed with our records as an application for the enrollment of said child.

Respectfully,
SIGNED

Tams Bixby
Chairman.

Choc New Born 170
   Mabel Burns
   (Born March 20, 1903)

BIRTH AFFIDAVIT.

DEPARTMENT OF THE INTERIOR.
COMMISSION TO THE FIVE CIVILIZED TRIBES.

IN RE APPLICATION FOR ENROLLMENT, as a citizen of the Choctaw Nation, of Mabel Burns, born on the 20th day of March, 1903

Name of Father: Alexander Burns   a citizen of the Choctaw Nation.
Name of Mother: Ollie Burns   a citizen of the Choctaw Nation.

Postoffice   McAlester, I.T.

Applications for Enrollment of Choctaw Newborn
Act of 1905   Volume III

AFFIDAVIT OF MOTHER.

UNITED STATES OF AMERICA, Indian Territory, }
Central   DISTRICT.

    I, Ollie Burns, on oath state that I am 25 years of age and a citizen by marriage, of the Choctaw Nation; that I am the lawful wife of Alexander Burns, who is a citizen, by blood of the Choctaw Nation; that a female child was born to me on 20th day of March, 1903; that said child has been named Mabel Burns, and was living March 4, 1905.

                              Ollie Burns

Witnesses To Mark:
{

    Subscribed and sworn to before me this 20th day of March, 1905

                              Wirt Franklin
                              Notary Public.

AFFIDAVIT OF ATTENDING PHYSICIAN OR MID-WIFE.

UNITED STATES OF AMERICA, Indian Territory, }
Central   DISTRICT.

    I, Minnie Sawyers, a mid-wife, on oath state that I attended on Mrs. Ollie Burns, wife of Alexander Burns on the 20th day of March, 1903; that there was born to her on said date a female child; that said child was living March 4, 1905, and is said to have been named Mabel Burns

                              Minnie Sawyers

Witnesses To Mark:
{

    Subscribed and sworn to before me this 20th day of March, 1905

                              Wirt Franklin
                              Notary Public.

Applications for Enrollment of Choctaw Newborn
Act of 1905   Volume III

(The letter below does not belong with the current applicant.)

7-2586.

Muskogee, Indian Territory, April 26, 1905.

Jackson Burns,
    Massey, Indian Territory.

Dear Sir:

    Receipt is hereby acknowledged of the affidavits of Laura Burns and Sarah Williams, to the birth of William Burns, child of Jackson and Laura Burns, January 9, 1905, and the same have been filed with our records as an application for the enrollment of said child.

                  Respectfully,

                                          Chairman.

Choc New Born 171
    Rebecca Minehart
    (Born June 7, 1903)

NEW BORN AFFIDAVIT

No ....

CHOCTAW ENROLLING COMMISSION

    IN THE MATTER OF THE APPLICATION FOR ENROLLMENT as a citizen of the Choctaw Nation, of   Rebecca Minehart   born on the 7 day of June   190 3

    Name of father   George H. Minehart   a citizen of   Choctaw   Nation,
final enrollment No.   7514

    Name of mother   Sarah E. Minehart   a citizen of   white   Nation,
final enrollment No.   ———

                                                            _____Postoffice.

Applications for Enrollment of Choctaw Newborn
Act of 1905   Volume III

AFFIDAVIT OF MOTHER

UNITED STATES OF AMERICA }
    INDIAN TERRITORY
DISTRICT   Central

I   Sarah E. Minehart   , on oath state that I am   34   years of age and a citizen by ——— of the ——— Nation, and as such have been placed upon the final roll of the ——— Nation, by the Honorable Secretary of the Interior my final enrollment number being ——; that I am the lawful wife of   George H. Minehart , who is a citizen of the   Choctaw   Nation, and as such has been placed upon the final roll of said Nation by the Honorable Secretary of the Interior, his final enrollment number being   7514   and that a   female   child was born to me on the   7   day of   June   190 3 ; that said child has been named   Rebecca Minehart , and is now living.

WITNESSETH: Sarah E. Minehart
  Must be two witnesses { L.R. Moore
  who are citizens   { G W McClain

Subscribed and sworn to before me this, the   6   day of   February   1905

         James Bower
           Notary Public.

My Commission Expires:
  Sept. 23 - 1907

Affidavit of Attending Physician or Midwife

UNITED STATES OF AMERICA, }
    INDIAN TERRITORY,
  Central   DISTRICT

I,   Rebecca Lanier   a   Midwife on oath state that I attended on Mrs.   Sarah E. Minehart   wife of   George H. Minehart   on the   7   day of   June , 190 3 , that there was born to her on said date a   Female   child, that said child is now living, and is said to have been named   Rebecca Minehart

         her
       Rebecca x Lanier   M. D.
         mark

Subscribed and sworn to before me this the   6   day of   February   1905

        James Bower
          Notary Public.

WITNESSETH:
  Must be two witnesses { L.R. Moore
  who are citizens and
  know the child.   { G W McClain

Applications for Enrollment of Choctaw Newborn
Act of 1905   Volume III

We hereby certify that we are well acquainted with Rebecca Lanier a **Midwife** and know her to be reputable and of good standing in the community.

Must be two citizen witnesses. { L.R. Moore
G W McClain

BIRTH AFFIDAVIT.

DEPARTMENT OF THE INTERIOR.
COMMISSION TO THE FIVE CIVILIZED TRIBES.

IN RE APPLICATION FOR ENROLLMENT, as a citizen of the Choctaw Nation, of Rebecca Minehart, born on the 7th day of June, 1903

Name of Father: George H. Minehart   a citizen of the Choctaw Nation.
Name of Mother: Sarah E Minehart   a citizen of the United States Nation.

Postoffice   Braden I.T.

AFFIDAVIT OF MOTHER.

UNITED STATES OF AMERICA, Indian Territory,
Central   DISTRICT.

I, Sarah E Minehart, on oath state that I am 33 years of age and a citizen by ...., of the United States Nation; that I am the lawful wife of George H Minehart, who is a citizen, by Blood of the Choctaw Nation; that a Female child was born to me on 7th day of June, 1903; that said child has been named Rebecca Minehart, and was living March 4, 1905.

Sarah E Minehart

Witnesses To Mark:
{

Subscribed and sworn to before me this 3rd day of April, 1905

W E Harrell
MY COMMISSION EXPIRES AUG. 6, 1908   Notary Public.

Applications for Enrollment of Choctaw Newborn
Act of 1905 Volume III

AFFIDAVIT OF ATTENDING PHYSICIAN OR MID-WIFE.

UNITED STATES OF AMERICA, Indian Territory, } Central DISTRICT.

I, Rebecca Lanier, a Midwife, on oath state that I attended on Mrs. Sarah E Minehart, wife of George H Minehart on the 7th day of June, 1903; that there was born to her on said date a Female child; that said child was living March 4, 1905, and is said to have been named Rebecca Minehart

Witnesses To Mark:
{ (Name Illegible)
{ (Name Illegible)

her
Rebecca x Lanier
mark

Subscribed and sworn to before me this 3rd day of April, 1905

W E Harrell
Notary Public.

MY COMMISSION EXPIRES AUG. 6, 1908

BIRTH AFFIDAVIT.

DEPARTMENT OF THE INTERIOR.
COMMISSION TO THE FIVE CIVILIZED TRIBES.

IN RE APPLICATION FOR ENROLLMENT, as a citizen of the Choctaw Nation, of Rebecca Minehart, born on the 7th day of June, 1903

Name of Father: George H. Minehart   a citizen of the Choctaw Nation.
Name of Mother: Sarah E Minehart   a citizen of the United States Nation.

Postoffice Braden Ind. Ter.

AFFIDAVIT OF MOTHER.

UNITED STATES OF AMERICA, Indian Territory, } Central DISTRICT.

I, Sarah E Minehart, on oath state that I am 33 years of age and a citizen by ———, of the United States ~~Nation~~; that I am the lawful wife of George H Minehart, who is a citizen, by blood of the Choctaw Nation; that a female child was born to me on 7th day of June, 1903; that said child has been named Rebecca Minehart, and was living March 4, 1905.

Sarah E Minehart

Applications for Enrollment of Choctaw Newborn
Act of 1905 Volume III

Witnesses To Mark:

Subscribed and sworn to before me this 10 day of April , 1905

MY COMMISSION EXPIRES AUG. 6, 1908   W E Harrell
                                        Notary Public.

AFFIDAVIT OF ATTENDING PHYSICIAN OR MID-WIFE.

UNITED STATES OF AMERICA, Indian Territory,
Central   DISTRICT.

I, Rebecca Lanier, a Midwife, on oath state that I attended on Mrs. Sarah E Minehart, wife of George H Minehart on the 7th day of June, 1903; that there was born to her on said date a female child; that said child was living March 4, 1905, and is said to have been named Rebecca Minehart

                            her
                Rebecca x Lanier
                            mark

Witnesses To Mark:
 W E Harrell
 E L Hickman

Subscribed and sworn to before me this 10 day of April , 1905

MY COMMISSION EXPIRES AUG. 6, 1908   W E Harrell
                                        Notary Public.

BIRTH AFFIDAVIT.

DEPARTMENT OF THE INTERIOR,
COMMISSION TO THE FIVE CIVILIZED TRIBES.

IN RE Application for Enrollment, as a citizen of the Choctaw Nation, of Rebecca Minehart[sic] , born on the 7th day of June , 1903

Name of Father: George H. Minehart   a citizen of the Choctaw Nation.
Name of Mother: Sarah E. Minehart   a citizen of the Choctaw Nation.

                Post-Office: Braden, Ind. Ter.

Applications for Enrollment of Choctaw Newborn
Act of 1905 Volume III

AFFIDAVIT OF MOTHER.

UNITED STATES OF AMERICA,
INDIAN TERRITORY.
Central   District.

I,   Sarah E Minehart   , on oath state that I am   32   years of age and a citizen by   Adoption   , of the Choctaw   Nation; that I am the lawful wife of   George H. Minehart   , who is a citizen, by   Blood   of the Choctaw Nation; that a   female   child was born to me on   7th   day of   June   , 1903 , that said child has been named   Rebecca Minehart   , and is now living.

Sarah E. Minehart

WITNESSES TO MARK:

Subscribed and sworn to before me this   20th   day of   October   , 1903

J Wesley Smith
NOTARY PUBLIC.

AFFIDAVIT OF ATTENDING PHYSICIAN OR MID-WIFE.

UNITED STATES OF AMERICA,
INDIAN TERRITORY.
Central   District.

I,   Dr. C. E. Jones   , a   physician   , on oath state that I attended on Mrs.   Sarah E Mineheart[sic]   , wife of   George H. Mineheart   on the   7th   day of   June   , 1903 ; that there was born to her on said date a   female   child; that said child is now living and is said to have been named   Rebecca Mineheart

C. E. Jones

WITNESSES TO MARK:

Subscribed and sworn to before me this   19th   day of   October   , 1903

J. Wesley Smith
NOTARY PUBLIC.

Applications for Enrollment of Choctaw Newborn
Act of 1905 Volume III

COPY

N. B. 171

Muskogee, Indian Territory, April 4, 1905.

George H. Minehart,
    Braden, Indian Territory.

Dear Sir:

    There is inclosed you herewith for execution application for the enrollment of your infant child, Rebecca Minehart, born June 7, 1903.

    The affidavits heretofore filed with the Commission show the child was living on October 19, 1903. It is necessary, for the child to be enrolled, that she was living on March 4, 1905.

    In having these affidavits executed care should be exercised to see that all names are written in full, as they appear in the body of the affidavit, and in the event that either of the persons signing the affidavit are unable to write, signatures by mark must be attested by two witnesses. Each affidavit must be executed before a Notary Public and the notarial seal and signature of the officer must be attached to each separate affidavit.

                      Respectfully,
                        SIGNED
                      T. B. Needles.

LM 4-14.   Commissioner in Charge.

Choctaw 2589.

Muskogee, Indian Territory, April 8, 1905.

George H. Minehart,
    Braden, Indian Territory.

Dear Sir:

    Receipt is hereby acknowledged of the affidavits of Sarah E. Minehart and Rebecca Lanier to the birth of Rebecca Minehart, daughter of George H. and Sarah E. Minehart, June 7, 1903, and the same have been filed with our records as an application for the enrollment of said child.

                        Respectfully,

                        Commissioner in Charge.

Applications for Enrollment of Choctaw Newborn
Act of 1905   Volume III

COPY

Choctaw N.B.171.

Muskogee, Indian Territory, April 13, 1905.

George H. Minehart,
    Braden, Indian Territory.

Dear Sir:

    Receipt is hereby acknowledged of the affidavits of Sarah E. Minehart and Rebecca Lanier to the birth of Rebecca Minehart, daughter of George H. and Sarah E. Minehart, June 7, 1903, and the same have been filed with our records in the matter of the enrollment of said child.

                  Respectfully,
                  SIGNED
                  T. B. Needles.
                  Commissioner in Charge.

<u>Choc New Born 172</u>
    George Washington Blaylock
    (Born Nov. 17, 1904)

BIRTH AFFIDAVIT.

DEPARTMENT OF THE INTERIOR.
COMMISSION TO THE FIVE CIVILIZED TRIBES.

    IN RE APPLICATION FOR ENROLLMENT, as a citizen of the   Choctaw   Nation, of George Washington Blaylock , born on the 17 day of Nov , 1904

Name of Father: Henry Blaylock   a citizen of the .... Nation.
Name of Mother: Rutha Blaylock   a citizen of the   Choctaw   Nation.

                  Postoffice   McCurtain I.T.

Applications for Enrollment of Choctaw Newborn
Act of 1905 Volume III

AFFIDAVIT OF MOTHER.

UNITED STATES OF AMERICA, Indian Territory,
Central DISTRICT.

I, Rutha Blaylock, on oath state that I am 28 years of age and a citizen by Birth, of the Choctaw Nation; that I am the lawful wife of Henry Blaylock, who is a citizen, by marriage of the Choctaw Nation; that a male child was born to me on 17" day of Nov, 1904, that said child has been named George Washington Blaylock, and is now living.

                                      her
                            Rutha x Blaylock
Witnesses To Mark: mark
{ CW Moore
  G M Gunter

Subscribed and sworn to before me this 20" day of Jan, 1905.

                              LB Johnson
                              Notary Public.

AFFIDAVIT OF ATTENDING PHYSICIAN OR MID-WIFE.

UNITED STATES OF AMERICA, Indian Territory,
Central DISTRICT.

I, Jane Overton, a midwife, on oath state that I attended on Mrs. Rutha Blaylock, wife of Henry Blaylock on the 17 day of Nov, 1904; that there was born to her on said date a male child; that said child is now living and is said to have been named George Washington Blaylock

                              Jane Overton
Witnesses To Mark:

{

Subscribed and sworn to before me this .... day of ....,190....

                              Notary Public.

Applications for Enrollment of Choctaw Newborn
Act of 1905   Volume III

NEW-BORN AFFIDAVIT.

Number..............

...Choctaw Enrolling Commission...

IN THE MATTER OF THE APPLICATION FOR ENROLLMENT, as a citizen of the Choctaw Nation, of Geo Washington Blaylock

born on the 17 day of November 1904

Name of father   Henry Blaylock   a citizen of   Choctaw
Nation final enrollment No. ———
Name of mother   Rutha Blaylock   a citizen of   Choctaw
Nation final enrollment No. 7540

Postoffice   McCurtain I.T.

AFFIDAVIT OF MOTHER.

UNITED STATES OF AMERICA
INDIAN TERRITORY
Central   DISTRICT

I   Ruth A[sic] Blaylock   , on oath state that I am 28 years of age and a citizen by blood of the Choctaw Nation, and as such have been placed upon the final roll of the Choctaw Nation, by the Honorable Secretary of the Interior my final enrollment number being 7540 ; that I am the lawful wife of   Henry Blaylock   , who is a citizen of the Choctaw Nation, and as such has been placed upon the final roll of said Nation by the Honorable Secretary of the Interior, his final enrollment number being ——— and that a boy child was born to me on the 17 day of November 1904 ; that said child has been named Geo Washington Blaylock , and is now living.

                                                      her
Witnesseth.   Rutha x Blaylock
  Must be two   ⎱ Thos. M. Dobson   mark
  Witnesses who ⎰
  are Citizens.   Thomas Foster

Subscribed and sworn to before me this 25 day of Feb 1905

                                J. L. Lewis
                                      Notary Public.

My commission expires:
  My commission expires Mar. 15, 1905

Applications for Enrollment of Choctaw Newborn
Act of 1905   Volume III

AFFIDAVIT OF ATTENDING PHYSICIAN OR MIDWIFE

UNITED STATES OF AMERICA
INDIAN TERRITORY
Central   DISTRICT

I, Amanda Talburt a midwife on oath state that I attended on Mrs. Ruth A[sic] Blaylock wife of Henry Blaylock on the 17 day of November, 190 4, that there was born to her on said date a boy child, that said child is now living, and is said to have been named Geo. Washington

            her
         Amanda x Talburt   M.D.
WITNESSETH: mark   midwife
Must be two witnesses who are citizens and know the child.
{ Thos. M. Dobson
  Thomas Foster

Subscribed and sworn to before me this, the 25 day of February 190 5

J. L. Lewis   Notary Public.

We hereby certify that we are well acquainted with Amanda Talburt a midwife and know her to be reputable and of good standing in the community.

{ Thos. M. Dobson
  Thomas Foster

BIRTH AFFIDAVIT.

DEPARTMENT OF THE INTERIOR.
COMMISSION TO THE FIVE CIVILIZED TRIBES.

IN RE APPLICATION FOR ENROLLMENT, as a citizen of the Choctaw Nation, of Geo. Washington Blaylock, born on the 17 day of Nov, 1904

Name of Father: Henry Blaylock   a citizen of the Choctaw Nation.
Name of Mother: Ruth A. Blaylock   a citizen of the Choctaw Nation.

Postoffice McCurtain, I.T.

Applications for Enrollment of Choctaw Newborn
Act of 1905   Volume III

AFFIDAVIT OF MOTHER.

UNITED STATES OF AMERICA, Indian Territory, }
  Central   DISTRICT.

I,   Ruth A. Blaylock   , on oath state that I am   28   years of age and a citizen by   blood   , of the   Choctaw   Nation; that I am the lawful wife of   Henry Blaylock   , who is a citizen, by   marriage   of the   Choctaw   Nation; that a   boy   child was born to me on   17   day of   November   , 1904; that said child has been named   Geo. Washington Blaylock   , and was living March 4, 1905.

                                          her
                              Ruth A. x Blaylock

Witnesses To Mark: mark
  { V.V. Cray
    G.W. Adams

Subscribed and sworn to before me this   4   day of   April   , 1905

                              J. L. Lewis
                              Notary Public.

AFFIDAVIT OF ATTENDING PHYSICIAN OR MID-WIFE.

UNITED STATES OF AMERICA, Indian Territory, }
  Central   DISTRICT.

I,   M. E. Talburt   , a   Midwife   , on oath state that I attended on Mrs.   Ruth A. Blaylock   , wife of   Henry Blaylock   on the 17 day of Nov. , 1904; that there was born to her on said date a   boy   child; that said child was living March 4, 1905, and is said to have been named Geo. Washington Blaylock

                                    her
                            M. E. x Talburt
                            mark

Witnesses To Mark:
  { V.V. Cray
    G.W. Adams

Subscribed and sworn to before me this   4   day of   April   , 1905

                              J. L. Lewis

My commission expires Mar. 11, 1909   Notary Public.

Applications for Enrollment of Choctaw Newborn
Act of 1905   Volume III

7-2602

Muskogee, Indian Territory, January 28, 1905.

Rutha Blaylock,
    McCurtain, Indian Territory.

Dear Madam:

    Receipt is hereby acknowledged of your affidavit and the affidavit of Jane Overton relative to the birth of George Washington Blaylock infant son of Rutha and Henry Blaylock, November 17, 1904, which it is presumed have been forwarded as an application for the enrollment of said child.

    You are advised that under the provisions of the act of Congress approved July 1, 1902, no children born to citizens of the Choctaw and Chickasaw Nations subsequent to September 25, 1902, the date of the ratification of said act, are entitled to enrollment and allotment in the Choctaw and Chickasaw Nations.

Respectfully,

Chairman.

COPY

N. B. 172

Muskogee, Indian Territory, April 7, 1905.

Henry Blaylock,
    McCurtain, Indian Territory.

Dear Sir:

    There is inclosed you herewith for execution application for the enrollment of your infant child, George Washington Blaylock, born November 17, 1904.

    The affidavits heretofore filed with the Commission show the child was living on January 20, 1905. It is necessary, for the child to be enrolled, that he was living on March 4, 1905. You will please insert the age of the mother in space left blank for that purpose.

    In having these affidavits executed care should be exercised to see that all names are written in full, as they appear in the body of the affidavit, and in the event that either of the persons signing the affidavit are unable to write, signatures by mark must be attested by two witnesses. Each affidavit must be executed before a Notary Public and the notarial seal and signature of the officer must be attached to each separate affidavit.

Applications for Enrollment of Choctaw Newborn
Act of 1905 Volume III

LM 7-1

Respectfully,
SIGNED
T. B. Needles.
Commissioner in Charge.

Choctaw 2602.

Muskogee, Indian Territory, April 10, 1905.

Henry Blaylock,
    McCurtain, Indian Territory.

Dear Sir:

    Receipt is hereby acknowledged of the affidavits of Ruth A. Blaylock and M. E. Talburt to the birth of Geo. Washington Blaylock, son of Henry and Ruth A. Blaylock, November 17, 1904, and the same have been filed with our records as an application for the enrollment of said child.

Respectfully,

Commissioner in Charge.

Applications for Enrollment of Choctaw Newborn
Act of 1905   Volume III

Choc New Born 173
   (Lillie M. Gregory)
   (Born May 22, 1904)

BIRTH AFFIDAVIT.

DEPARTMENT OF THE INTERIOR,
COMMISSION TO THE FIVE CIVILIZED TRIBES.

In Re Application for Enrollment, as a citizen of the   Choctaw   Nation, of   Lillie M. Gregory   , born on the   22   day of   May   , 1904

Name of Father: E. S. Gregory   a citizen of the   Choctaw   Nation.
Name of Mother: Algie[sic] R. Gregory   a citizen of the   Choctaw   Nation.

                Post-office   Pocola I.T.

AFFIDAVIT OF MOTHER.

UNITED STATES OF AMERICA,
   INDIAN TERRITORY,
   Central   District.

    I,   Algie R. Gregory , on oath state that I am   25   years of age and a citizen by   Intermarriage   , of the   Choctaw   Nation; that I am the lawful wife of   E. S. Gregory   , who is a citizen, by Blood of the   Choctaw   Nation; that a   female   child was born to me on   22   day of   May   , 1904 , that said child has been named   Lillie M. Gregory   , and is now living.

                          Algia[sic] r[sic] gregory[sic]

WITNESSES TO MARK:

    Subscribed and sworn to before me this   11   day of   Oct , 1904

                            W. F. Lester
                              NOTARY PUBLIC.

Applications for Enrollment of Choctaw Newborn
Act of 1905   Volume III

AFFIDAVIT OF ATTENDING PHYSICIAN OR MID-WIFE.

UNITED STATES OF AMERICA,
    INDIAN TERRITORY,
    Central   District.

I, Mary C. Gregory, a Midwife, on oath state that I attended on Mrs. Algie R. Gregory, wife of E.S. Gregory on the 22 day of May, 1904; that there was born to her on said date a female child; that said child is now living and is said to have been named Lillie M. Gregory.

                M. C. Gregory

WITNESSES TO MARK:

Subscribed and sworn to before me this 11 day of Oct, 1904

                W. F. Lester
                    NOTARY PUBLIC.

NEW-BORN AFFIDAVIT.

Number..............

...Choctaw Enrolling Commission...

IN THE MATTER OF THE APPLICATION FOR ENROLLMENT, as a citizen of the Choctaw Nation, of Lillie M. Gregory

born on the 22 day of ___May___ 190 4

Name of father Edwin S. Gregory   a citizen of   Choctaw
Nation final enrollment No. 7551
Name of mother Algia R. Gregory   a citizen of   Choctaw
Nation final enrollment No. 250 InterM

                Postoffice   Pocola I.T.

AFFIDAVIT OF MOTHER.

UNITED STATES OF AMERICA
INDIAN TERRITORY
    Central   DISTRICT

I Algia R. Gregory, on oath state that I am 25 years of age and a citizen by InterM of the Choctaw

Applications for Enrollment of Choctaw Newborn
Act of 1905 Volume III

Nation, and as such have been placed upon the final roll of the Choctaw Nation, by the Honorable Secretary of the Interior my final enrollment number being 250 ; that I am the lawful wife of Edwin S. Gregory , who is a citizen of the Choctaw Nation, and as such has been placed upon the final roll of said Nation by the Honorable Secretary of the Interior, his final enrollment number being 7551 and that a Female child was born to me on the 22 day of May 190 4 ; that said child has been named Lillie May Gregory , and is now living.

Witnesseth. Algia r[sic]. gregory[sic]

Must be two Witnesses who are Citizens. } Mary I. McClain

Viola Karl

Subscribed and sworn to before me this 15 day of Feb 190 5

William. F. Lester
Notary Public.

My commission expires: Feb 1st 1906

AFFIDAVIT OF ATTENDING PHYSICIAN OR MIDWIFE

UNITED STATES OF AMERICA
INDIAN TERRITORY
Central DISTRICT

I, Mary C. Gregory a midwife on oath state that I attended on Mrs. Algia R Gregory wife of Edwin S. Gregory on the 22 day of May , 190 4 , that there was born to her on said date a Female child, that said child is now living, and is said to have been named Lillie May Gregory

Mary C. Gregory M.W.

Subscribed and sworn to before me this, the 15 day of Feb. 190 5

WITNESSETH: William F. Lester Notary Public.

Must be two witnesses who are citizens { Mary I McClain

Viola Karl

We hereby certify that we are well acquainted with Mrs Mary C. Gregory a Midwife and know her to be reputable and of good standing in the community.

Mary I. McClain Viola Karl

Applications for Enrollment of Choctaw Newborn
Act of 1905 Volume III

BIRTH AFFIDAVIT.

DEPARTMENT OF THE INTERIOR.
COMMISSION TO THE FIVE CIVILIZED TRIBES.

IN RE APPLICATION FOR ENROLLMENT, as a citizen of the Choctaw Nation, of Lillie M. Gregory, born on the 21[sic] day of May, 1904

Name of Father: Edward[sic] S. Gregory   a citizen of the Choctaw Nation.
Name of Mother: Algie R. Gregory   a citizen of the Choctaw Nation.

Postoffice   Pocola Ind Ter

AFFIDAVIT OF MOTHER.

UNITED STATES OF AMERICA, Indian Territory,
Central DISTRICT.

I, Algie R. Gregory, on oath state that I am 25 years of age and a citizen by Intermarriage, of the Choctaw Nation; that I am the lawful wife of Edward[sic] S. Gregory, who is a citizen, by Blood of the Choctaw Nation; that a Female child was born to me on 21[sic] day of May, 1904; that said child has been named Lillie M. Gregory, and was living March 4, 1905.

Algia r[sic] gregory[sic]

Witnesses To Mark:
{

Subscribed and sworn to before me this 27 day of March, 1905

W.F. Lester
Notary Public.

AFFIDAVIT OF ATTENDING PHYSICIAN OR MID-WIFE.

UNITED STATES OF AMERICA, Indian Territory,
Central DISTRICT.

I, Mary C. Gregory, a midwife, on oath state that I attended on Mrs. Algie R Gregory, wife of Edward S Gregory on the 21 day of May, 1904; that there was born to her on said date a Female child; that said child was living March 4, 1905, and is said to have been named Lillie M Gregory

Mary C Gregory

Witnesses To Mark:
{

Applications for Enrollment of Choctaw Newborn
Act of 1905   Volume III

Subscribed and sworn to before me this   27 day of   March   , 1905

W.F. Lester
Notary Public.

Choctaw-2606.

Muskogee, Indian Territory, April 1, 1905.

Edwin S. Gregory,
Pocola, Indian Territory.

Dear Sir:

Receipt is hereby acknowledged of the affidavits of Algia R. Gregory and Mary C. Gregory to the birth of Lillie M. Gregory, daughter of Edwin S. and Algia R. Gregory, May 21, 1904, and the same have been filed with our records as an application for the enrollment of said child.

Respectfully,

Chairman.

---

7 N.B. 173.

Muskogee, Indian Territory, May 29, 1905.

Edwin S. Gregory,
Pocola, Indian Territory.

Dear Sir:

Receipt is hereby acknowledged of your letter of May 22, asking if you can file for your child, Lily[sic] M. Gregory, for whom you made application recently.

In reply to your letter you are advised that the name of your child, Lillie M. Gregory, has been placed upon a schedule of citizens by blood of the Choctaw Nation which has been prepared for forwarding to the Secretary of the Interior, and you will be further advised when her enrollment is approved by him.

However, pending the approval of her enrollment by the Secretary of the Interior, no selection of allotment can be made in her behalf.

Respectfully,

Chairman.

Applications for Enrollment of Choctaw Newborn
Act of 1905   Volume III

Choc New Born 174
    Edith Johnson
    (Born Oct. 2, 1902)
    Lena Johnson
    (Born Sep. 12, 1904)

BIRTH AFFIDAVIT.

Department of the Interior,
COMMISSION TO THE FIVE CIVILIZED TRIBES.

IN RE APPLICATION FOR ENROLLMENT, as a citizen of the Choctaw Nation, of Edith Johnson, born on the 2 day of Oct., 190 2

Name of Father: Van B Johnson   a citizen of the Choctaw Nation.
Name of Mother: Ida Johnson   a citizen of the Choctaw Nation.

Post-Office: Tamaha

AFFIDAVIT OF ~~MOTHER~~. father

UNITED STATES OF AMERICA,
  INDIAN TERRITORY,
  Central District.

I, Van B Johnson, on oath state that I am 27 years of age and a citizen by marriage, of the Choctaw Nation; that I am the lawful ~~wife~~ husband of Ida Johnson, who is a citizen, by blood of the Choctaw Nation; that a female child was born to ~~me~~ us on 2 day of October, 190 2, that said child has been named Edith Johnson, and is now living.

                         V B Johnson

WITNESSES TO MARK:
{

Subscribed and sworn to before me this 16 day of December, 190 2.

                         P.C. Bolger
                             Notary Public.

Applications for Enrollment of Choctaw Newborn
Act of 1905   Volume III

NEW-BORN AFFIDAVIT.

Number..............

...Choctaw Enrolling Commission...

IN THE MATTER OF THE APPLICATION FOR ENROLLMENT, as a citizen of the Choctaw Nation, of Edith Johnson

born on the 2 day of October 190 2

Name of father   Van B. Johnson   a citizen of   Choctaw
Nation final enrollment No.   252
Name of mother   Ida Johnson   a citizen of   Choctaw
Nation final enrollment No.   252

Postoffice   Tamaha

AFFIDAVIT OF MOTHER.

UNITED STATES OF AMERICA
INDIAN TERRITORY
   Central   DISTRICT

I   Ida Johnson   , on oath state that I am 22 years of age and a citizen by Blood of the Choctaw Nation, and as such have been placed upon the final roll of the Choctaw Nation, by the Honorable Secretary of the Interior my final enrollment number being 252 ; that I am the lawful wife of Van B. Johnson , who is a citizen of the Choctaw Nation[sic] Nation, and as such has been placed upon the final roll of said Nation by the Honorable Secretary of the Interior, his final enrollment number being 252 and that a Female child was born to me on the 2 day of October 190 2; that said child has been named Edith Johnson , and is now living.

Witnesseth.   Ida Johnson
   Must be two ⎤ Albert Deshon
   Witnesses who ⎥
   are Citizens. ⎦ Albert Harrison

Subscribed and sworn to before me this 5 day of Jany 190 5

                                      W B Davidson
                                         Notary Public.

My commission expires: 11ᵗʰ May 1907

Applications for Enrollment of Choctaw Newborn
Act of 1905 Volume III

AFFIDAVIT OF ATTENDING PHYSICIAN OR MIDWIFE

UNITED STATES OF AMERICA
INDIAN TERRITORY
Central   DISTRICT

I,   A. T. Hill   a   Physician on oath state that I attended on Mrs.   Ida Johnson   wife of   Van B Johnson on the   2   day of   October   , 190 2 , that there was born to her on said date a   female child, that said child is now living, and is said to have been named   Edith Johnson

Subscribed and sworn to before me this, the   5   day of 5th January   190 5   A.T. Hill M.D.

WITNESSETH: WB Davidson   Notary Public.
Must be two witnesses { Albert Deshon
who are citizens   { Albert Harrison

We hereby certify that we are well acquainted with   A.T. Hill a   Physician   and know   him   to be reputable and of good standing in the community.

Iva A. Deshon   Albert Deshon

Albert Harrison   W.B. Davidson

BIRTH AFFIDAVIT.
DEPARTMENT OF THE INTERIOR.
COMMISSION TO THE FIVE CIVILIZED TRIBES.

IN RE APPLICATION FOR ENROLLMENT, as a citizen of the   Choctaw   Nation, of Edith Johnson   , born on the   2   day of   October   , 1902

Name of Father: Van B. Johnson   a citizen of the   Choctaw   Nation.
Name of Mother: Ida Johnson   a citizen of the   Choctaw   Nation.

Postoffice   Tamaha, I.T.

AFFIDAVIT OF MOTHER.

UNITED STATES OF AMERICA, Indian Territory, }
Central   DISTRICT.

I,   Ida Johnson   , on oath state that I am   22   years of age and a citizen by blood   , of the   Choctaw   Nation; that I am the lawful wife of   Van B. Johnson   ,

Applications for Enrollment of Choctaw Newborn
Act of 1905   Volume III

who is a citizen, by intermarriage of the Choctaw Nation; that a female child was born to me on 2 day of October , 1902; that said child has been named Edith Johnson , and was living March 4, 1905.

                                              Ida Johnson

Witnesses To Mark:

{

    Subscribed and sworn to before me this 18 day of April , 1905

My commission expires   W. B. Davidson
11th May 1907   Notary Public.

AFFIDAVIT OF ATTENDING PHYSICIAN OR MID-WIFE.

UNITED STATES OF AMERICA, Indian Territory,
    Central   DISTRICT.

    I, A. T. Hill , a Physician , on oath state that I attended on Mrs. Ida Johnson , wife of Van B. Johnson on the 2 day of October , 1902; that there was born to her on said date a female child; that said child was living March 4, 1905, and is said to have been named Edith Johnson

                                              A.T. Hill MD

Witnesses To Mark:

{

    Subscribed and sworn to before me this 18 day of April , 1905

My commission expires   W. B. Davidson
11th May 1907   Notary Public.

Applications for Enrollment of Choctaw Newborn
Act of 1905   Volume III

NEW-BORN AFFIDAVIT.

Number..............

...Choctaw Enrolling Commission...

IN THE MATTER OF THE APPLICATION FOR ENROLLMENT, as a citizen of the Choctaw Nation, of   Lena Johnson

born on the 12 day of September   190 4

Name of father   Van B. Johnson   a citizen of   Choctaw Nation
Nation final enrollment No. _____
Name of mother   Ida Johnson   a citizen of   Choctaw
Nation final enrollment No. 252

Postoffice   Tamaha

AFFIDAVIT OF MOTHER.

UNITED STATES OF AMERICA
INDIAN TERRITORY
  Central   DISTRICT

I   Ida Johnson   , on oath state that I am   22   years of age and a citizen by   Blood   of the   Choctaw Nation, and as such have been placed upon the final roll of the   Choctaw Nation, by the Honorable Secretary of the Interior my final enrollment number being   252 ; that I am the lawful wife of   Van B. Johnson   , who is a citizen of the Choctaw Nation[sic]   Nation, and as such has been placed upon the final roll of said Nation by the Honorable Secretary of the Interior, his final enrollment number being   252   and that a   Female   child was born to me on the   12   day of   September   190 4; that said child has been named   Lena Johnson   , and is now living.

Witnesseth.   Ida Johnson
  Must be two ⎫ Albert Deshon
  Witnesses who ⎬
  are Citizens. ⎭ Albert Harrison

Subscribed and sworn to before me this   5   day of   Jany   190 5

W B Davidson
Notary Public.

My commission expires:
  11th May 1907

Applications for Enrollment of Choctaw Newborn
Act of 1905   Volume III

BIRTH AFFIDAVIT.

DEPARTMENT OF THE INTERIOR.
COMMISSION TO THE FIVE CIVILIZED TRIBES.

IN RE APPLICATION FOR ENROLLMENT, as a citizen of the Choctaw Nation, of Lena Johnson, born on the 12 day of September, 1904

Name of Father: Van B. Johnson   a citizen of the Choctaw Nation.
Name of Mother: Ida Johnson   a citizen of the Choctaw Nation.

Postoffice   Tamaha, I.T.

AFFIDAVIT OF MOTHER.

UNITED STATES OF AMERICA, Indian Territory,
Central   DISTRICT.

I, Ida Johnson, on oath state that I am 22 years of age and a citizen by Blood, of the Choctaw Nation; that I am the lawful wife of Van B. Johnson, who is a citizen, by Intermarriage of the Choctaw Nation; that a Female child was born to me on 12 day of September, 1904; that said child has been named Lena Johnson, and was living March 4, 1905.

                               Ida Johnson

Witnesses To Mark:
{

Subscribed and sworn to before me this 18 day of April, 1905

My commission expires   W. B. Davidson
11th May 1907   Notary Public.

AFFIDAVIT OF ATTENDING PHYSICIAN OR MID-WIFE.

UNITED STATES OF AMERICA, Indian Territory,
Central   DISTRICT.

I, A. T. Hill, a Physician, on oath state that I attended on Mrs. Ida Johnson, wife of Van B. Johnson on the 12 day of September, 1904; that there was born to her on said date a female child; that said child was living March 4, 1905, and is said to have been named Lena Johnson

                               A.T. Hill MD

Witnesses To Mark:
{

Applications for Enrollment of Choctaw Newborn
Act of 1905 Volume III

Subscribed and sworn to before me this 18 day of April , 1905

My commission expires W. B. Davidson
11th May 1907 Notary Public.

AFFIDAVIT OF ATTENDING PHYSICIAN OR MIDWIFE

UNITED STATES OF AMERICA
INDIAN TERRITORY
Central   DISTRICT

I, A. T. Hill a Physician on oath state that I attended on Mrs. Ida B.[sic] Johnson wife of Van B Johnson on the 12 day of September , 190 4 , that there was born to her on said date a female child, that said child is now living, and is said to have been named Lena Johnson

Subscribed and sworn to before me this, the 5 day of January 190 5   A.T. Hill M.D.

WITNESSETH: WB Davidson Notary Public.
Must be two witnesses who are citizens { Albert Deshon
  Albert Harrison

We hereby certify that we are well acquainted with A.T. Hill a Physician and know him to be reputable and of good standing in the community.

Iva A. Deshon Albert Deshon

Albert Harrison W.B. Davidson

7-251?.

Muskogee, Indian Territory, January 6, 1903.

Van B. Johnson,
  Tamaha, Indian Territory.

Dear Sir:

Referring to the application for enrollment as a citizen of the Choctaw Nation of Edith Johnson, infant daughter of Van B. and Ida Johnson, born October 2, 1902; you are advised that the Commission is without authority to enroll this child as a citizen of the Choctaw Nation, it appearing that said child was born October 2, 1902, subsequent to the

Applications for Enrollment of Choctaw Newborn
Act of 1905   Volume III

ratification by the citizens of the Choctaw and Chickasaw Nations September 25, 1902, of an act of Congress approved July 1, 1902 (32 Stats., 641).

Section twenty-eight thereof provided as follows:

"The names of all persons living on the date of the final ratification of this agreement entitled to be enrolled as provided in section 27 hereof shall be placed upon the rolls made by said Commission; and no child born thereafter to a citizen or freedman and no person intermarried thereafter to a citizen shall be entitled to enrollment or to participate in the distribution of the tribal property of the Choctaws and Chickasaws."

Respectfully,

Acting Chairman.

COPY

N. B. 174

Muskogee, Indian Territory, April 6, 1905.

Van B. Johnson,
Tamaha, Indian Territory.

Dear Sir:

There is inclosed you herewith for execution application for the enrollment of your infant child, Edith Johnson, born October 2, 1902.

The papers heretofore filed with the Commission were incomplete in that they contained neither the affidavit of the mother nor that of the attending physician or midwife. Your affidavit which is on file in this office show[sic] that the applicant was living on December 16, 1902. It is necessary, for the child to be enrolled, that she was living on March 4, 1905.

In the event that the mother is dead, or that there was no physician or midwife in attendance, it will be necessary that you procure the affidavits of two persons who have actual knowledge of the fact, that the child was born, was living on March 4, 1905, and that Ida Johnson was her mother.

In having these affidavits executed care should be exercised to see that all names are written in full, as they appear in the body of the affidavit, and in the event that either of the persons signing the affidavit are unable to write, signatures by mark must be attested by two witnesses. Each affidavit must be executed before a Notary Public and the notarial seal and signature of the officer must be attached to each separate affidavit.

Applications for Enrollment of Choctaw Newborn
Act of 1905 Volume III

LM 5-11

Respectfully,
SIGNED
T. B. Needles.
Commissioner in Charge.

Choctaw 2610.

Muskogee, Indian Territory, April 26, 1905.

Van B. Johnson,
Tamaha, Indian Territory.

Dear Sir:

Receipt is hereby acknowledged of the affidavits of Ida Johnson and A. T. Hill to the birth of Lena Johnson, daughter of Van B. and Ida Johnson, September 12, 1904, and the same have been filed with our records as an application for the enrollment of said child.

Respectfully,

Chairman.

Choc New Born 175
    Clarence Mason
    (Born March 28, 1903)

BIRTH AFFIDAVIT.

DEPARTMENT OF THE INTERIOR.
COMMISSION TO THE FIVE CIVILIZED TRIBES.

IN RE APPLICATION FOR ENROLLMENT, as a citizen of the Choctaw Nation, of Clarence Mason, born on the 28 day of March, 1903

Name of Father: John Mason   a citizen of the Choctaw Nation.
Name of Mother: Susie Mason   a citizen of the Choctaw Nation.

Postoffice Fort Smith Ark. R.F.D. No 3

Applications for Enrollment of Choctaw Newborn
Act of 1905 Volume III

AFFIDAVIT OF MOTHER.

UNITED STATES OF AMERICA, Indian Territory, }
Central DISTRICT.

I, Susie Mason , on oath state that I am 24 years of age and a citizen by blood , of the Choctaw Nation; that I am the lawful wife of John Mason , who is a citizen, by .... of the Choctaw Nation; that a male child was born to me on 28 day of March , 1903, that said child has been named Clarence Mason , and is now living.

                                              Susie Masson[sic]

Witnesses To Mark:
{

Subscribed and sworn to before me this 16 day of November , 1904.

                                               H.M. Ashworth
                                               Notary Public.

AFFIDAVIT OF ATTENDING PHYSICIAN OR MID-WIFE.

UNITED STATES OF AMERICA, Indian Territory, }
Central DISTRICT.

I, Arau Morris , a midwife , on oath state that I attended on Mrs. Susie Mason , wife of John Mason on the 28 day of March , 1903; that there was born to her on said date a male child; that said child is now living and is said to have been named Clarence Mason

                                             her
                                    Arau x Morris

Witnesses To Mark: mark
{ Clara Lena Fulsom
  H.D. Stuckey

Subscribed and sworn to before me this 16 day of November , 1904.

                                              H.M. Ashworth
                                              Notary Public.

Applications for Enrollment of Choctaw Newborn
Act of 1905 Volume III

BIRTH AFFIDAVIT.

DEPARTMENT OF THE INTERIOR.
COMMISSION TO THE FIVE CIVILIZED TRIBES.

IN RE APPLICATION FOR ENROLLMENT, as a citizen of the Choctaw Nation, of Clarence Mason, born on the 28 day of March, 1903

Name of Father: John Mason   a citizen of the U.S. Nation.
Name of Mother: Susan Mason   a citizen of the Choctaw Nation.

Postoffice   Fort Smith, Ark - R.F.D. No 3

AFFIDAVIT OF MOTHER.

UNITED STATES OF AMERICA, Indian Territory,
Central DISTRICT.

I, Susan Mason, on oath state that I am 27 years of age and a citizen by blood, of the Choctaw Nation; that I am the lawful wife of John Mason, who is a citizen, by .... of the U.S. Nation; that a male child was born to me on 28 day of March, 1903; that said child has been named Clarence Mason, and was living March 4, 1905.

Susan Masson[sic]

Witnesses To Mark:
{

Subscribed and sworn to before me this 20th day of April, 1905.

H.M. Ashworth
Notary Public.

AFFIDAVIT OF ATTENDING PHYSICIAN OR MID-WIFE.

UNITED STATES OF AMERICA, Indian Territory,
Central DISTRICT.

I, Arah[sic] Ann Morris, a midwife, on oath state that I attended on Mrs. Susan Mason, wife of John Mason on the 28 day of March, 1903; that there was born to her on said date a male child; that said child was living March 4, 1905, and is said to have been named Clarence Mason

her
Arah Ann x Morris
mark

262

Applications for Enrollment of Choctaw Newborn
Act of 1905 Volume III

Witnesses To Mark:
  { Francis Call
  { Marthie Henderson

Subscribed and sworn to before me this 20th day of April , 1905

H.M. Ashworth
Notary Public.

COPY

N. B. 175

Muskogee, Indian Territory, April 6, 1905.

John Mason,
  R. F. D. #3,
    Fort Smith, Arkansas.

Dear Sir:

There is inclosed you herewith for execution application for the enrollment of your infant child, Clarence Mason, born March 28, 1903.

The affidavits heretofore filed with the Commission show the child was living on November 16, 1904. It is necessary, for the child to be enrolled, that he was living on March 4, 1905. You will please insert the age of the mother in space left blank for that purpose.

In having these affidavits executed care should be exercised to see that all names are written in full, as they appear in the body of the affidavit, and in the event that either of the persons signing the affidavit are unable to write, signatures by mark must be attested by two witnesses. Each affidavit must be executed before a Notary Public and the notarial seal and signature of the officer must be attached to each separate affidavit.

Respectfully,
SIGNED
T. B. Needles.
Commissioner in Charge.

LM 5-10.

Applications for Enrollment of Choctaw Newborn
Act of 1905   Volume III

COPY

7-NB-175.

Muskogee, Indian Territory, April 25, 1905.

John Mason,
    R. F. D. No. 3,
        Fort Smith, Arkansas.

Dear Sir:

    Receipt is hereby acknowledged of the affidavits of Susan Mason and Arah Ann Morris, to the birth of Clarence Mason, child of John and Susan Mason, March 28, 1903, and the same have been filed with our records in the matter of the enrollment of said child.

                Respectfully,
                SIGNED

                Tams Bixby
                Chairman.

---

7 NB 175

Muskogee, Indian Territory, June 16, 1905.

Susan Mason,
    R.F.D. No. 3, Box 116,
        Fort Smith, Arkansas.

Dear Madam:

    Receipt is hereby acknowledged of your letter of June 2, 1905, asking if Clarence Mason is approved so you can secure his allotment.

    In reply to your letter you are advised that the name of your son Clarence Mason has been placed upon a schedule of citizens by blood of the Choctaw Nation which has been forwarded the Secretary of the Interior, but the Commission has not yet been advised of Departmental action thereon. You will be notified when his enrollment is approved by the Secretary of the Interior.

                Respectfully,

                      Chairman.

Applications for Enrollment of Choctaw Newborn
Act of 1905 Volume III

Choc New Born 176
    Clara Lee LeFlore
    (Born Sep. 24, 1904)

No. 1838

Form No. 593.

MARRIAGE LICENSE.
UNITED STATES OF AMERICA,)
THE INDIAN TERRITORY,   )
CENTRAL DISTRICT.   )

TO ANY PERSON AUTHORIZED BY LAW TO SOLEMNIZE MARRIAGE - - GREETING:

You are hereby commanded to solemnize the Rite and publish the BANNS OF MATRIMONY between Mr. Turner Leflore of Milton in the Indian Territory, aged 19 years, and Miss Lena Abernathy of Milton in the Indian Territory, aged 19 years, according to law, and do you officially sign and return this License to the parties therein named.

WITNESS my hand and official seal, this 22" day of July, A.D. 1903.

(S E A L)   (signed)   E. J. Fannie
                                   Clerk of the United States Court
By T. T. Varner
    Deputy.

CERTIFICATE OF MARRIAGE.

UNITED STATES OF AMERICA)
THE INDIAN TERRITORY,   ) SS: I, W. F. Davidson a Minister of the
CENTRAL DISTRICT.   )   Gospel do hereby CERTIFY, that on
the 24 day of July, A. D. 1903, I did duly and according to law, as commanded in the foregoing License, solemnize the Rite and publish the BANNS OF MATRIMONY between the parties therein named.

Witness my hand this 24 day of July, A. D. 1903
My credentials are recorded in the office of the Clerk of the United States Court in the Indian Territory, Central District, Book M, Page 125,

                              (signed)   W. F. Davidson

                              a   Minister.

Applications for Enrollment of Choctaw Newborn
Act of 1905   Volume III

ENDORSED ON BACK AS FOLLOWS:

No. 1838
CERTIFICATE OF RECORD OF MARRIAGES.

UNITED STATES OF AMERICA,)
   THE INDIAN TERRITORY,) SCT:
   CENTRAL DISTRICT)

I, E. J. Fannin, Clerk of the United Dtates[sic] Court in the Indian Territory and District aforesaid, do hereby CERTIFY that the License for and Certificate of the Marriage of Mr. Turner Leflore and Miss Lena Abernathy was filed in my office in said Territory and District the 27 day of July, A. D. 1903, and duly recorded in Book 2 of Marriage Record Page 301
     Witness my hand and seal of said Court, at Poteau this 27 day of July A. D. 1903

                        E. J. Fannin
                              Clerk
                    by T. T. Varner Deputy.

DEPARTMENT OF THE INTERIOR,
COMMISSION TO THE FIVE CIVILIZED TRIBES.
   F I L E D
     MAY 17 1905
       Tams Bixby Chairman.

I, Lola Mann, a stenographer to the Commissioner to the Five Civilized Tribes, hereby certify that I copies the above License and certificate of marriage and that the same is a true and correct copy of the original
                              Lola Mann

Subscribed and sworn to before me this 14th day of July, 1905.

                            Myron White
                            Notary Public.

Applications for Enrollment of Choctaw Newborn
Act of 1905 Volume III

BIRTH AFFIDAVIT.

DEPARTMENT OF THE INTERIOR,
COMMISSION TO THE FIVE CIVILIZED TRIBES.

IN RE Application for Enrollment, as a citizen of the   Choctaw   Nation, of   Clara Lee Leflore   , born on the   24   day of   Sept   , 1904

Name of Father: T. L. Leflore   a citizen of the   Choctaw Nation.
Name of Mother: Lena Leflore   a citizen of the   ————Nation.

Post-Office: Milton, I.T.

AFFIDAVIT OF MOTHER.

UNITED STATES OF AMERICA, }
   INDIAN TERRITORY.
  Central   District.

I,   Lena Leflore   , on oath state that I am   20   years of age and a citizen by   marriage   , of the Choctaw Nation; that I am the lawful wife of   Turner Leflore , who is a citizen, by   blood   of the Choctaw Nation; that a   girl   child was born to me on   24th   day of Sept.   , 1904 , that said child has been named Clara Lee Leflore, and is now living.

                            Lena Leflore

WITNESSES TO MARK:
{

Subscribed and sworn to before me this   13   day of   Dec   , 1904

                            J. L. Lewis
                              NOTARY PUBLIC.

AFFIDAVIT OF ATTENDING PHYSICIAN OR MID-WIFE.

UNITED STATES OF AMERICA, }
   INDIAN TERRITORY.
  Central   District.

I,   T. L. Hedgecock   , a   physician   , on oath state that I attended on Mrs.   Lena Leflore   , wife of   T. L. Leflore   on the   24   day of Sept   , 1904 ; that there was born to her on said date a   female   child; that said child is now living and is said to have been named   Clara Lee Leflore

Applications for Enrollment of Choctaw Newborn
Act of 1905   Volume III

T. L. Hedgecock M.D.

WITNESSES TO MARK:
{

Subscribed and sworn to before me this   2   day of   Dec   , 1904

J. L. Lewis

My commission expires Mar. 15, 1905   *NOTARY PUBLIC.*

Milton I.T.

NEW-BORN AFFIDAVIT.

Number..................

...Choctaw Enrolling Commission...

IN THE MATTER OF THE APPLICATION FOR ENROLLMENT, as a citizen of the Choctaw   Nation, of   Clara Lee Leflore

born on the   24   day of   September   190 4

Name of father   Turner Leflore   a citizen of   Choctaw
Nation final enrollment No. 7623   by marriage
Name of mother   Lena Leflore   a citizen^of   Choctaw
Nation final enrollment No. ——

Postoffice   Milton, I. Ty.

AFFIDAVIT OF MOTHER.

UNITED STATES OF AMERICA
INDIAN TERRITORY
   Central   DISTRICT

I   Lena Leflore   , on oath state that I am   20   years of age and a citizen by   Marriage   of the   Choctaw   Nation, and as such have been not[sic] placed upon the final roll of the   Choctaw   Nation, by the Honorable Secretary of the Interior my final enrollment number being —— ; that I am the lawful wife of   Turner Leflore   , who is a citizen of the   Choctaw   Nation, and as such has been placed upon the final roll of said Nation by the Honorable Secretary of the Interior, his final enrollment number being   7623   and that a   girl   child was born to me on the   24   day of   September   190 4 ; that said child has been named   Clara Lee Leflore   , and is now living.

Lena Leflore

Applications for Enrollment of Choctaw Newborn
Act of 1905 Volume III

Witnesseth.

Must be two Witnesses who are Citizens. } J. W. Leflore

L. E. Leflore

Subscribed and sworn to before me this   14   day of   Feb   190 5

J.L. Lewis

My commission expires Mar. 15, 1905   Notary Public.
My commission expires:

AFFIDAVIT OF ATTENDING PHYSICIAN OR MIDWIFE

UNITED STATES OF AMERICA
INDIAN TERRITORY
Central   DISTRICT

I,   T. L. Hedgecock   a   physician on oath state that I attended on Mrs.   Lena Leflore   wife of   Turner Leflore on the   24   day of   September , 190 4 , that there was born to her on said date a   girl child, that said child is now living, and is said to have been named   Clara Lee Leflore

T. L. Hedgecock   M.D.

WITNESSETH:

Must be two witnesses who are citizens and know the child. { Thomas Foster

J.W. Leflore

Subscribed and sworn to before me this, the   14   day of   February   190 5

J. L. Lewis   Notary Public.

We hereby certify that we are well acquainted with   Dr T. L. Hedgecock   a   physician   and know   him   to be reputable and of good standing in the community.

{ Thomas Foster

J. W. Leflore

Applications for Enrollment of Choctaw Newborn
Act of 1905 Volume III

BIRTH AFFIDAVIT.

DEPARTMENT OF THE INTERIOR.
COMMISSION TO THE FIVE CIVILIZED TRIBES.

IN RE APPLICATION FOR ENROLLMENT, as a citizen of the Choctaw Nation, of Clara Lee LeFlore, born on the 24 day of Sept, 1904

Name of Father: Turner LeFlore   a citizen of the Choctaw Nation.
Name of Mother: Lena LeFlore   a citizen of the U.S. Nation.

Postoffice   Milton, I.T.

AFFIDAVIT OF MOTHER.

UNITED STATES OF AMERICA, Indian Territory, } DISTRICT.

I, Lena LeFlore, on oath state that I am 20 years of age and a citizen by ~~~~~~~~~, of the U.S. Nation; that I am the lawful wife of Turner LeFlore, who is a citizen, by blood of the Choctaw Nation; that a female child was born to me on 24" day of Sept, 1904; that said child has been named Clara Lee LeFlore, and was living March 4, 1905.

                         Lena Leflore

Witnesses To Mark:
{

Subscribed and sworn to before me this 10 day of April, 1905.

                         J. L. Lewis
                         Notary Public.

AFFIDAVIT OF ATTENDING PHYSICIAN OR MID-WIFE.

UNITED STATES OF AMERICA, Indian Territory, } Central DISTRICT.

I, T. L. Hedgecock, a physician, on oath state that I attended on Mrs. Lena LeFlore, wife of Turner LeFlore on the 24" day of Sept, 1904; that there was born to her on said date a .... child; that said child was living March 4, 1905, and is said to have been named Clara Lee LeFlore

                         T. L. Hedgecock M.D.

Witnesses To Mark:
{

Applications for Enrollment of Choctaw Newborn
Act of 1905   Volume III

Subscribed and sworn to before me this 10 day of   Apr   , 1905

J. L. Lewis

My commission expires Mar. 15, 1905   Notary Public.

COPY

N. B. 176

Muskogee, Indian Territory, April 6, 1905.

Turner LeFlore,
    Milton, Indian Territory.

Dear Sir:

    There is inclosed you herewith for execution application for the enrollment of your infant child, Clara Lee LeFlore, born September 24, 1904.

    The affidavits heretofore filed with the Commission show the child was living on December 2, 1904. It is necessary, for the child to be enrolled, that he was living on March 4, 1905. You will please insert the age of the mother in the space provided for the purpose.

    In having these affidavits executed care should be exercised to see that all names are written in full, as they appear in the body of the affidavit, and in the event that either of the persons signing the affidavit are unable to write, signatures by mark must be attested by two witnesses. Each affidavit must be executed before a Notary Public and the notarial seal and signature of the officer must be attached to each separate affidavit.

Respectfully,
SIGNED
T. B. Needles.

LM 8-9   Commissioner in Charge.

Choctaw N.B. 176

COPY

Muskogee, Indian Territory, April 13, 1905.

Turner Leflore,
    Milton, Indian Territory.

Dear Sir:

    Receipt is hereby acknowledged of the affidavits of Lena LeFlore and T. L. Hedgecock to the birth of Clara Lee Leflore, daughter of Turner and Lena LeFlore,

Applications for Enrollment of Choctaw Newborn
Act of 1905 Volume III

September 24, 1904, and the same have been filed in the matter of the enrollment of said child.

                Respectfully,
                SIGNED
                T. B. Needles.
                Commissioner in Charge.

                7-N.B. 176.

        Muskogee, Indian Territory, May 10, 1905.

Turner LeFlore,
    Milton, Indian Territory.

Dear Sir:

    Referring to the application for the enrollment of your infant child, Clara Lee LeFlore, born September 24, 1904, it noted that the applicant claims through you.

    If this is the case, it will be necessary for you to file with the Commission either the original or a certified copy of the license and certificate of your marriage to the applicant's mother, Lena LeFlore.

    Please give this matter your immediate attention.

                Respectfully,

                        Chairman.

---

                7 NB 176

        Muskogee, Indian Territory, May 18, 1905.

Turner LeFlore,
    Milton, Indian Territory.

Dear Sir:

    Receipt is hereby acknowledged of the marriage license and certificate between Turner LeFlore and Lena Abernathy which you offer in support of the application for the enrollment of your child Clara Lee LeFlore and the same have been filed with the record in this office.

                Respectfully,

                        Chairman.

Applications for Enrollment of Choctaw Newborn
Act of 1905   Volume III

7 NB 176

Muskogee, Indian Territory, September 7, 1905.

Turner Le Flore[sic],
    Milton, Indian Territory.

Dear Sir:
    Receipt is hereby acknowledged of your letter of August 31st, inquiring as to the enrollment of your child Clara Lee LeFlore as a citizen of the Choctaw Nation.

    You are advised that on August 22, 1905, the enrollment of your minor child, Clara Lee LeFlore as a new-born citizen by blood of the Choctaw Nation was approved by the Secretary of the Interior and her name placed upon the roll of such citizens opposite number 1277.

    An allotment may now be selected for this child at the land office for the nation in which the prospective allotment is located.

                    Respectfully,

                                    Acting Commissioner.

Choc New Born 177
    James Hiarker
    (Born Jan. 18, 1903)
    Estes Hiarker
    (Born Feb. 24, 1905)

DEPARTMENT OF THE INTERIOR,
COMMISSION TO THE FIVE CIVILIZED TRIBES.

    Record in the matter of the application for enrollment as a citizen by blood of the Choctaw Nation of :

        JAMES HIARKER   7-NB-177.

Applications for Enrollment of Choctaw Newborn
Act of 1905 Volume III

BIRTH AFFIDAVIT.

DEPARTMENT OF THE INTERIOR,
COMMISSION TO THE FIVE CIVILIZED TRIBES.

IN RE Application for Enrollment, as a citizen of the Choctaw Nation, of James Hiarker , born on the 18 day of January , 1903

Name of Father: Frank R Hiarker   a citizen of the Choctaw Nation.
Name of Mother: Sarah Hiarker   a citizen of the Choctaw Nation.

Post-Office: Spiro, Ind. Ter.

AFFIDAVIT OF MOTHER.

UNITED STATES OF AMERICA,
INDIAN TERRITORY.
Central   District.

I, Sarah Hiarker , on oath state that I am 23 years of age and a citizen by Marriage , of the Choctaw Nation; that I am the lawful wife of Frank R. Hiarker , who is a citizen, by blood of the Choctaw Nation; that a male child was born to me on 18th day of January , 190 3, that said child has been named James Hiarker , and is now living.

                               her
                     Mrs Sarah x Hiarker

WITNESSES TO MARK: mark
   J. Wesley Smith
   N. J. Willkett

Subscribed and sworn to before me this 5 *day of* December , 1903

                     J Wesley Smith
                         NOTARY PUBLIC.

AFFIDAVIT OF ATTENDING PHYSICIAN OR MID-WIFE.

UNITED STATES OF AMERICA,
INDIAN TERRITORY.
Central   District.

I, Mrs N. J. Wilkett[sic] , a Midwife , on oath state that I attended on Mrs. Sarah Hiarker , wife of Frank R. Hiarker on the 18th day of January , 1903 ; that there was born to her on said date a male child; that said child is now living and is said to have been named James Hiarker

Applications for Enrollment of Choctaw Newborn
Act of 1905   Volume III

N. J. Willkett

WITNESSES TO MARK:
{

Subscribed and sworn to before me this   5   day of   December   , 1903.

J Wesley Smith
NOTARY PUBLIC.
My Com Expires Oct 29 1905

BIRTH AFFIDAVIT.

DEPARTMENT OF THE INTERIOR.
COMMISSION TO THE FIVE CIVILIZED TRIBES.

IN RE APPLICATION FOR ENROLLMENT, as a citizen of the   Choctaw   Nation, of Estes Hiarker   , born on the   24   day of   Feb.   , 1905

Name of Father: Frank R Hiarker   a citizen of the   Choctaw   Nation.
Name of Mother: Sarah Hiarker   a citizen of the   Choctaw   Nation.

Postoffice   Spiro Ind Ter

AFFIDAVIT OF MOTHER.

UNITED STATES OF AMERICA, Indian Territory, }
Central   DISTRICT.

I,   Sarah Hiarker   , on oath state that I am   24   years of age and a citizen by Marriage   , of the   Choctaw   Nation; that I am the lawful wife of   Frank R Hiarker   , who is a citizen, by Blood   of the   Choctaw   Nation; that a female   child was born to me on 24   day of   February   , 1905; that said child has been named   Estes Hiarker   , and was living March 4, 1905.

her
Sarah x Hiarker
mark

Witnesses To Mark:
{ Edwin L. Hickman
  W E Harrell

Subscribed and sworn to before me this   27   day of   Mar   , 1905

W.E. Harrell
MY COMMISSION EXPIRES AUG. 6, 1908.   Notary Public.

275

Applications for Enrollment of Choctaw Newborn
Act of 1905   Volume III

AFFIDAVIT OF ATTENDING PHYSICIAN OR MID-WIFE.

UNITED STATES OF AMERICA, Indian Territory, }
Central   DISTRICT.

I, Mrs. M. J. Willkett, a Midwife, on oath state that I attended on Mrs. Sarah Hiarker, wife of Frank R Hiarker on the 24 day of Feb, 1903; that there was born to her on said date a female child; that said child was living March 4, 1905, and is said to have been named Estes Hiarker

Mrs M J. Willkett

Witnesses To Mark:
{

Subscribed and sworn to before me this 27 day of Mar, 1905

W.E. Harrell
MY COMMISSION EXPIRES AUG. 6, 1908.   Notary Public.

COPY

N. B. 177

Muskogee, Indian Territory, April 6, 1905.

[sic]
Spiro, Indian Territory.

Dear Sir:

There is inclosed you herewith for execution application for the enrollment of your infant child, James Hiarker, born January 18, 1903.

The affidavits heretofore filed with the Commission show the child was living on December 5, 1903. It is necessary, for the child to be enrolled, that he was living on March 4, 1905.

In having these affidavits executed care should be exercised to see that all names are written in full, as they appear in the body of the affidavit, and in the event that either of the persons signing the affidavit are unable to write, signatures by mark must be attested by two witnesses. Each affidavit must be executed before a Notary Public and the notarial seal and signature of the officer must be attached to each separate affidavit.

Respectfully,
SIGNED
T. B. Needles.
LM 6-3   Commissioner in Charge.

Applications for Enrollment of Choctaw Newborn
Act of 1905 Volume III

(The letter below typed as given.)

Spiro, I.T.
April 13, 1905.

Commission to the five civilized tribe
Muscogee Ind Terr

Dear Sir

I received the application from you. and it Read that James Hiarker my son had to be living on March 4, 1905, and he aint living on that date mentioned above James Hiarker died October 22, 1904 and I cant fill the application unless I can fill one in 1904 when he was living if so let me no at once.

Yours Respectfully,

Frank R. Hiarker
Spiro, I.T.

COPY

7 NB 177.

Muskogee, Indian Territory, April 19, 1905.

Frank R. Hiarker,
Spiro, Indian Territory.

Dear Sir:

Receipt is hereby acknowledged of your letter of April 13, 1905, in which you refer to the application recently forwarded you to be executed in the matter of the enrollment of your son James Hiarker in which it was stated that your son was living on March 4, 1905; you state that the child was not living on that date as he died October 15, 1904.

In reply to your letter you are advised that under the provisions of the act of Congress approved March 3, 1905, the Commission is authorized for a period of sixty days from the date to receive applications for the enrollment of children born to enrolled citizens by blood of the Choctaw and Chickasaw Nations between September 25, 1902, and March 4, 1905, and living on said latter date. You will therefore see that as your son James Hiarker died prior to March 4, 1905, the Commission is without authority to enroll said child.

Applications for Enrollment of Choctaw Newborn
Act of 1905 Volume III

There is inclosed herewith a blank form for proof of death which you are requested to have executed and returned to this office as early as practicable showing the correct date of the death of your child.

Respectfully,
SIGNED

Tams Bixby
Chairman.

D. C.

DEPARTMENT OF THE INTERIOR.
COMMISSION TO THE FIVE CIVILIZED TRIBES.

In the matter of the death of James Hiarker Deceased a citizen of the Choctaw Nation, who formerly resided at or near Spiro , Ind. Ter., and died on the 22 day of October , 1904

AFFIDAVIT OF RELATIVE.

UNITED STATES OF AMERICA, Indian Territory,
Central   DISTRICT.

I, Frank Hiarker , on oath state that I am 31 years of age and a citizen by blood , of the Choctaw Nation; that my postoffice address is Spiro , Ind. Ter.; that I am Father of James Hiarker deceased who was a citizen, by blood , of the Choctaw Nation and that said James Hiarker died on the 22nd day of October , 1904

Frank R Hiarker

Witnesses To Mark:

Subscribed and sworn to before me this 22 day of April , 1905.

WE Harrell
MY COMMISSION EXPIRES AUG. 6, 1908.   Notary Public.

AFFIDAVIT OF ACQUAINTANCE.

UNITED STATES OF AMERICA, Indian Territory,
Central   DISTRICT.

I, T. B. Kennedy , on oath state that I am 30 years of age, and a citizen by United States Nation; that my postoffice address is Spiro , Ind. Ter.; that I was personally acquainted with James Hiarker deceased who was a citizen, by blood,

Applications for Enrollment of Choctaw Newborn
Act of 1905   Volume III

of the Choctaw Nation; and that said James Hiarker died on the 22 day of October , 1904

T.B. Kennedy

Witnesses To Mark:

{

Subscribed and sworn to before me this 22 day of April , 1905.

WE Harrell
Notary Public.
MY COMMISSION EXPIRES AUG. 6, 1908.

COPY

7-NB-177.

Muskogee, Indian Territory, April 26, 1905.

Frank R. Hiarker,
    Spiro, Indian Territory.

Dear Sir:

    Receipt is hereby acknowledged of your affidavit and the affidavit of T. B. Kennedy, to the death of your son, James Hiarker, which occured[sic] October 22, 1904.

    Referring to the application heretofore forwarded for the enrollment of said child, you are advised that the Commission is authorized, by the Act of Congress approved March 5[sic], 1905, for a period of sixty days from that date, to receive applications for enrollment of children born to enrolled citizens by blood of the Choctaw Nation, between September 25, 1902 and March 4, 1905, and living on the latter date. You will therefore see that the Commission is without authority to enroll your child, who died October 22, 1904.

Respectfully,
SIGNED

Tams Bixby
Chairman.

Applications for Enrollment of Choctaw Newborn
Act of 1905   Volume III

W.F.
7-NB-177.

DEPARTMENT OF THE INTERIOR,
COMMISSION TO THE FIVE CIVILIZED TRIBES.

In the matter of the application for the enrollment of James Hiarker as a citizen by blood of the Choctaw Nation.

---oOo---

It appears from the record herein that on March 4, 1905 there was filed with the Commission application for the enrollment of James Hiarker as a citizen by blood of the Choctaw Nation.

It further appears from the record in this case and the records of the Commission that the applicant was born January 18, 1903; that he is a son of Frank R. Hiarker, a recognized and enrolled citizen by blood of the Choctaw Nation whose name appears as number 7648 upon the final roll of citizens by blood of the Choctaw Nation, approved by the Secretary of the Interior on January 17, 1903, and Sarah Hiarker, a recognized and enrolled citizen by intermarriage of the Choctaw Nation whose name appears as number 257 upon the final roll of citizens by intermarriage of the Choctaw Nation, approved by the Secretary of the Interior on September 12, 1903; and that said applicant died on October 22, 1904.

The Act of Congress approved March 3, 1905 (Public No. 212) among other things provides:

"That the Commission to the Five Civilized Tribes is authorized for sixty days after the date of the approval of this act to receive and consider applications for enrollment of children born subsequent to September twenty-fifth, nineteen hundred and two, and prior to March fourth, nineteen hundred and five, and who were living on said latter date, to citizens by blood of the Choctaw and Chickasaw tribes of Indians whose enrollment has been approved by the Secretary of the Interior prior to the date of the approval of this act; and to enroll and make allotments to such children."

It is, therefore, hereby ordered that the application for the enrollment of James Hiarker as a citizen by blood of the Choctaw Nation be dismissed in accordance with the order of the Commission of March 31, 1905.

COMMISSION TO THE FIVE CIVILIZED TRIBES,

Tams Bixby
Chairman.

Muskogee, Indian Territory.
JUN 13 1905

Applications for Enrollment of Choctaw Newborn
Act of 1905 Volume III

7-NB-177

Muskogee, Indian Territory, June 15, 1905.

Frank R. Hiarker,   **COPY**
    Spiro, Indian Territory.

Dear Sir:

    Inclosed herewith you will find a copy of the order of this Commission, dated June 15, 1905, dismissing the application for the enrollment of your infant child, James Hiarker, as a citizen by blood of the Choctaw Nation.

                Respectfully,
                SIGNED

                Tams Bixby
Registered.   Chairman.
Incl. 7-NB-177

---

7 NB 177

Muskogee, Indian Territory, June 15, 1905.

Mansfield, McMurray & Cornish,
    Attorneys for Choctaw and Chickasaw Nations,
        South McAlester, Indian Territory.   **COPY**

Gentlemen:

Inclosed herewith you will find a copy of the order of this Commission, dated June 15, 1905, dismissing the application for the enrollment of your infant child, James Hiarker, as a citizen by blood of the Choctaw Nation.

                Respectfully,
                SIGNED

                Tams Bixby
Incl. 7-NB177[sic]   Chairman.

Applications for Enrollment of Choctaw Newborn
Act of 1905   Volume III

7-2630

Muskogee, Indian Territory, December 10, 1903.

J. Wesley Smith,
    Spiro, Indian Territory.

Dear Sir:

    Receipt is hereby acknowledged of your letter of the 5th inst., enclosing the affidavits of Sarah Hiarker and N. J. Wilkett relative to the birth of James Hiarker, infant son of Frank R. and Sarah Hiarker, January 18, 1903, which it is presumed have been forwarded to this office as an application for enrollment of the above named child as a citizen by blood of the Choctaw Nation.

    You are informed that under the provision of the Act of Congress approved July 1, 1902 (32 Stats., 641), the Commission is now without authority to receive or consider the original application for enrollment of any person whomsoever as a citizen of the Choctaw or Chickasaw Nation.

    Respectfully,

    Chairman.

7-2630

Muskogee, Indian Territory, April 7, 1905.

Frank R. Hiarker,
    Spiro, Indian Territory.

Dear Sir:

    Receipt is hereby acknowledged of the affidavits of Sarah Hiarker and Mrs. M. J. Willkett, to the birth of Estes Hiarker, daughter of Frank R. and Sarah Hiarker, February 24, 1905, and the same have been filed with our records as an application for the enrollment of said child.

    Respectfully,

    Commissioner in Charge.

Applications for Enrollment of Choctaw Newborn
Act of 1905 Volume III

Choc New Born 178
    Commodore Stewart
    (Born December 14, 1902)

BIRTH AFFIDAVIT.

Department of the Interior,
COMMISSION TO THE FIVE CIVILIZED TRIBES.

IN RE APPLICATION FOR ENROLLMENT, as a citizen of the Choctaw Nation, of Comoto Walter , born on the 14 day of December , 190 2

Name of Father: William Stewart   a citizen of the Choctaw Nation.
Name of Mother: Isabella Stewart   a citizen of the Choctaw Nation.

Post-Office: Lathem Ind Ty

AFFIDAVIT OF MOTHER.

UNITED STATES OF AMERICA,
  INDIAN TERRITORY,
    Central   District.

I, Isabella Stewart , on oath state that I am 17 years of age and a citizen by Blood , of the Choctaw Nation; that I am the lawful wife of William Stewart , who is a citizen, by Adoption of the Choctaw Nation; that a male child was born to me on 14 day of December , 1902, that said child has been named Comoto Walter , and is now living.

                           Isabella Stewart

WITNESSES TO MARK:

Subscribed and sworn to before me this 18 *day of* December , *1902*

                           Frank D. Inman
My commission expires Mar. 9, 1904   *Notary Public.*

Applications for Enrollment of Choctaw Newborn
Act of 1905 Volume III

AFFIDAVIT OF ATTENDING PHYSICIAN OR MID-WIFE.

UNITED STATES OF AMERICA, }
   INDIAN TERRITORY,
  Central   District.

I, Abbie Choate, a Midwife, on oath state that I attended on Mrs. Isabella Stewart, wife of William Stewart on the 14 day of December, 190 2; that there was born to her on said date a male child; that said child is now living and is said to have been named Comoto Walter

                         her
                     Abbie x Choate

WITNESSES TO MARK: mark
  { J. C. Eubanks
    A. J. Hornback

Subscribed and sworn to before me this 18 *day of* December, 1902

                      Frank D. Inman
My commission expires Mar. 9, 1904   *Notary Public.*

NEW-BORN AFFIDAVIT.

      Number..................

...Choctaw Enrolling Commission...

IN THE MATTER OF THE APPLICATION FOR ENROLLMENT, as a citizen of the Choctaw Nation, of Commodore Stewart

born on the 14 day of ___December___ 190 2
                          freedman
Name of father Willie Stuart   a^citizen of   Choctaw
Nation final enrollment No. 1568   Shoat[sic])
Name of mother Isabella Stuart (nee Isabella a citizen of   Choctaw
Nation final enrollment No. 7654

                          Postoffice   Broyel I.T.

Applications for Enrollment of Choctaw Newborn
Act of 1905   Volume III

AFFIDAVIT OF MOTHER.

UNITED STATES OF AMERICA
INDIAN TERRITORY
Central   DISTRICT

I   Isabella Stuart   , on oath state that I am 19 years of age and a citizen by   blood   of the   Choctaw Nation, and as such have been placed upon the final roll of the   Choctaw Nation, by the Honorable Secretary of the Interior my final enrollment number being   7654 ; that I am the lawful wife of   Willie Stuart   , who is a citizen of the   Choctaw Nation, and as such has been placed upon the final roll of said Nation by the Honorable Secretary of the Interior, his final enrollment number being   1568   and that a male   child was born to me on the   14th day of   December   190 2; that said child has been named   Commodore Stuart   , and is now living.

Witnesseth.

Must be two Witnesses who are Citizens.   L R Moore
John Taylor

  her
Isabella x Stuart (nee Isabella Shoat)
  mark

Subscribed and sworn to before me this   31st day of   Jan   190 5

Edwin L Hickman
Notary Public.

My commission expires:
Feb 5 1905

AFFIDAVIT OF ATTENDING PHYSICIAN OR MIDWIFE

UNITED STATES OF AMERICA
INDIAN TERRITORY
Central   DISTRICT

I,   Abbie Shoat   a   Midwife on oath state that I attended on Mrs. Isabelle[sic] Stuart   wife of   Willie Stuart on the   14th day of   December   , 190 2, that there was born to her on said date a   Male child, that said child is now living, and is said to have been named   Commodore Stuart

Subscribed and sworn to before me this,   the   31st day of
January   190 5   Abbie x Shoat
  mark
WITNESSETH: Edwin L Hickman   Notary Public.

Must be two witnesses who are citizens   L R Moore
John Taylor

We hereby certify that we are well acquainted with   Abby Shoat a   Midwife   and know _____ to be reputable and of good standing in the community.

285

Applications for Enrollment of Choctaw Newborn
Act of 1905   Volume III

L R Moore

John Taylor

BIRTH AFFIDAVIT.

DEPARTMENT OF THE INTERIOR.
COMMISSION TO THE FIVE CIVILIZED TRIBES.

IN RE APPLICATION FOR ENROLLMENT, as a citizen of the Choctaw Nation, of Commodore Stewart, born on the 14th day of December, 1902

Name of Father: Willie Stewart   a ~~citizen~~ freedman of the Choctaw Nation.
Name of Mother: Isabella Stewart (nee Choate)   a citizen of the Choctaw Nation.

Postoffice   Brazil Ind Ter

AFFIDAVIT OF MOTHER.

UNITED STATES OF AMERICA, Indian Territory,
Central   DISTRICT.

I, Isabelle Stewart, on oath state that I am 20 years of age and a citizen by blood, of the Choctaw Nation; that I am the lawful wife of Willie Stewart, who is a ~~citizen, by~~ freedman of the Choctaw Nation; that a male child was born to me on 14th day of December, 1902; that said child has been named Commodore Stewart, and was living March 4, 1905.

Isabell Stewart

Witnesses To Mark:
  Turner Williams
  Henry Choate

Subscribed and sworn to before me this 5th day of April, 1905

My commission   J.C. Eubanks
will expire Jan 29. 09   Notary Public.

Applications for Enrollment of Choctaw Newborn
Act of 1905 Volume III

AFFIDAVIT OF ATTENDING PHYSICIAN OR MID-WIFE.

UNITED STATES OF AMERICA, Indian Territory,
Central DISTRICT.

I, Abbie Choate, a midwife, on oath state that I attended on Mrs. Isabelle Stewart, wife of Willie Stewart on the 14th day of December, 1902; that there was born to her on said date a male child; that said child was living March 4, 1905, and is said to have been named Commodore Stewart

Witnesses To Mark:
    { Turner Williams
    { Henry Choate

                                        her
                                    Abbie x Choate
                                      mark

Subscribed and sworn to before me this 5th day of April, 1905.

My commission will   J.C. Eubanks
expire Jan 29-09   Notary Public.

BIRTH AFFIDAVIT.

DEPARTMENT OF THE INTERIOR.
COMMISSION TO THE FIVE CIVILIZED TRIBES.

IN RE APPLICATION FOR ENROLLMENT, as a citizen of the Choctaw Nation, of Comoto Walter Stewart, born on the 14" day of December, 1902

Name of Father: William Stewart   a citizen of the U. S. Nation.
Name of Mother: Isabelle Stewart -R-7654   a citizen of the Choctaw Nation.

                            Postoffice   Latham Ind Ter

AFFIDAVIT OF MOTHER.

UNITED STATES OF AMERICA, Indian Territory,
Central DISTRICT.

I, Isabelle Stewart, on oath state that I am 19 years of age and a citizen by Blood, of the Choctaw Nation; that I am the lawful wife of William Stewart, who is a citizen, by .... of the United States Nation; that a male child was born to me on 14" day of December, 1902; that said child has been named Comoto Walter Stewart, and was living March 4, 1905.

                                      Isabelle Stewart

Applications for Enrollment of Choctaw Newborn
Act of 1905   Volume III

Witnesses To Mark:

Subscribed and sworn to before me this   12   day of   April   , 1905

Lacey P Bobo
Notary Public.

AFFIDAVIT OF ATTENDING PHYSICIAN OR MID-WIFE.

UNITED STATES OF AMERICA, Indian Territory,
Central   DISTRICT.

I,   Abbie Choate   , a   mid-wife   , on oath state that I attended on Mrs.   Isabelle Stewart   , wife of   William Stewart   on the   14"   day of   December   , 1902; that there was born to her on said date a   Male   child; that said child was living March 4, 1905, and is said to have been named Comoto Walter Stewart

her
Abbie x Choate
mark

Witnesses To Mark:
J.W. Homes
Jalce Choate

Subscribed and sworn to before me this   12th   day of   April   , 1905

Lacey P Bobo
Notary Public.

7-2632.

Muskogee, Indian Territory, January 26, 1903.

William Stewart,
Lathem[sic], Indian Territory.

Dear Sir

It appears from our records that on December 13[sic], 1902, there was received at this office an application for enrollment as a citizen of the Choctaw Nation of Comoto Walter Stewart, infant son of William and Isabella Stewart, born December 14, 1902.

It appearing from the affidavit of the mother that she is a citizen by blood of the Choctaw Nation, under date of December 31, 1902, you were requested to state when, where and under what name she was listed for enrollment as such, together with the names of her parents and other members of her family who appeared at the same time, in

Applications for Enrollment of Choctaw Newborn
Act of 1905 Volume III

order that the Commission might be able to identify her as being duly listed for enrollment as a citizen by blood of the Choctaw Nation.

Receipt is hereby acknowledged of your letter of the 5th inst., stating that the mother of this child, Isabelle Stewart, is the daughter of Henry and Abbie Choate and that she was listed for enrollment at Spiro, Indian Territory.

The information contained in your letter has enabled the Commission to identify the mother of the child as having been listed for enrollment June 14, 1899, as a citizen by blood of the Choctaw Nation under the name of Isabelle Choate.

Referring to the application for enrollment of your infant child, your attention is invited to section 28 of the Act of Congress approved July 1, 1902, which was ratified by the citizens of the Choctaw and Chickasaw Nation, September 25, 1902, as follows:

"The names of all persons living on the date of the final ratification of this agreement entitled to be enrolled as provided in section 27 hereof shall be placed upon the rolls made by said Commission; and no child born thereafter to a citizen or freedman and no person intermarried thereafter to a citizen shall be entitled to enrollment or to participate in the distribution of the tribal property of the Choctaws and Chickasaws."

Under the above legislation, the Commission is without authority to enroll this child.

Respectfully,

Acting Chairman.

COPY N. B. 178

Muskogee, Indian Territory, April 6, 1905.

William Stewart,
    Latham, Indian Territory.

Dear Sir:

There is inclosed you herewith for execution application for the enrollment of your infant child, Comoto Walter Stewart, born December 14, 1902.

The affidavits heretofore filed with the Commission show the child was living on December 18, 1902. It is necessary, for the child to be enrolled, that he was living on March 4, 1905.

In having these affidavits executed care should be exercised to see that all names are written in full, as they appear in the body of the affidavit, and in the event that either

Applications for Enrollment of Choctaw Newborn
Act of 1905   Volume III

of the persons signing the affidavit are unable to write, signatures by mark must be attested by two witnesses. Each affidavit must be executed before a Notary Public and the notarial seal and signature of the officer must be attached to each separate affidavit.

LM 6-5.

Respectfully,
SIGNED
T. B. Needles.
Commissioner in Charge.

COPY   7 NB 178

Muskogee, Indian Territory, April 19, 1905.

William Stewart,
　Latham, Indian Territory.

Dear Sir:

　Receipt is hereby acknowledged of the affidavits of Isabelle Stewart and Abbie Choat[sic] to the birth of Comoto Walter Stewart, son of William and Isabella Stewart, December 14, 1902, and the same have been filed with our records as an application for the enrollment of said child.

Respectfully,
SIGNED
Tams Bixby
Chairman.

Choc New Born 179
　Loyd Levi Allen
　(Born Jan 14, 1903)

BIRTH AFFIDAVIT.

DEPARTMENT OF THE INTERIOR,
COMMISSION TO THE FIVE CIVILIZED TRIBES.

IN RE Application for Enrollment, as a citizen of the　　Choctaw　　Nation, of　Loyd Levi　, born on the　14　day of　Jan　, 1903

Applications for Enrollment of Choctaw Newborn
Act of 1905   Volume III

Name of Father: John K Allen   a citizen of the   Choctaw   Nation.
Name of Mother: Lue Ella Allen   a citizen of the ....Nation.

Post-Office: Cheek I.T.

AFFIDAVIT OF MOTHER.

UNITED STATES OF AMERICA, }
   INDIAN TERRITORY.
   Southern   District.

I,   Lue Ella Allen   , on oath state that I am   23   years of age and a citizen by   - - - , of the   — —   — Nation; that I am the lawful wife of   John K Allen   , who is a citizen, by   Birth   of the   Choctaw   Nation; that a   male   child was born to me on   14   day of   Jan   , 1903 , that said child has been named   Loyd Levi   , and is now living.

Lou Ella Allen

WITNESSES TO MARK:
{ Ado Bagle
  Annie Winston

Subscribed and sworn to before me this   21   day of   March   , 1903

Chas H. Bigby
NOTARY PUBLIC.

AFFIDAVIT OF ATTENDING PHYSICIAN OR MID-WIFE.

UNITED STATES OF AMERICA, }
   INDIAN TERRITORY.
   Southern   District.

I,   S. P. Winston   , a   Physician   , on oath state that I attended on Mrs.   Lue Ella Allen   , wife of   John K. Allen   on the   14   day of   Jan   , 1903 ; that there was born to her on said date a   male   child; that said child is now living and is said to have been named   Loyd Levi

S. P. Winston M.D.

WITNESSES TO MARK:
{ Ado Bagle
  Annie Winston

Subscribed and sworn to before me this   21   day of   March   , 1903

Chas H. Bigby
NOTARY PUBLIC.

Applications for Enrollment of Choctaw Newborn
Act of 1905   Volume III

BIRTH AFFIDAVIT.

DEPARTMENT OF THE INTERIOR.
COMMISSION TO THE FIVE CIVILIZED TRIBES.

IN RE APPLICATION FOR ENROLLMENT, as a citizen of the Choctaw Nation, of Lloyd Levy Allen, born on the 14 day of Jan, 1903

Name of Father: John K. Allen   a citizen of the Choctaw Nation.
Name of Mother: Lue Ella Allen   a citizen of the Choctaw Nation.

Postoffice   Cheek I.T.

AFFIDAVIT OF MOTHER.

UNITED STATES OF AMERICA, Indian Territory, }
Southern DISTRICT.

I, Lue Ella Allen, on oath state that I am 25 years of age and a citizen by Marriage, of the Choctaw Nation; that I am the lawful wife of John K. Allen, who is a citizen, by birth of the Choctaw Nation; that a male child was born to me on 14 day of January, 1903; that said child has been named Lloyd Levi Allen, and was living March 4, 1905.

Lue Ella Allen

Witnesses To Mark:
{ Florence Colston
{ A. Overstreet

Subscribed and sworn to before me this 3 day of April, 1905.

E.S. Hammond
Notary Public.

AFFIDAVIT OF ATTENDING PHYSICIAN OR MID-WIFE.

UNITED STATES OF AMERICA, Indian Territory, }
Southern DISTRICT.

I, Mrs. Bettie Payne, a Mid-wife, on oath state that I attended on Mrs. Lue Ella Allen, wife of John K. Allen on the 14 day of Jan, 1903; that there was born to her on said date a male child; that said child was living March 4, 1905, and is said to have been named Lloyd Levi Allen

Applications for Enrollment of Choctaw Newborn
Act of 1905 Volume III

Mrs. Betty Payne

Witnesses To Mark:
{ Florence Colston
{ A. Overstreet

Subscribed and sworn to before me this 3 day of April , 1905

E.S. Hammond
Notary Public.

COPY

N. B. 179

Muskogee, Indian Territory, April 6, 1905.

John K. Allen,
    Cheek, Indian Territory.

Dear Sir:

    There is inclosed you herewith for execution application for the enrollment of your infant child, Loyd Levi Allen, born January 14, 1903.

    The affidavits heretofore filed with the Commission show the child was living on March 21, 1903. It is necessary, for the child to be enrolled, that he was living on March 4, 1905.

    In having these affidavits executed care should be exercised to see that all names are written in full, as they appear in the body of the affidavit, and in the event that either of the persons signing the affidavit are unable to write, signatures by mark must be attested by two witnesses. Each affidavit must be executed before a Notary Public and the notarial seal and signature of the officer must be attached to each separate affidavit.

Respectfully,
SIGNED
T. B. Needles.
Commissioner in Charge.

LM 6-1

Applications for Enrollment of Choctaw Newborn
Act of 1905 Volume III

COPY

7 NB 179

Muskogee, Indian Territory, May 8, 1905.

John K. Allen,
    Cheek, Indian Territory.

Dear Sir:

    Receipt is hereby acknowledged of your letter of May 2, 1905, asking if your son Loyd Levi Allen has been approved.

    In reply to your letter you are advised that the affidavits heretofore forwarded to the birth of your son Loyd Levi Allen have been filed with our records as an application for the enrollment of said child, but his name has not yet been placed upon a schedule of citizens by blood of said Nation prepared for forwarding of the Secretary of the Interior.

                  Respectfully,
                  SIGNED
                  T. B. Needles.
                  Commissioner in Charge.

Choc New Born 180
    Lola McCarley
    (Born Aug. 7, 1903)

BIRTH AFFIDAVIT.

DEPARTMENT OF THE INTERIOR.
COMMISSION TO THE FIVE CIVILIZED TRIBES.

    IN RE APPLICATION FOR ENROLLMENT, as a citizen of the Choctaw Nation, of Lola McCarley, born on the 7th day of Aug, 1903

Name of Father: James McCarley   a citizen of the U. S. Nation.
Name of Mother: Katie McCarley nee Ross   a citizen of the Choctaw Nation.

                Postoffice   Medill, Ind. Ter.

Applications for Enrollment of Choctaw Newborn
Act of 1905 Volume III

AFFIDAVIT OF MOTHER.

UNITED STATES OF AMERICA, Indian Territory, }
Southern   DISTRICT.

I, Katie McCarley, on oath state that I am 24 years of age and a citizen by blood, of the Choctaw Nation; that I am the lawful wife of James McCarley, who is a citizen, by .... of the U. S. Nation; that a female child was born to me on 7th day of Aug, 1903, that said child has been named Lola McCarley, and ~~is now~~ was living. on March 4th 1905 and died on March 11th 1905

Katie McCarley

Witnesses To Mark:
{

Subscribed and sworn to before me this 17th day of March, 1905.

(Illegible) Hardy
Notary Public.

AFFIDAVIT OF ATTENDING PHYSICIAN OR MID-WIFE.

UNITED STATES OF AMERICA, Indian Territory, }
Southern   DISTRICT.

I, J. S. Welch, a Physician, on oath state that I attended on Mrs. Katie McCarley (nee Ross), wife of James McCarley on the 7th day of Aug, 1903; that there was born to her on said date a female child; that said child ~~is now~~ was living on March 4th 1905 and died on March 11th 1905 and is said to have been named Lola McCarley

J.S. Welch M.D.

Witnesses To Mark:
{

Subscribed and sworn to before me this 17th day of March, 1905.

(Illegible) Hardy
Notary Public.

Applications for Enrollment of Choctaw Newborn
Act of 1905 Volume III

COPY

7 NB 180

Muskogee, Indian Territory, April 20, 1905

Katie McCarley,
    Madill, Indian Territory.

Dear Madam:

    Receipt is hereby acknowledged of your letter of April 15, 1905, stating that you have forwarded application for the enrollment of your child and ask if these are sufficient.

    In reply to your letter you are informed that the affidavits heretofore forwarded to the birth of your child Lola McCarley have been filed with our records as an application for the enrollment of said child.

    In event further evidence is necessary to enable the Commission to determine her right to enrollment you will be duly notified.

                  Respectfully,
                  SIGNED

                    Tams Bixby
                    Chairman.

COPY

7 NB 180

Muskogee, Indian Territory, April 21, 1905.

Katie McCarley,
    Madill, Indian Territory.

Dear Madam:

    Receipt is hereby acknowledged of your letter of April 15, 1905, stating that you have forwarded application for the enrollment of your child and ask if these are sufficient.

    In reply to your letter you are informed that the affidavits heretofore forwarded to the birth of your child Lola McCarley have been filed with our records as an application for the enrollment of said child.

    In event further evidence is necessary to enable the Commission to determine her right to enrollment you will be duly notified.

Applications for Enrollment of Choctaw Newborn
Act of 1905 Volume III

Respectfully,
SIGNED

Tams Bixby
Chairman.

Choc New Born 181
    Roland Cox
    (Born July 21, 1903)

BIRTH AFFIDAVIT.

DEPARTMENT OF THE INTERIOR,
COMMISSION TO THE FIVE CIVILIZED TRIBES.

In Re Application for Enrollment, as a citizen of the Choctaw Nation, of Roland Cox , born on the 21st day of July , 1903

Name of Father: Cale[sic] Cox   a citizen of the United States Nation.
Name of Mother: Mary Cox   a citizen of the Choctaw Nation.

Post-office   Poteau Ind Ter

AFFIDAVIT OF MOTHER.

UNITED STATES OF AMERICA, }
    INDIAN TERRITORY,
    Central   District.

I, Mary Cox , on oath state that I am 24 years of age and a citizen by Blood , of the Choctaw Nation; that I am the lawful wife of Cale Cox , who is a citizen, by .... of the United States ~~Nation~~; that a male child was born to me on 21 day of July , 190 3, that said child has been named Roland - Cox , and is now living.

                                  Mary Cox

WITNESSES TO MARK:

Subscribed and sworn to before me this 5th day of Sept , 1908[sic]

                                R.D. Turman
                                    NOTARY PUBLIC.

Applications for Enrollment of Choctaw Newborn
Act of 1905   Volume III

AFFIDAVIT OF ATTENDING PHYSICIAN OR MID-WIFE.

UNITED STATES OF AMERICA, }
   INDIAN TERRITORY,
Central   District. }

I,   Elizabeth Franklin   , a   midwife   , on oath state that I attended on Mrs.   Mary Cox , wife of   Cale Cox   on the   21   day of   July , 1903 ; that there was born to her on said date a   male   child; that said child is now living and is said to have been named   Roland Cox
                         her
                        Elizabeth x Franklin

WITNESSES TO MARK: mark
{ W M Hopkins
{ *(Name Illegible)*

Subscribed and sworn to before me this 5th day of   Sept , 1908[sic]

                          R.D. Turman
                          NOTARY PUBLIC.

NEW-BORN AFFIDAVIT.

          Number...............

...Choctaw Enrolling Commission...

IN THE MATTER OF THE APPLICATION FOR ENROLLMENT, as a citizen of the Choctaw   Nation, of   Roland Cox

born on the 21st day of   July   190 3

Name of father   Caleb Cox   a citizen of   United States
Nation final enrollment No. ——
Name of mother   Mary Cox nee Bohanan   a citizen of   Choctaw
Nation final enrollment No.   7785

                      Postoffice   Shady Point Ind T.

Applications for Enrollment of Choctaw Newborn
Act of 1905   Volume III

AFFIDAVIT OF MOTHER.

UNITED STATES OF AMERICA
INDIAN TERRITORY
Central   DISTRICT

I, Mary Cox, on oath state that I am 25 years of age and a citizen by blood of the Choctaw Nation, and as such have been placed upon the final roll of the Choctaw Nation, by the Honorable Secretary of the Interior my final enrollment number being 7785; that I am the lawful wife of Caleb Cox, who is a citizen of the United States Nation, and as such has been placed upon the final roll of said Nation by the Honorable Secretary of the Interior, his final enrollment number being ——— and that a Male child was born to me on the 21st day of July 190 3; that said child has been named Roland Cox, and is now living.

Witnesseth.   Mary Cox

Must be two Witnesses who are Citizens.
- Sam Bohanan
- Tom Wall

Subscribed and sworn to before me this 16th day of February 190 5.

Malcolm E. Rosser
Notary Public.

My commission expires: Dec 11 1906

AFFIDAVIT OF ATTENDING PHYSICIAN OR MIDWIFE

UNITED STATES OF AMERICA
INDIAN TERRITORY
Central   DISTRICT

I, Elizabeth Franklin a midwife on oath state that I attended on Mrs. Mary Cox wife of Caleb Cox on the 21st day of July, 190 3, that there was born to her on said date a male child, that said child is now living, and is said to have been named Roland Cox

Elizabeth x Franklin   Midwife
her mark

WITNESSETH:
Must be two witnesses who are citizens and know the child.
- Sam Bohanan
- Tom Wall

Subscribed and sworn to before me this, the 16th day of February 190 5

Malcolm E Rosser   Notary Public.

Applications for Enrollment of Choctaw Newborn
Act of 1905 Volume III

We hereby certify that we are well acquainted with Elizabeth Franklin a Midwife and know her to be reputable and of good standing in the community.

{ Sam Bohanan
{ Tom Wall

BIRTH AFFIDAVIT.

DEPARTMENT OF THE INTERIOR.
COMMISSION TO THE FIVE CIVILIZED TRIBES.

IN RE APPLICATION FOR ENROLLMENT, as a citizen of the Choctaw Nation, of Roland Cox, born on the 21 day of July, 1903

Name of Father: Caleb Cox   a citizen of the U S Nation.
Name of Mother: Mary Cox nee Bohanan   a citizen of the Choctaw Nation.

Postoffice Poteau I T

AFFIDAVIT OF MOTHER.

UNITED STATES OF AMERICA, Indian Territory,
Central DISTRICT.

I, Mary Cox nee Bohanan, on oath state that I am 25 years of age and a citizen by Blood, of the Choctaw Nation; that I am the lawful wife of Caleb Cox, who is a citizen, by .... of the United States ~~Nation~~; that a Male child was born to me on 21 day of July, 1903; that said child has been named Roland Cox, and was living March 4, 1905.

Mary Cox

Witnesses To Mark:
{ Sam Bohanan
{ JB Jackson

Subscribed and sworn to before me this 30 day of March, 1905

WH Phillips
Notary Public.

Applications for Enrollment of Choctaw Newborn
Act of 1905 Volume III

AFFIDAVIT OF ATTENDING PHYSICIAN OR MID-WIFE.

UNITED STATES OF AMERICA, Indian Territory,
Central DISTRICT.

I, Elizabeth Franklin, a Midwife, on oath state that I attended on Mrs. Mary Cox nee Bohanan, wife of Caleb Cox on the 21 day of July, 1903; that there was born to her on said date a male child; that said child was living March 4, 1905, and is said to have been named Roland Cox

                          her
                        Elizabeth x Franklin midwife

Witnesses To Mark: mark
   { Sam Bohanan
     JB Jackson

Subscribed and sworn to before me this 30 day of March, 1905

                          WH Phillips
                              Notary Public.

BIRTH AFFIDAVIT.

DEPARTMENT OF THE INTERIOR.
COMMISSION TO THE FIVE CIVILIZED TRIBES.

IN RE APPLICATION FOR ENROLLMENT, as a citizen of the Choctaw Nation, of Roland Cox, born on the 21" day of July, 1903

Name of Father: Cale Cox   a citizen of the   U S   Nation.
Name of Mother: Mary Cox (Bohanan)   a citizen of the   Choctaw   Nation.

                  Postoffice   Poteau Ind Ter

AFFIDAVIT OF MOTHER.

UNITED STATES OF AMERICA, Indian Territory,
Central DISTRICT.

I, Mary Cox (Bohanan), on oath state that I am 24 years of age and a citizen by Blood, of the Choctaw Nation; that I am the lawful wife of Cale Cox, who is a citizen, by ——— of the United States Nation; that a Male child was born to me on 21" day of July, 1903; that said child has been named Roland Cox, and was living March 4, 1905.

                                Mary Cox

Applications for Enrollment of Choctaw Newborn
Act of 1905   Volume III

Witnesses To Mark:
{

Subscribed and sworn to before me this 11th day of April, 1905

Malcolm E Rosser
Notary Public.

AFFIDAVIT OF ATTENDING PHYSICIAN OR MID-WIFE.

UNITED STATES OF AMERICA, Indian Territory, }
Central   DISTRICT.

I, Elizabeth Franklin, a midwife, on oath state that I attended on Mrs. Mary Cox (Roland[sic]), wife of Cale Cox on the 21" day of July, 1903; that there was born to her on said date a Male child; that said child was living March 4, 1905, and is said to have been named Roland Cox

            her
         Elizabeth x Franklin
Witnesses To Mark: mark
{ John L *(Illegible)*
{ Sam Bohanan

Subscribed and sworn to before me this 11th day of April, 1905

Malcolm E Rosser
Notary Public.

Blank 731.

CHOCTAW ROLL. CITIZENS BY BLOOD.

New Born.

Act of Congress Approved March 3rd, 1905. (Public No. 212.)

No.	Name	ge[sic]	Sex	Blood	Card No.
182	Cox, Roland	2	M	1/4	181

Applications for Enrollment of Choctaw Newborn
Act of 1905 Volume III

DEPARTMENT OF THE INTERIOR Blank 744.
United States Indian Service
Five Civilized Tribes
Muskogee, Oklahoma.

This is to certify that I am the officer having the custody of the records pertaining to the enrollment of the members of the members of the Choctaw, Chickasaw, Cherokee, Creek and Seminole tribes of Indians, and the disposition of the land of said tribes, and the following described papers, attached hereto, are true and correct copies of the entire enrollment record on file in this office in connection with the application of

Roland Cox

Roll No. __182, N-B,__ for enrollment as a   New Born Citizen   of the __Choctaw__ Nation:

Census Card No. 181 ; 5-Birth Affidavits; Letters Dated

April 8, 1905, April 18, 1905; Copy of Approved Roll

No. 182-NB.

H. H. FISKE, Inspector in Charge.

BY E.C. Funk CLERK
IN CHARGE Choctaw RECORDS
DATE 7-13-28
MEC.

COPY

N. B. 181

Muskogee, Indian Territory, April 6, 1905.

Cale Cox,
    Poteau, Indian Territory.

Dear Sir:

There is inclosed you herewith for execution application for the enrollment of your infant child, Roland Cox, born July 21, 1903.

The affidavits heretofore filed with the Commission show the child was living on September 5, 1903. It is necessary, for the child to be enrolled, that he was living on March 4, 1905.

Applications for Enrollment of Choctaw Newborn
Act of 1905 Volume III

In having these affidavits executed care should be exercised to see that all names are written in full, as they appear in the body of the affidavit, and in the event that either of the persons signing the affidavit are unable to write, signatures by mark must be attested by two witnesses. Each affidavit must be executed before a Notary Public and the notarial seal and signature of the officer must be attached to each separate affidavit.

LM 6-2

Respectfully,
SIGNED
T. B. Needles.
Commissioner in Charge.

Choctaw N.B. 181.
COPY
Muskogee, Indian Territory, April 18, 1905.

Cale Cox,
    Poteau, Indian Territory.

Dear Sir:

Receipt is hereby acknowledged of the affidavits of Mary Cox and Elizabeth Franklin to the birth of Roland Cox, son of Cale and Mary Cox (Roland), July 21, 1903, and the same have been filed with our records in the matter of the enrollment of the above named child.

Respectfully,
SIGNED
Tams Bixby
Chairman.

Applications for Enrollment of Choctaw Newborn
Act of 1905 Volume III

Choc New Born 182
    Jewell V. Long
    (Born Feb. 11, 1904)

BIRTH AFFIDAVIT.

DEPARTMENT OF THE INTERIOR,
COMMISSION TO THE FIVE CIVILIZED TRIBES.

IN RE **Application for Enrollment,** as a citizen of the Choctaw Nation, of Jewell V. Long, born on the 11 day of Feb, 1904

                                                intermarried

Name of Father: Wm I. Long   a citizen of the Choctaw Nation.
Name of Mother: Flaurah B. Long   a citizen of the Choctaw Nation.

                Post-Office: Brazil Ind Ter

AFFIDAVIT OF MOTHER.

UNITED STATES OF AMERICA,
    INDIAN TERRITORY.
    Central   District.

    I, Ja[sic] Flaurah B Long, on oath state that I am 22 years of age and a citizen by blood, of the Choctaw Nation; that I am the lawful wife of W^m I Long, who is a citizen, by intermarriage of the Choctaw Nation; that a male child was born to me on 11th day of February, 1904, that said child has been named Jewell V Long, and is now living.

                                      Flaurah B Long

WITNESSES TO MARK:

{

    Subscribed and sworn to before me this 28 day of Jan, 1905.

                                    Jno R Smoot
                                        NOTARY PUBLIC.

Applications for Enrollment of Choctaw Newborn
Act of 1905   Volume III

AFFIDAVIT OF ATTENDING PHYSICIAN OR MID-WIFE.

UNITED STATES OF AMERICA,
   INDIAN TERRITORY.
Central District.

I, F C Parrot, a physician, on oath state that I attended on Mrs. Flaurah B Long, wife of Wm I. Long on the 11th day of Feb, 1904; that there was born to her on said date a male child; that said child is now living and is said to have been named Jewell V Long

F C Parrott M.D.

WITNESSES TO MARK:

{

Subscribed and sworn to before me this 28th day of Jan, 1905.

John R Smoot
NOTARY PUBLIC.

2/11/1904/ male

AFFIDAVIT OF ATTENDING PHYSICIAN OR MIDWIFE

UNITED STATES OF AMERICA
INDIAN TERRITORY
_____ DISTRICT

I, F C Parrott a physician on oath state that I attended on Mrs. Flaurah B Long wife of William I Long on the 11th day of February, 190 4, that there was born to her on said date a male child, that said child is now living, and is said to have been named Jewell V Long

F.C. Parrott   M.D.

WITNESSETH:

Must be two witnesses who are citizens and know the child. { James Taylor
C. B. Ward

Subscribed and sworn to before me this, the 7th day of March 1905

John R Smoot   Notary Public.

We hereby certify that we are well acquainted with Dr. F. C. Parrott a practicing physician and know him to be reputable and of good standing in the community.

W.O.B.
7-2695

{ James Taylor
C. B. Ward

Applications for Enrollment of Choctaw Newborn
Act of 1905 Volume III

7-2695

DEPARTMENT OF THE INTERIOR,
COMMISSION TO THE FIVE CIVILIZED TRIBES.
BOKOSHE, INDIAN TERRITORY APRIL 4, 1905.

In the matter of the application for the enrollment of Jewell V. Long as a citizen by blood of the Choctaw Nation.

William I. Long being first duly sworn testifies as follows:

EXAMINATION BY THE COMMISSION:

Q What is your name? A William I. Long.
Q What is your age? A I am twenty-nine as well as I remember the 26th day of last January.
Q Post office address? A Brazil.
Q Are you a citizen of the Choctaw Nation? A No, sir, I am not.
Q You present here a letter addressed to you by the Commission to the Five Civilized Tribes wherein they acknowledge receipt of the affidavit of F. C. Parrott to the birth of Jewell V. Long said letter being dated March 11, 1905. Is Jewell V. Long your son?
A Yes, sir, my wife says he is.
Q What is the name of this child's mother? A Flaurah B. Long.
Q She is a citizen by blood of the Choctaw Nation? A Yes, sir.
Q You have heretofore sent in a Birth affidavit to the Commission? A Yes, sir.
Q When was that affidavit sent in? Prior to March 4, 1905? A Yes, sir.
Q When was that child born? A It was born February 11, 1904.
Q Is it living now? A Yes, sir.

Witness excused.

Chas. T. Difendafer being first duly sworn states that the above and foregoing is a full, true and correct transcript of his stenographic notes taken in said cause on said date.

Chas. T. Difendafer

Subscribed and sworn to before me this 4th day of April - 1905.

OL Johnson
Notary Public.

Applications for Enrollment of Choctaw Newborn
Act of 1905   Volume III

BIRTH AFFIDAVIT.

DEPARTMENT OF THE INTERIOR.
COMMISSION TO THE FIVE CIVILIZED TRIBES.

IN RE APPLICATION FOR ENROLLMENT, as a citizen of the Choctaw Nation, of Jewell V. Long, born on the 11th day of Feb, 1904

Name of Father: Will I Long   a citizen of the Choctaw Nation.
Name of Mother: Flaurah B. Long   a citizen of the Choctaw Nation.

Postoffice   Brazil Ind Ter

AFFIDAVIT OF MOTHER.

UNITED STATES OF AMERICA, Indian Territory,
Central   DISTRICT.

I, Flaurah B Long, on oath state that I am 22 years of age and a citizen by blood, of the Choctaw Nation; that I am the lawful wife of Will I Long, who is a citizen, by residence of the Choctaw Nation; that a male child was born to me on 11th day of February, 1904; that said child has been named Jewell V Long, and was living March 4, 1905.

Flaurah B Long

Witnesses To Mark:
{

Subscribed and sworn to before me this 17th day of Apr, 1905

John R Smoot
Notary Public.

com expire July 21st 1906.

AFFIDAVIT OF ATTENDING PHYSICIAN OR MID-WIFE.

UNITED STATES OF AMERICA, Indian Territory,
Central   DISTRICT.

I, F E[sic] Parrott, a physician, on oath state that I attended on Mrs. Flaurah B Long, wife of Will I Long on the 11th day of Feb, 1904; that there was born to her on said date a male child; that said child was living March 4, 1905, and is said to have been named Jewell V Long

F C Parrott, M.D.

Applications for Enrollment of Choctaw Newborn
Act of 1905   Volume III

Witnesses To Mark:
{

    Subscribed and sworn to before me this 17th day of Apr , 1905

John R Smoot
Notary Public.
com expire July 21st 1906.

7-2695

Muskogee, Indian Territory, March 11, 1905.

Will I. Long,
    Milton, Indian Territory.

Dear Sir:

    Receipt is hereby acknowledged of the affidavit of F. C. Parrott to the birth of Jewell V. Long, infant son of William I. and Flaurah B. Long, February 11, 1904, and the same has been filed in connection with the affidavits heretofore forwarded as an application for the enrollent[sic] of said child.

Respectfully,

Chairman.

COPY   Choctaw N.B. 182.

Muskogee, Indian Territory, April 21, 1905.

Will I. Long,
    Brazil, Indian Territory.

Dear Sir:

    Receipt is hereby acknowledged of the affidavits of Flaurah B. Long and F. E[sic]. Parrott to the birth of Jewel[sic] V. Long, son of Will D[sic]. and Flaurah B. Long, February 11, 1904, and the same have been filed with our records in the matter of the enrollment of said child.

Respectfully,
SIGNED

Tams Bixby
Chairman.

Applications for Enrollment of Choctaw Newborn
Act of 1905   Volume III

Choc New Born 183
  Lena Ola Ward
  (Born Jan. 12, 1904)

No. 1771   Form No. 593

MARRIAGE LICENSE.

UNITED STATES OF AMERICA,)
THE INDIAN TERRITORY,   ) ss:
CENTRAL DISTRICT.   )

To any Person Authorized by Law to Solemnize Marriage--Greeting:

You are hereby commanded to solemnize the Rite and publish the BANNS OF MATRIMONY between Mr. C. B. Ward of Milton in the Indian Territory aged 52 years, and Miss Nealie Whalen of Milton in the Indian Territory, aged 20 years, according to law, and do you officially sign and return this License to the parties therein named.

WITNESS my hand and official seal, this 6" day of May, A. D. 1903

                    E. J. Fannin
(SEAL)   Clerk of the United States Court.

by T. T. Varner
       Deputy.

CERTIFICATE OF MARRIAGE.

UNITED STATES OF AMERICA,)
THE INDIAN TERRITORY,   ) ss: I,   J. R. Smith
CENTRAL DISTRICT.   )
                                a   Minister

do hereby CERTIFY, that on the 6 day of May, A. D. 1903, I did duly and according to law, as commanded in the foregoing License, solemnize the Rite and publish the BANNS OF MATRIMONY between the parties therein named.

Witness my hand this 6 day of May, A. D. 1903.

My credentials are recorded in the office of the Clerk of the United States Court in the Indian Territory, Central District, Book A. Page ------

                    J. R. Smith
                    a Minister.

Applications for Enrollment of Choctaw Newborn
Act of 1905   Volume III

NOTE.-- This License and Certificate of Marriage must be returned to the Office of the Clerk of the United States Court of the Indian Territory, from whence it was issued, within sixty days from the date thereof, or the party to whom the License was issued will be liable in the amount of One Hundred Dollars ($100.00).

No. 1771

CERTIFICATE OF RECORD OF MARRIAGES.

UNITED STATES OF AMERICA,)
   THE INDIAN TERRITORY,   ) SCT:
      CENTRAL DISTRICT.   )

I, E. J. Fannin, Clerk of the United States Court in the Indian Territory and District aforesaid, do hereby CERTIFY that the License for and Certificate of the Marriage of Mr. C. B. Ward and Miss Nealie Whalen was filed in my office in said Territory and District the 6" day of May, A. D. 1903 and duly recorded in Book 2 of Marriage Record, Page 268.

WITNESS my hand and seal of said Court, at Poteau this 6 day of May, A.D. 1903
(SEAL)
                              E. J. Fannin
                                  Clerk.

By T. T. Varner
      Deputy.

DEPARTMENT OF THE INTERIOR,
COMMISSION TO THE FIVE CIVILIZED TRIBES.
FILED Apr. 10, 1905.

I, Pat E. Trent, a clerk to the Commissioner to the Five Civilized Tribes do hereby certify that the above and foregiong[sic] is a true and correct copy of the original now on file with the records of this office.
                                        Pat E. Trent

Subscribed and sworn to before me this   14   day of   Nov   1907.

                                        Frances *(Illegible)*
                                        Notary Public.

Applications for Enrollment of Choctaw Newborn
Act of 1905 Volume III

(The affidavit below typed as given.)

April 18 A D 1904
Bokoshe I.T.

Know all Parties by these presents that I C B Ward of Bokoshe IT do state on my oath that there was a heir borned unto Me a Choctaw citizen on the 12 day of January A.D. 1904 by My lawful wife Nealie Ward And I prey the said *(illegible ...)* same heir by name Lenia Ola Ward which is now living.

C.B. Ward

Sworn to this 18 April 1904   JD Shaw
                                      Notary Public

On this day Personly appeared the tending Phisian of the family of the said C.B. Ward and state on his oath that he was at the afore named place Mr Wards & that he waited on the said Nealia Ward in case of *(illegible)* & that there was a heir borned[sic] to the Mr & Mrs Ward at the above state & time

E.F. Hodges M.D.

Subscribed and sworn to before me this sworn to this the 18 of April 1904

J.D. Shaw
Notary Public.

(The above affidavit given again.)

NEW-BORN AFFIDAVIT.

Number..............

...Choctaw Enrolling Commission...

IN THE MATTER OF THE APPLICATION FOR ENROLLMENT, as a citizen of the Choctaw Nation, of Lena Ola Ward

born on the 12 day of January   190 4

Name of father   Cyrus B. Ward   a citizen of _____
Nation final enrollment No. 7851
Name of mother   Nealie Ward   a citizen of _____
Nation final enrollment No. 7851

                                   chto[sic]
                        Postoffice   Bokoshe IT

312

Applications for Enrollment of Choctaw Newborn
Act of 1905 Volume III

AFFIDAVIT OF MOTHER.

UNITED STATES OF AMERICA
INDIAN TERRITORY
    Central   DISTRICT

I   Nelia[sic] Ward   , on oath state that I am 21 years of age and a citizen by   marage[sic]   of the   Choctaw Nation, and as such have not yet been been placed upon the final roll of the Choctaw Nation, by the Honorable Secretary of the Interior my final enrollment number being _____ ; that I am the lawful wife of   Cyrus B Ward   , who is a citizen of the   Choctaw Nation, and as such has been placed upon the final roll of said Nation by the Honorable Secretary of the Interior, his final enrollment number being   7851   and that a Female   child was born to me on the   12   day of   January   190 4   ; that said child has been named   Lena Ola Ward   , and is now living.

Witnesseth.   Nealie Ward

Must be two Witnesses who are Citizens.   James Taylor
                     Myrtle G. Statham

Subscribed and sworn to before me this   12   day of   Jan   190 5

                     J. D. Shaw
                           Notary Public.

My commission expires:
   Feb 7 1907

AFFIDAVIT OF ATTENDING PHYSICIAN OR MIDWIFE

UNITED STATES OF AMERICA
INDIAN TERRITORY
    Central   DISTRICT

I,   E F Hodges   a   Physician on oath state that I attended on Mrs. Nelia Ward   wife of   Cyrus B Ward on the   12   day of   January   , 190 4 , that there was born to her on said date a Female child, that said child is now living, and is said to have been named   Lena Ola Ward

                     E F Hodges   M.D.

Subscribed and sworn to before me this, the   12   day of January   190 5

WITNESSETH: J D Shaw   Notary Public.

Must be two witnesses who are citizens   James Taylor
                 ~~Jim Bagwell~~
                Myrtle G Statham

Applications for Enrollment of Choctaw Newborn
Act of 1905   Volume III

We hereby certify that we are well acquainted with   Cyrus B Ward   a   Choctaw Citizen   and know   him   to be reputable and of good standing in the community.

Myrtle G Statham   _____

S W James   _____

BIRTH AFFIDAVIT.

DEPARTMENT OF THE INTERIOR.
COMMISSION TO THE FIVE CIVILIZED TRIBES.

IN RE APPLICATION FOR ENROLLMENT, as a citizen of the   Choctaw   Nation, of   Lena Ola Ward   , born on the 12th day of   January   , 1904

Name of Father: Cyrus B Ward   a citizen of the   Choctaw   Nation.
Name of Mother: Nealie Ward   a citizen of the   non citizen   Nation.

Postoffice   Bokoshe

AFFIDAVIT OF MOTHER.

UNITED STATES OF AMERICA, Indian Territory, }
Central   DISTRICT. }

I,   Nealie Ward   , on oath state that I am   22   years of age and a citizen ~~by~~ non citizen   , of the   Choctaw   Nation; that I am the lawful wife of   Cyrus B Ward   , who is a citizen, by   blood   of the   Choctaw   Nation; that a female   child was born to me on   12th day of   January   , 1904, that said child has been named   Lena Ola Ward   , and is now living.

Nealie Ward

Witnesses To Mark:
{

Subscribed and sworn to before me this 13th day of   March   , 1905.

My Com. Exps.   C.M. Bagwell
March 29th 1908   Notary Public.

Applications for Enrollment of Choctaw Newborn
Act of 1905 Volume III

AFFIDAVIT OF ATTENDING PHYSICIAN OR MID-WIFE.

UNITED STATES OF AMERICA, Indian Territory, }
Central   DISTRICT.

    I, D F Hodges , a Physician , on oath state that I attended on Mrs. Nealie Ward , wife of Cyrus B Ward on the 12th day of January , 1904; that there was born to her on said date a female child; that said child is now living and is said to have been named Lena Ola Ward

                                     E. F. Hodges, M.D.

Witnesses To Mark:
{

    Subscribed and sworn to before me this 13th day of March , 1905.

My Com. Exps.   C.M. Bagwell
March 29th 1908   Notary Public.

BIRTH AFFIDAVIT.

DEPARTMENT OF THE INTERIOR.
COMMISSION TO THE FIVE CIVILIZED TRIBES.

    IN RE APPLICATION FOR ENROLLMENT, as a citizen of the Choctaw Nation, of Lena Ola Ward , born on the 12 day of January , 1904

Name of Father: Cyrus B Ward   a citizen of the Choctaw Nation.
Name of Mother: Nealie Ward   a citizen of the U. S. Nation.

                      Postoffice Bokoshe Ind. Ter.

AFFIDAVIT OF MOTHER.

UNITED STATES OF AMERICA, Indian Territory, }
Central   DISTRICT.

    I, Nealie Ward , on oath state that I am 21 years of age and a citizen by ———— , of the United States ~~Nation~~; that I am the lawful wife of Cyrus B. Ward, who is a citizen, by blood of the Choctaw Nation; that a female child was born to me on 12 day of January , 1904; that said child has been named Lena Ola Ward , and was living March 4, 1905.

                                Nealie Ward

Witnesses To Mark:
{

Applications for Enrollment of Choctaw Newborn
Act of 1905 Volume III

Subscribed and sworn to before me this 3rd day of   April   , 1905

                                OL Johnson
                                Notary Public.

AFFIDAVIT OF ATTENDING PHYSICIAN OR MID-WIFE.

UNITED STATES OF AMERICA, Indian Territory,
....DISTRICT.

I,   E. F. Hodges   , a   physician   , on oath state that I attended on Mrs.   Nealie Ward , wife of   Cyrus B Ward   on the 12 day of   January , 1904; that there was born to her on said date a   female   child; that said child was living March 4, 1905, and is said to have been named Lena Ola Ward

                                E. F. Hodges, M.D.

Witnesses To Mark:

Subscribed and sworn to before me this 4th day of   April   , 1905

                                OL Johnson
                                Notary Public.

                                        7-2698

                    Muskogee, Indian Territory, March 18, 1905.

Cyrus B. Ward,
    Bokoshe, Indian Territory.

Dear Sir:

    Receipt is hereby acknowledged of the affidavits of Nealie Ward and E. F. Hodges, M. D., to the birth of Lena Ola Ward, infant daughter of Cyrus B. and Nealie Ward, January 12, 1904, and the same have been filed with our records as an application for the enrollment of said child.

                    Respectfully,

                              Chairman.

Applications for Enrollment of Choctaw Newborn
Act of 1905 Volume III

Choc New Born 184
    Johnny Frances Merryman
    (Born April 4, 1903)

BIRTH AFFIDAVIT.

DEPARTMENT OF THE INTERIOR,
COMMISSION TO THE FIVE CIVILIZED TRIBES.

IN RE Application for Enrollment, as a citizen of the   Choctaw   Nation, of   John Francies[sic] Meryman[sic] , born on the   4   day of   April , 1903

Name of Father: James Francis Meryman   a citizen of the   Choctaw   Nation.
Name of Mother: Ruth Meryman   a citizen of the   Choctaw   Nation.

                 Post-Office: Bokoshe Ind Ter

AFFIDAVIT OF MOTHER.

UNITED STATES OF AMERICA,
    INDIAN TERRITORY.
    ....District.

     I,   Ruth Meryman   , on oath state that I am   Twenty-Three   years of age and a citizen by   Intermarriage   , of the   Choctaw   Nation; that I am the lawful wife of James Francies Meryman , who is a citizen, by   Blood   of the   Choctaw   Nation; that a   Female   child was born to me on   4   day of   April   , 1903 , that said child has been named   John Frances Meryman   , and is now living.

                                                Ruth Merryman

WITNESSES TO MARK:
    { J A *(Illegible)*
      S W James

       Subscribed and sworn to before me this .... *day of* ...., 190....

                                       ....
                                              NOTARY PUBLIC.

Applications for Enrollment of Choctaw Newborn
Act of 1905 Volume III

AFFIDAVIT OF ATTENDING PHYSICIAN OR MID-WIFE.

UNITED STATES OF AMERICA, }
INDIAN TERRITORY.
.............................District.

I, D P Barbour , a Physician , on oath state that I attended on Mrs. Ruth Meryman , wife of James F. Meryman on the 4 day of April , 1903 ; that there was born to her on said date a Female child; that said child is now living and is said to have been named John Francies Meryman

D. P. Barbour M.D.

WITNESSES TO MARK:
{ J A *(Illegible)*
S W James

Subscribed and sworn to before me this 18 day of Oct , 1904.

J D Shaw

NOTARY PUBLIC.

BIRTH AFFIDAVIT.

DEPARTMENT OF THE INTERIOR.
COMMISSION TO THE FIVE CIVILIZED TRIBES.

IN RE APPLICATION FOR ENROLLMENT, as a citizen of the Choctaw Nation, of Johnny Frances Merryman , born on the 4th day of April , 1903

Name of Father: James Francis Merryman a citizen of the Choctaw Nation.
Name of Mother: Ruth Merryman a citizen of the Choctaw Nation.

Postoffice Bokoshe, Ind. Ter.

AFFIDAVIT OF MOTHER.

UNITED STATES OF AMERICA, Indian Territory, }
Central DISTRICT.

I, Ruth Merryman , on oath state that I am 24 years of age and a citizen by intermarriage , of the Choctaw Nation; that I am the lawful wife of James Francis Merryman , who is a citizen, by blood of the Choctaw Nation; that a female child was born to me on 4th day of April , 1903; that said child has been named Johnny Frances Merryman , and was living March 4, 1905.

Ruth Merryman

Applications for Enrollment of Choctaw Newborn
Act of 1905 Volume III

Witnesses To Mark:
  { James Taylor
  { Jno R Smoot

Subscribed and sworn to before me this 3rd day of April , 1905

OL Johnson
Notary Public.

AFFIDAVIT OF ATTENDING PHYSICIAN OR MID-WIFE.

UNITED STATES OF AMERICA, Indian Territory, }
  Central   DISTRICT.

I, D. P. Barbour , a physician , on oath state that I attended on Mrs. Ruth Merryman , wife of James Francis Merryman on the 4th day of April , 1903; that there was born to her on said date a female child; that said child was living March 4, 1905, and is said to have been named Johnny Frances Merryman

D P Barbour

Witnesses To Mark:
  { James Taylor
  { Jno R Smoot

Subscribed and sworn to before me this 10th day of April , 1905

Jno R Smoot
Notary Public.

COPY

N. B. 184

Muskogee, Indian Territory, April 6, 1905.

James F. Merryman,
  Bokoshe, Indian Territory.

Dear Sir:

There is inclosed you herewith for execution application for the enrollment of your infant child, John Frances Merryman, born April 4, 1903.

The affidavit heretofore filed with the Commission show the child was living on October 18, 1904. It is necessary, for the child to be enrolled, that she was living on

Applications for Enrollment of Choctaw Newborn
Act of 1905   Volume III

March 4, 1905. You will please insert the age of the mother in space left blank for that purpose.

In having these affidavits executed care should be exercised to see that all names are written in full, as they appear in the body of the affidavit, and in the event that either of the persons signing the affidavit are unable to write, signatures by mark must be attested by two witnesses. Each affidavit must be executed before a Notary Public and the notarial seal and signature of the officer must be attached to each separate affidavit.

Respectfully,
SIGNED
T. B. Needles.
Commissioner in Charge.

LM 6-8

Choc New Born 185
   Ruth LeFlore
   (Born Dec. 17, 1902)
   Mable LeFlore
   (Born Feb. 3, 1904)

No. 1 dismissed June 15, 1905.

DEPARTMENT OF THE INTERIOR,
COMMISSION TO THE FIVE CIVILIZED TRIBES.

Record in the matter of the application for enrollment as a citizen by blood of the Choctaw Nation of:

RUTH LeFLORE   7-NB-185.

BIRTH AFFIDAVIT.

DEPARTMENT OF THE INTERIOR,
COMMISSION TO THE FIVE CIVILIZED TRIBES.

IN RE Application for Enrollment, as a citizen of the   Choctaw   Nation, of   Ruth LeFlore , born on the   17   day of   December , 1902

Name of Father: Greenwood F LeFlore   a citizen of the   Choctaw   Nation.
Name of Mother: Leona A LeFlore   a citizen of the   Choctaw   Nation.

Applications for Enrollment of Choctaw Newborn
Act of 1905 Volume III

Post-Office: Spiro Ind. Ter.

AFFIDAVIT OF MOTHER.

UNITED STATES OF AMERICA, ⎫
   INDIAN TERRITORY.   ⎬
  Central   District. ⎭

I, Leona A. LeFlore , on oath state that I am 27 years of age and a citizen by blood , of the Choctaw Nation; that I am the lawful wife of Greenwood F LeFlore , who is a citizen, by blood of the Choctaw Nation; that a female child was born to me on 17th day of December , 1902 , that said child has been named Ruth LeFlore , and is now living.

                                 Lana A Leflore[sic]

WITNESSES TO MARK:
{

Subscribed and sworn to before me this 14 *day of* January , 1903.

My Com Expires Oct 29 1909   J Wesley Smith
                                               NOTARY PUBLIC.

AFFIDAVIT OF ATTENDING PHYSICIAN OR MID-WIFE.

UNITED STATES OF AMERICA, ⎫
   INDIAN TERRITORY.   ⎬
  Central   District. ⎭

I, Dr W.C. Frederick , a physician , on oath state that I attended on Mrs. Leona A LeFlore , wife of Greenwood F LeFlore on the 17 day of December , 1902 ; that there was born to her on said date a female child; that said child is now living and is said to have been named Ruth LeFlore

                                 W.C. Frederick

WITNESSES TO MARK:
{

Subscribed and sworn to before me this 15th *day of* Jan , 1903

                                 J Wesley Smith
                                      NOTARY PUBLIC.

Applications for Enrollment of Choctaw Newborn
Act of 1905 Volume III

NEW BORN AFFIDAVIT

No

CHOCTAW ENROLLING COMMISSION

IN THE MATTER OF THE APPLICATION FOR ENROLLMENT as a citizen of the Choctaw Nation, of Mabel Leflore   born on the 3^d day of February 190 4

Name of father F. Greenwood Leflore   a citizen of Choctaw Nation, final enrollment No. 8023
Name of mother Leona A. Leflore   a citizen of Choctaw Nation, final enrollment No. 8024

Spiro, Ind. Ter.   Postoffice.

AFFIDAVIT OF MOTHER

UNITED STATES OF AMERICA
INDIAN TERRITORY
DISTRICT   Central

I   Leona A Leflore   , on oath state that I am   30   years of age and a citizen by   Blood   of the   Choctaw   Nation, and as such have been placed upon the final roll of the   Choctaw   Nation, by the Honorable Secretary of the Interior my final enrollment number being   8024 ; that I am the lawful wife of   F. Greenwood Leflore   , who is a citizen of the   Choctaw   Nation, and as such has been placed upon the final roll of said Nation by the Honorable Secretary of the Interior, his final enrollment number being   8023   and that a female   child was born to me on the 3^d day of   February   190 4 ; that said child has been named   Mable Leflore   , and is now living.

WITNESSETH: Leona A Leflore
Must be two witnesses { L.R. Moore
who are citizens   { E.L. Hickman

Subscribed and sworn to before me this, the 3^d day of March 1905

J Wesley Smith
Notary Public.

My Commission Expires: Oct 29, 1905

Applications for Enrollment of Choctaw Newborn
Act of 1905   Volume III

Affidavit of Attending Physician or Midwife

UNITED STATES OF AMERICA,
INDIAN TERRITORY,
Central   DISTRICT

I,   Charles H. Mahar   a   physician on oath state that I attended on Mrs. Leona A Leflore   wife of   F. Greenwood Leflore on the   3ᵈ   day of   February   , 190 4 , that there was born to her on said date a female   child, that said child is now living, and is said to have been named   Mable Leflore

My Com ex Oct 29, 1909   Charles H. Mahar   M. D.

Subscribed and sworn to before me this the   3ᵈ   day of   March   1905

J Wesley Smith
Notary Public.

WITNESSETH:
Must be two witnesses
who are citizens and   { Thomas D. Ainsworth
know the child.   J.W. Underwood

We hereby certify that we are well acquainted with   Charles H. Mahar a   physician   and know   Him   to be reputable and of good standing in the community.

Must be two citizen   { Thomas D Ainsworth
witnesses.   J.W. Underwood

BIRTH AFFIDAVIT.

DEPARTMENT OF THE INTERIOR.
COMMISSION TO THE FIVE CIVILIZED TRIBES.

IN RE APPLICATION FOR ENROLLMENT, as a citizen of the   Choctaw   Nation, of Mable Leflore   , born on the   3   day of   Feb   , 1904

Name of Father: F Greenwood Leflore   a citizen of the   Choctaw   Nation.
Name of Mother: Leona A Leflore   a citizen of the   Choctaw   Nation.

Postoffice   Spiro Ind. Ter

Applications for Enrollment of Choctaw Newborn
Act of 1905 Volume III

AFFIDAVIT OF MOTHER.

UNITED STATES OF AMERICA, Indian Territory,
Central   DISTRICT.

I, Leona A. Leflore , on oath state that I am .... years of age and a citizen by blood , of the Choctaw Nation; that I am the lawful wife of F Greenwood Leflore , who is a citizen, by blood of the Choctaw Nation; that a Female child was born to me on 3 day of February , 1904; that said child has been named Mable Leflore , and was living March 4, 1905.

Leona A Leflore

Witnesses To Mark:
{

Subscribed and sworn to before me this 22 day of Mar , 1905

W.E. Harrell
MY COMMISSION EXPIRES AUG 6, 1908   Notary Public.

AFFIDAVIT OF ATTENDING PHYSICIAN OR MID-WIFE.

UNITED STATES OF AMERICA, Indian Territory,
Central   DISTRICT.

I, Dr C H Mahar , a Practicing Physician , on oath state that I attended on Mrs. Leona A Leflore , wife of F Greenwood Leflore on the .... day of ...., 190....; that there was born to her on said date a Female child; that said child was living March 4, 1905, and is said to have been named Mable Leflore

C. H. Mahar M.D.
Witnesses To Mark:
{

Subscribed and sworn to before me this 22 day of Mar , 1905

W.E. Harrell
MY COMMISSION EXPIRES AUG 6, 1908   Notary Public.

Applications for Enrollment of Choctaw Newborn
Act of 1905 Volume III

BIRTH AFFIDAVIT.

DEPARTMENT OF THE INTERIOR.
COMMISSION TO THE FIVE CIVILIZED TRIBES.

IN RE APPLICATION FOR ENROLLMENT, as a citizen of the Choctaw Nation, of Mable LeFlore, born on the 3 day of Feby, 1904

Name of Father: F Greenwood LeFlore   a citizen of the Choctaw Nation.
Name of Mother: Leona A LeFlore   a citizen of the Choctaw Nation.

Postoffice   Spiro, I. T.

AFFIDAVIT OF MOTHER.

UNITED STATES OF AMERICA, Indian Territory, } Central DISTRICT.

I, Leona A. LeFlore, on oath state that I am 31 years of age and a citizen by blood, of the Choctaw Nation; that I am the lawful wife of F. Greenwood LeFlore, who is a citizen, by blood of the Choctaw Nation; that a female child was born to me on 3 day of Feby, 1904; that said child has been named Mable LeFlore, and was living March 4, 1905.

                     Leona A LeFlore

Witnesses To Mark:
{

Subscribed and sworn to before me this 17 day of April, 1905

                     W.E. Harrell

MY COMMISSION EXPIRES AUG 6, 1908   Notary Public.

AFFIDAVIT OF ATTENDING PHYSICIAN OR MID-WIFE.

UNITED STATES OF AMERICA, Indian Territory, } Central DISTRICT.

I, Mrs. L J McKensey, a Midwife, on oath state that I attended on Mrs. Leona A LeFlore, wife of F. Greenwood LeFlore on the 3" day of Feby, 1904; that there was born to her on said date a female child; that said child was living March 4, 1905, and is said to have been named Mable LeFlore

                            her
                     Mrs. L J M^c x Kensey
                           mark

Applications for Enrollment of Choctaw Newborn
Act of 1905 Volume III

Witnesses To Mark:
{ (Name Illegible)
{ W.E. Harrell

Subscribed and sworn to before me this   17   day of   April   , 1905

MY COMMISSION EXPIRES AUG 6, 1908   W.E. Harrell
                                               Notary Public.

DEPARTMENT OF THE INTERIOR.
COMMISSION TO THE FIVE CIVILIZED TRIBES.

In the matter of the death of   Ruth Leflore   a citizen of the   Choctaw   Nation, who formerly resided at or near   Oak Lodge   , Ind. Ter., and died on the   24th day of   January , 1903

AFFIDAVIT OF RELATIVE.

UNITED STATES OF AMERICA, Indian Territory, }
       Central;   DISTRICT. }

I,   F G Leflore   , on oath state that I am   Thirty five   years of age and a citizen by   Blood , of the   Choctaw   Nation; that my postoffice address is   Oak Lodge , Ind. Ter.; that I am   the father   of   Ruth Leflore   who was a citizen, by   Blood , of the   Choctaw   Nation and that said   Ruth Leflore   died on the   24th   day of   January   , 1903

                                   F Greenwood Leflore
Witnesses To Mark:
{
{

Subscribed and sworn to before me this   28th   day of   April   , 1905.

My Commission Expires March 3rd 1906   Jas. H. Bowman
                                             Notary Public.

AFFIDAVIT OF ACQUAINTANCE.

UNITED STATES OF AMERICA, Indian Territory, }
       Central   DISTRICT. }

I,   Caroline Bowman   , on oath state that I am   66   years of age, and a citizen by   Blood   of the   Choctaw   Nation; that my postoffice address is   Oak Lodge , Ind. Ter.; that I ~~was personally acquainted with~~   am the Grand Mother Ruth Leflore

Applications for Enrollment of Choctaw Newborn
Act of 1905 Volume III

who was a citizen, by Blood, of the Choctaw Nation; and that said Ruth Leflore died on the 24th day of January, 1903

Caroline Bowman

Witnesses To Mark:
{

Subscribed and sworn to before me this 28th day of April, 1905.

My Commission Expires March 3rd 1906   Jas. H. Bowman
                                              Notary Public.

2742
NB 185

COPY
Muskogee, Indian Territory, May 3, 1905.

F. Greenwood LeFlore,
    Oak Lodge, Indian Territory.

Dear Sir:

Receipt is hereby acknowledged of your affidavit and the affidavit of Caroline Bowman to the death of your daughter, Ruth LeFlore, January 24, 1903.

Referring to the affidavits heretofore filed in the matter of the enrollment of this child, you are advised that the Commission is authorized by the Act of Congress approved March 3, 1905, for a period of sixty days from that date to receive applications for the enrollment of children born to enrolled citizens by blood of the Choctaw and Chickasaw Nations between September 25, 1902 and March 4, 1905, and living on the latter date.

You will therefore see that the Commission is without authority to enroll children born subsequent to September 25, 1902, who were not living on March 4, 1905.

                    Respectfully,
                    SIGNED

                    Tams Bixby
                    Chairman.

Applications for Enrollment of Choctaw Newborn
Act of 1905 Volume III

W.F.
7-NB-185.

DEPARTMENT OF THE INTERIOR,
COMMISSION TO THE FIVE CIVILIZED TRIBES.

In the matter of the application for the enrollment of Ruth LeFlore as a citizen by blood of the Choctaw Nation.

---oOo---

It appears from the record herein that on March 4, 1905 there was filed with the Commission application for the enrollment of Ruth LeFlore as a citizen by blood of the Choctaw Nation.

It further appears from the record in this case and the records of the Commission that the applicant was born on December 17, 1902; that she is a daughter of F. Greenwood LeFlore and Leona A. LeFlore, recognized and enrolled citizens by blood of the Choctaw Nation whose names appear as numbers 8023 and 8024, respectively, upon the final roll of citizens by blood of the Choctaw Nation, approved by the Secretary of the Interior January 17, 1903; and that said applicant died on January 24 1903.

The Act of Congress approved March 3, 1905 (Public No. 212) among other things provides:

"That the Commission to the Five Civilized Tribes is authorized for sixty days after the date of the approval of this act to receive and consider applications for enrollment of children born subsequent to September twenty-fifth, nineteen hundred and two, and prior to March fourth, nineteen hundred and five, and who were living on said latter date, to citizens by blood of the Choctaw and Chickasaw tribes of Indians whose enrollment has been approved by the Secretary of the Interior prior to the date of the approval of this act; and to enroll and make allotments to such children."

It is, therefore, hereby ordered that the application for the enrollment of Ruth LeFlore as a citizen by blood of the Choctaw Nation be dismissed in accordance with the order of the commission of March 31, 1905.

COMMISSION TO THE FIVE CIVILIZED TRIBES,

Tams Bixby
Chairman.

Muskogee, Indian Territory.
JUN 15 1905

Applications for Enrollment of Choctaw Newborn
Act of 1905   Volume III

7 NB 185

Muskogee, Indian Territory, June 15, 1905.

F. Greenwood LeFlore, **COPY**
    Oaklodge, Indian Territory.

Dear Sir:

    Inclosed herewith you will find a copy of the order of this Commission, dated June 15, 1905, dismissing the application for the enrollment of your infant child, Ruth LeFlore as a citizen by blood of the Choctaw Nation.

    Respectfully,

SIGNED   *Tams Bixby*

Registered. Chairman.
Incl. 7-NB-185

---

7 NB 185

Muskogee, Indian Territory, June 15, 1905.

Mansfield, McMurray & Cornish,
    Attorneys for Choctaw and Chickasaw Nations,
        South McAlester, Indian Territory.   **COPY**

Gentlemen:

    Inclosed herewith you will find a copy of the order of this Commission, dated June 15, 1905, dismissing the application for the enrollment of your infant child, Ruth LeFlore as a citizen by blood of the Choctaw Nation.

    Respectfully,
    SIGNED

Tams Bixby

Incl. 7-NB-185 Chairman.

Applications for Enrollment of Choctaw Newborn
Act of 1905   Volume III

COPY

N. B. 185

Muskogee, Indian Territory, April 6, 1905.

F. Greenwood LeFlore,
    Spiro, Indian Territory.

Dear Sir:

    There is inclosed you herewith for execution application for the enrollment of your infant children, Ruth LeFlore and Mable LeFlore, born December 17, 1902 and February 3, 1904, respectively.

    The affidavits heretofore filed with the Commission show Ruth LeFlore was living on January 15, 1903. It is necessary, for the child to be enrolled, that she was living on March 4, 1905. It is also noted that in the application for the enrollment of Mable LeFlore the date of her birth was left blank in the physician's affidavit. You will please insert the age of the mother in the place provided for the purpose.

    In having these affidavits executed care should be exercised to see that all names are written in full, as they appear in the body of the affidavit, and in the event that either of the persons signing the affidavit are unable to write, signatures by mark must be attested by two witnesses. Each affidavit must be executed before a Notary Public and the notarial seal and signature of the officer must be attached to each separate affidavit.

                           Respectfully,
                           SIGNED
                           T. B. Needles.
                           Commissioner in Charge.

LM 6-4

COPY

Choctaw N.B. 185.

Muskogee, Indian Territory, April 21, 1905.

F. Greenwood LeFlore,
    Spiro, Indian Territory.

Dear Sir:

    Receipt is hereby acknowledged of your letter of April 17 transmitting the affidavits of Leona A. Leflore[sic] and Mrs. L. J. McKensey to the birth of Mable LeFlore, daughter of F. Greenwood and Leona A. LeFlore, February 3, 1904, and the

Applications for Enrollment of Choctaw Newborn
Act of 1905 Volume III

same have been filed with our records in the matter of the enrollment of the above named child.

You state that you have destroyed the affidavit forwarded you for Ruth LeFlore, as she died prior to March 5, 1905, and according to the rules is not entitled to enrollment.

For the purpose of making the date of the death of Ruth LeFlore a matter of record There is enclosed you herewith for execution application for the enrollment of your infant child, herewith a blank form of proof of death which you are requested to have executed and returned to this office as early as practicable.

Respectfully,
SIGNED

Tams Bixby
Chairman.

Index

ABERNATHY
  Lena 265,266,273
ADAMS
  G W 244
AINSWORTH
  Martha 135
  Martha E 136
  Thomas D 323
ALLEN
  Andrew 122
  Andrew J 119,120,121,122
  Andy 119,121
  John K 291,292,293,294
  Kate 119,120,121,122
  Katie 119
  L D 6,179
  Lloyd Levi 292
  Lloyd Levy 292
  Lou Ella 291
  Loyd 290
  Loyd Levi 290,291,293,294
  Lue Ella 291,292
  S W 20
  Theodore Claton 119,121
  Theodore Clayton 119
  Therdore Claton 120,121,122
ASHER
  L A 31,32
ASHWORTH
  H M 261,262,263

BAGLE
  Ado 291
BAGWELL
  C M 314,315
  Jim 313
BAKER
  Gracie 174,175,177,178
  Mrs Rosa 175
  Rosa 174,175,176,177
  W L 174,175,176,177,178
  Willie Alma 174,176,178
BALDWIN
  M 68
BARBOUR
  D P 318,319
  D P, MD 318

BATEMAN
  W H 210
BECKETT
  A L 205,206
BENCH
  J D 143
BENNETT
  A L 2
BIGBY
  Chas H 291
BIGGS
  J J 148,149,152,153
BIXBY
  Tams 7,41,78,110,111,117,122,
    132,134,162,193,198,204,208,209,211,
    212,216,220,225,230,231,264,266,
    278,279,280,281,290,296,297,304,309,
    327,328,329,331
BLAYLOCK
  Geo Washington 242,243,244,246
  George Washington 240,241,245
  Henry 240,241,242,243,244,245,246
  Ruth A 242,243,244,246
  Rutha 240,241,242,245
BOATRIGHT
  Joseph 201,202,203
  Lou E 201,202
  Milton Elias 201,202,203
BOATWRIGHT
  Joseph 200,201,202,204
  Lou E 202,204
  Lu E 200,201
  Milton Elias 200,201,202,204
  Susie E 204
BOBO
  Lacey P 288
BOHANAN
  Mary 298,300,301
  Sam 299,300,301,302
BOLGER
  P C 63,252
BOWER
  James 5,67,75,150,158,180,181,
    182,234
BOWMAN
  Caroline 326,327
  Jas H 159,160,326,327

Index

BRADY
- Joanna.......... 194,195,196,197,198,199
- R G 194
- R J 197
- Robert G 195,196,197,198,199
- Selina 195,196,197,198,199
- Selina C 194
- Selina Ross 198

BRASHEARS
- Tobias 139

BRINK
- S G 165

BROCK
- Henry 20

BROWN
- David W 102,103
- Eliza 90
- H 90

BRYANT
- Raymond 53,57,60

BURGEVIN
- F E 12
- F E, MD 12
- Frances E 9,13
- Frances E, MD 9,13
- Francis E 14

BURNS
- Alexander 231,232
- Henry 75,76
- Jackson 103,233
- Laura 233
- Mabel 231,232
- Ollie 231,232
- William 233

BUSH
- F D 116
- F D, MD 113
- Francis D 112
- Francis D, MD 112,113

BUTLER
- Sam H 217

BYNUM
- J H 111

CALFEE
- Lee P 155

CALL

Francis 263

CASEY
- Duel Joe 156,157,158,159,160,161
- Eliza 156,157,158,159,160,161
- J F 156,157
- John F 156,157,158,159,160,161

CHASTAIN
- J D 24,25

CHOAT
- Abbie 290

CHOATE
- Abbie 284,287,288,289
- Henry 286,287,289
- Isabella 286
- Jalce 288

CHUBBER
- Austin 96

CLARK
- Edwin O 183,184,185,186,188

CLAYTON
- Wm H H 165

COKER
- G C 221,222,226
- George 225
- George C 220,223,224,225
- Lula 220,221,222,223,224,225
- Palina T 221,222
- Paulina 225
- Paulina T 220,223,225,226
- T C 222
- Willie V E 225

COLLIER
- Martha 140,143

COLLIN
- Malida 155
- Melinda 155

COLLINS
- S D 70,71

COLSTON
- Florence 292,293

CONSER
- Lou 6
- Lue 4,5

COOPER
- Henry 89
- James 180,181,182,183

COX

334

Cale 297,298,301,302,303,304
Caleb 298,299,300,301
Constant E 4
Eunice 1,2,3,4
J E 3,4
John 3
John E 1,2
Mary 297,298,299,300,301,302,304
Matilda 1,2,3,4
Maude 3
Ona Leo 4
Roland 297,298,299,300,301, 302,303,304
CRAY
   V V 244
CROMWELL
   Carrie 228,230,231
   Carrie O 227,229
   Corrie O 226,227
   James D 226,227,228,229,231
   James H 230,231
   Verna T 226,228,230,231
   Verne T 229
   Verner T 226,227
   Vernie T 227,229
CROSBY
   Lydia Ane 189,193
CROUTHAMEL
   A H 113,200,201,202

DAVIDSON
   W B 253,254,255,256,257,258
   W F 265
DAVIS
   A B 62,214,215,216
   Dr A B 214
   S P 145,146
DEBORD
   Kate 189
DESHON
   Albert 253,254,256,258
   Iva A 254
DIFENDAFER
   Chas T 307
DOBSON
   Thos M 242,243
DOOLE
   Bernice A 189
DUNMAN
   B E 141,146
   B E, MD 141
DYER
   E E 123,124

EAKIN
   Geo M 113
ESTES
   W M 3
EUBANKS
   J C 284,286,287
FANNIE
   E J 310
FANNIN
   E J 41,42,165,265,266,311
   W S 79
FARRIS
   Minnie 181
FERGUSON
   Lucy A 79
FISKE
   H H 303
FITE
   F B 206,210
   F B, MD 206
FITZER
   Ellen D 142,143
   Frances 139,140,141,142,143,144, 145,146,147
   Francis 140
   Iverey Elen D 143,144
   Ivery Elen D 139,141,144,146,147
   Ivery Ellen D 146
   Ivrey Elen 140
   James 139,140,142,143,146
   James H 141,143,144,145,146,147
   Jim H 140
   Loucinda 142
   Raymon W 139,145,147
   Raymon Wesley 139,140
FOLSOM
   S J 1,2
FORREST
   Alice 180,182,183

Index

FOSTER
  Thomas 242,243,269
FOWLER
  Rev J C 42
FRANKLIN
  Elizabeth 298,299,300,301,302,304
  Wirt 7,9,49,50,51,69,70,128,151,
    155,172,232
FREDERICK
  Dr W C 321
  W C 321
FULSOM
  Clara Lena 261
FUNK
  E C 303

GARDNER
  R H 165
GERMON
  John F 129,134
GILL
  Jno J 46,48
  Jno J, MD 46,48,49,50
  John J 49,50
GOIN
  Jefferson 30,31
GOLD
  S M 111
GOODWIN
  G W 16
GRACE
  B F 144
GRAHAM
  Mary 29
GRAY
  Dorris 213,214,215,216
  Josephine 213,214,215,216
  Oscar 213,214,215,216
GREEN
  Stewart F 91,126,127
GREGORY
  Agie R 248
  Algia R 247,248,249,250,251
  Algie R 247,250
  E S 247,248
  Edward S 250
  Edwin S 248,249,251

Lillie M 247,248,250,251
Lillie May 249
Lily M 251
M C 248
Mary C 248,249,250,251
GRIFFIN
  J F 179
GRIFFITH
  Ida L 62,63,65
  Ida Lee 61
GUNTER
  G M 241
GUYNES
  Wm 20
HAMMOND
  E S 292,293
HAMMONS
  Mrs John 179
HARL
  W B 20,21
HARRELL
  W E 13,235,236,237,275,276,278,
    279,324,325,326
HARRIS
  Aaron 154,155
  Charles James 154,155
  Sillin 154,155
  W L 76,77
HARRISON
  Albert 253,254,256,258
  W H 61
HAWKINS
  S, MD 221
HAZEL
  Ane Crosby 190,191,192,193
  Arthur O 189,190,191,192,193
  J Crosby 189,190,191,192,193
HEDGECOCK
  Dr T L 269
  T L 267,268,269,270,271
  T L, MD 269,270
HENDERSON
  Marthie 263
HERRON
  George C 224
  Lula 221,222,223,224,225

Paulina T 224
HIARKER
  Ester 282
  Estes 273,275,276
  Frank 278
  Frank R 274,275,276,277,278,279, 280,281,282
  James 273,274,276,277,278,279, 280,281,282
  Sarah 274,275,276,280,282
HICKMAN
  E L 237,322
  Edwin L 10,11,12,275,285
  Robt T 13
HILL
  E P 27
  Ester 68
  Floy May 111,112,113,114,115, 116,117,118
  Jeff W 111,112,118
  Jefferson 114
  Jefferson W .. 112,113,115,116,117,118
  Jennie 111,112,113,114,115,116,117
  A T 254,255,257,258,260
  A T, MD 254,255,257,258
HODGES
  E F 313,315,316
  E F, MD 312,313,315,316
HOLDER
  Catherine 180,181,182,183,184,185,186,187,188
  Ed 178,179,185,188
  Edris Emma Jane 180,182
  Edris Imogen 184,185,187,188
  Edris Imogene 186,187
  Edward 183,184,185,186,187
  Elnora 178
  G E 180,181,182
  Idris Imogen 178
  Katie 178,179
  Wilmot Elnora 183,184,186,187,188
  Wilmoth Elnorah 178,179,185
  Wilmoth L 181
HOLLEY
  G A 89
HOMES

J W 288
HOOVER
  J T 175,176,177
HOPKINS
  W M 298
HORNBACK
  A J 284
HOWARD
  Ida J 227
HOWLAND
  L E 205,206
HYDEN
  F S 219
INMAN
  Frank D 283,284
ISAAC
  James 82,83,101
  Kizzie 83,84
JACKSON
  J B 300,301
  Jack 103
  Sarah 169
JAMES
  S W 314,317,318
JOHNSON
  Alex 85
  B J 30,31,32
  Dr Emmett 6
  E 7,8
  E, MD 7
  Edith 252,253,254,255,258,259
  Emmett 5
  Emmett, MD 5
  Ida 252,253,254,255,256,257,260
  Ida B 258
  L B 241
  Lena 252,256,257,258,260
  O L 43,152,228,229,307,316,319
  Van B 252,253,254,255,256,257, 258,259,260
JOHNSTON
  D R 33,34,35,36
JONES
  C E 10,33,35,238
  C E, MD 10,34

Charley 66,67,150
Dr C E 238
John 163,165
Leoni 72
Loeni 71
Louina 69
Louise 67
Lousie 67
Lwena 67
Sarah 163,164,167
Tom 80,81
KARL
  Viola 249
KELLEY
  Nora 194,195
KELLY
  Nora 197,199
KENNEDY
  T B 278,279
KING
  Anne 80,173
  Annie 80,81,82,83,84,85,87
  Betsey 80,81,82,83,84,85,86,87
  Betsy 173
  N M 81,82
  Nichodemas M 83,84
  Nichodemus M 173
  Nicodemas 80,81
  Nicodemus 86,87,100,101,106
  Nicodemus M 85
KINSEY
  John W 68
KYLE
  S H 17,18,124

LANE
  Allie 87,88,89,90,91,93
  Damie Ophelia 93
  Damie Ophelie 91,94
  Dannie Ophelie 92
  Dawie Ophelie 87,88,89,90,91,93,94
  J P 87,88,89,90,91,92,93
LANIER
  Rebecca 234,235,236,237,239,240
LANKFORD
  Douglas Newton 19,20,21,22,23

Mary 19,20,21,22,23
Thomas A 23
Thomas N 19,20,21,22
LAUDERMAN
  A 88
LE FLORE
  Turner 273
LEE
  J B 221
  Robert E 28,29,73,74,75
LEFLORE
  Clara Lee 265
LEFLORE
  Clara Lee 267,268,269,270
LEFLORE
  Clara Lee 271
LEFLORE
  Clara Lee 273
LEFLORE
  Clara Lee 273
LEFLORE
  F G 326
  F Greenwood 322,323,324
LEFLORE
  F Greenwood 325
LEFLORE
  F Greenwood 326
LEFLORE
  F Greenwood 327,328,329,330
LEFLORE
  Felix 158,159
LEFLORE
  Greenwood F 320,321
LEFLORE
  J W 269
  L E 269
  Lana A 321
  Lena 267,268,269,270,271
LEFLORE
  Lena 273
  Leona A 320,321
LEFLORE
  Leona A 322,323,324
LEFLORE
  Leona A 325,328
LEFLORE
  Leona A 330

Index

Mabel 322
LEFLORE
  Mable 320
LEFLORE
  Mable 323,324
LEFLORE
  Mable 325,330
LEFLORE
  Mary 103,110
  Noel 96,104,110
LEFLORE
  Ruth 320,321
LEFLORE
  Ruth 326
LEFLORE
  Ruth 327,328,329,330,331
LEFLORE
  T L 267
LEFLORE
  Turner 265
LEFLORE
  Turner 266,268,269,270
LEFLORE
  Turner 271
LEFLORE
  Turner 271
LEFLORE
  Turner 273
LESTER
  W F 247,248,250,251
  William F 249
LEWIS
  Frank 79
  J L 242,243,244,267,268,269,
  270,271
LINDSAY
  Emma 189
LINZ
  John M 140,142,143,144
LOCKS
  Victor M, Jr 69,70,155
LONG
  Flaurah B 305,306,307,308,309
  Jewel V 309
  Jewell V 305,306,307,308,309
  Le Roy 27
  LeRoy 27

Will D 309
Will I 308,309
William I 306,307,309
Wm I 305,306
LOWERY
  Josephine 213,214
LUCE
  Herbert ... 95,96,97,98,99,100,103,104,
  107,109,110
  Lester 95,100,101,102,103,104,105,
  106,108,109,110
  Salina 107,108,109
  Saline 95,96,100
  Selina
    95,96,97,98,99,100,102,103,104,105,
    106,107,110
  Seline 101
  Thomas 97,100,101,106,107,
  108,109,110
  Thoms 105
  Thos 95,96,97,98,99,100,101,103,
  104,105,109
  Tom 102,103,107
LUCUS
  Josh 82,83
LUNSFORD
  T B 130
LUNTZ
  John M 140
LYLE
  J P 189
LYTLE
  Mary 143,144,147

McARTHUR
  C L 138,193
  Claire L 137,191,192
McBRIAN
  C A 114
McCARLEY
  James 294,295
  Katie 294,295,296
  Lola 294,295,296
McCLAIM
  Edward George 170
McCLAIN
  C 135

339

Index

C M 136
Edward George 170,171,172,173
G W 234,235
James R 173
James T 170,171,172
James Thomas 171,172
Mary I 249
Susan 170,171,172
McCLELLAN
   Kittie.. 222
McCLELLON
   Kittie.. 223
McCLELON
   Kitty... 222
McCURTAIN
   David C 26,27
   Green 7,8
   Greenwood Mitchell 26,27
   Katherine N 26,27
   Louisa 73,74,76,77,78
   Mitchell 75,76
   Salley 77,78
   Sallie 74,75,76,77
   Thomas 73,74,75,76,77,78
   William 73,74,75,76,77,78
McGILBREY
   Martha 108
McGILLBERRY
   Martha 103
McGILLBREY
   Martha 103
McKENSEY
   Mrs L J 325,330
McKINNY
   S W 5,6
McMORRIET
   L W 222,223
MAHAR
   C H, MD 324
   Charles H 171,172,323
   Charles H, MD 171,323
   Dr C H 324
MANN
   Lola 266
MANSFIELD, McMURRAY &
   CORNISH 212,281,329
MARRYMAN
   Marriene Frances 28
MARTIN
   Annie 179
MASON
   Clarence 260,261,262,263
   John 260,261,262,263,264
   Susan 262,264
   Susie 260,261
MASSON
   Susan 262
   Susie 261
MATHIES
   C C 2,4
MAY
   Robt 135,136
MERRYMAN
   Abraham 28,29,30,31,32
   Cordilia E 29
   D C 54,57
   David C 54,60
   James F 319
   James Francis 318,319
   John Frances 319
   Johnny Frances 317,318,319
   Marion Francis 28,29,30,31,32
   Maron Francis 31
   Marriene Frances 28,29
   Ora 28,29,30,31,32
   Ruth 318,319
MERYMAN
   James F 318
   James Francies 317
   James Francis 317
   John Frances 317
   John Francies 317,318
   Ruth 317,318
MILLS
   James 69,70
MILLUS
   Jno B 31,32
   Ruth 29,31
   Rutha 30,32
MILTON
   G C 117
MINEHART
   George H 233,234,235,236,237,238,
   239,240

Index

Rebecca 233,234,235,236,237,238, 239,240
Sarah E 233,234,235,236,237,238, 239,240
MINEHEART
Rebecca 237
MITCHEL
C T.. 168
MITCHELL
H Gaines 16,17,18,19
Virginia P 16,17,18,19
William L 16,17,18,19
McGILBERY
Martha 101
MOORE
C W 241
E A 11,12
H M 5,6
Henry 127
James William A 131,132,134
James William Arthur.................... 127
Jas William A 126,127,128,129, 130,133,134
John Henry 126,128,129,130,131, 132,133,134
Jon Henry 126,127
L R 158,234,235,285,286,322
Louena.. 131
Louvena E....................................... 129
Louvina... 132
Louvina E 127,128,129,130,131, 133,134
Louvinia E 132
Luvenay.................................... 126,127
Maude... 1,2
MORGAN
Thomas M................................175,177
Thos M 176
Thos M, MD 175,176
MORRIS
Arah Ann 262,264
Arau.. 261
Clarence.. 264
MOSBY
Martha J.. 202
MOSEBY
Martha J.. 201

MOSELEY
Martha I...204
MOSELY
Martha I...202
MUSE
Kentucky A 35,36
NAIL
Louvina 131
Louvina E........................ 129,130,132
Louvinia E......................................131
NALE
Elvira...165
NEEDLES
T B 14,15,22,23,36,44,60,61,64,86, 110,122,133,134,153,161,174,186,187, 193,203,207,225,230,239,240,246, 260,263,271,272,276,290,293,294,304, 320,330
NEWMAN
M W 80,81,82,95,96,98,99,100, 101,103,104,105,106,107,163
N W......................................83,84,85
NORMAN
H T 112

OVERSTREET
A..292,293
OVERTON
Jane...241,245

PARROT
F C...306
PARROTT
Dr F C..306
F C............. 38,40,43,227,228,229,230, 231,307,309
F C, MD 38,40,227,306,308
F E..308,309
PAYNE
Bettie...292
Betty..293
John K..292
Lloyd Levi.......................................292
Lue Ella..292
PERRY
Dan...102,103

Index

Elizabeth ... 169
Lyman ... 169
Stephen ... 102
PETER
  Barnabas ... 69,70,71,72,150
  Barnabus ... 66,67
  Emaline ... 66,67
  Emeline ... 69,70,71,72
  Levina ... 66,67,72
  Levine ... 66
  Leviney ... 66,69,70,71,72
PETERS
  Barnabas ... 67,68
  Emaline ... 67,68
  Vina ... 68
  Wina ... 67
PHILLIPS
  H M ... 224,225
  Mrs H M ... 224
  W H ... 300,301
PILGREEN
  Hosea S ... 128,129,130
  J B ... 128,134
POLLOCK
  A S ... 62,63,65
  A S, MD ... 62,63
POTTS
  Ada ... 52,53,54,55,56,57,58,59,60
  Ada B ... 54,55,59
  Forbis ... 52,53,54,55,56,57,58,59,60
  Forbis B ... 59
  Jane ... 53
  Margaret J ... 53,59
  Margaret Jane ... 52,53,54,55,56,59,60
  Martha A ... 52,59
  Martha Ann ... 52,54,55,57,58,59,60
POUNDS
  Margaret T ... 131
  Margret T ... 127,131,132
  Margrette T ... 127
POWELL
  Edgar F ... 37
  Hubbard ... 33,34,35,36,37
  Kannie ... 36
  Kannie Muse ... 35
  Kemie ... 36
  Kenney ... 36

Kenney Muse ... 33,34,35,36
Kenney Must ... 37
Kennie Muse ... 33
Kenny Must ... 37
Lizzie M ... 33,34,35,36,37
Murtle G ... 41
Myrtle G ... 42,44
RALSTON
  Benj W ... 190,192,193
  Benj W, MD ... 191,192
REAGAN
  Phebe ... 45,46,47,48
  Robert L ... 45,46,47,48
REED
  J E ... 113,114
REID
  J E ... 117
REXROAT
  Estella B ... 217
  Estella Belle ... 216,217,218
  Estelle B ... 219
  Opal Delana ... 216,217,218,219
  U T ... 213,214,215,216,217,218,219
RICKTS
  B C ... 214
RIGG
  J J ... 68
RIGGS
  J D ... 71
  J J ... 70
RISTEEN
  H C ... 52,53
RITTER
  Dr J N ... 140
  J N ... 140,145,147
  J N, MD ... 140,145
ROBERTS
  Sam T, Jr ... 53,54,55,56,57,58
ROBINSON
  Jno W ... 24,25
RODDEN
  A J ... 141
ROGERS
  Jos A ... 88
ROLAND
  Mary ... 302,304

Index

ROSS
  Katie 294,295
  S E 199
  Selina 196,199
  Selina C 194,197

ROSSER
  Malcolm E 299,302

ROWLEY
  H G 223,224

RUSHING
  G M 17,18,19
  G M, MD 17,18

RUSSELL
  Campbell 204,205,206,207,208,209, 210,211,212
  Campbell, Jr. 204,206,207,208,209, 210,211,212
  Mary A 205,206,207,208,210

SAKIKI
  Linnie 83,84

SAMES
  W W 24,25,26
  W W, MD 24

SAWYERS
  Minnie 232

SCOTT
  David 103

SEXTON
  Ben 123,124
  Benj F 124,125
  Lou 123,124,125
  Rual Finton 123,124
  Ruel Finton 123,124,125
  Thos J 123,124

SHAW
  J D 227,312,313,318

SHIFFEY
  Dr E E 149,153
  E E 149,150,151,154
  E E, MD 150,151

SHOAT
  Abbie 285
  Abby 285
  Isabella 284,285

SHONEY
  W A 123

SHULER
  Dr 124
  Dr J L 124
  Jas L 125
  Jas L, MD 124

SIMS
  Edith 148,149,150,151,152,153,154
  Lula 148,149,150,151,152,153,154
  T J 149,150
  Thomas 151
  Thomas J 148,149,151,152,153,154

SINGER
  Alexander 23,24,25,26
  Mary 23,24,25,26
  Mitchell 23,24,25,26

SMITH
  C D 135,136,137
  Charles D 136,138
  Chas 137
  Ella G 136,137,138
  Ella Gertrude 135,136,137
  J H 34
  J R 310
  J Wesley 170,171,238,274,275,282, 321,322,323
  Joseph P 190,191
  Martha 135,136
  Martha Ainsworth 137
  Martha E 137
  Martha E Ainsworth 137,138
  V 119,120,121
  W 63

SMOOT
  Jno R 38,305,319
  John R 39,40,306,308,309

SOCKEY
  Hanah 84,173
  Hannah 82,83,85,87
  Ned 30,31

SPINDLE
  W A 20,21,22,23

SPRING
  B J 4,5,6,7,8
  Benjamin 5
  Benjamin J 4,5,6
  Elma Edith 4,5,6,7,8
  Lou 6,7,8

Index

Lue... 5
SPROWLS
  W T.. 125
STATHAM
  Everet F 37,39,40,44
  Everett F 38,39,42,43,44
  James F 37,38,39,40,41,42,43,44
  Myrtle G 37,38,39,40,42,43,313,314
STATLE
  Price.. 196
STATLER
  Price... 194,195,197
STEWART
  Commodore 283,284,286,287
  Comoto Walter
    283,284,287,288,289,290
  Isabella 283,284,286,288,290
  Isabelle 286,287,288,289,290
  William........ 283,284,287,288,289,290
  Willie... 286,287
STHATHAM
  Everet F 38
STIGLER
  J S.. 89
STINSON
  R F.. 62
STUART
  Commodore 285
  Isabella 284,285
  Isabelle 285
  Willie..284,285
STUCKEY
  H D.. 261
SUCKY
  Hannah 81,85
SUMPTER
  W K.. 20
SWANSON
  H 88
SWITZER
  Martin 164,165

TALBURT
  Amanda 243
  M E...244,246
TAYLOR
  James 39,40,306,313,319

John 285,286
THOMPSON
  Alice...199
  Allice 194,195,197
  G B 197,199
  Geo B 196,198
  George B 199
  Green..16,17
  S A 196,197,198,199
TOKKUBBEE...87
TOKKWBBEE...87
  Annie..84,87
TRENT
  Pat E..311
TUCKER
  J W 121,122
  J W, MD...121
  James W 121
  Jas W 119
  Jas W, MD...120
TURMAN
  R D 297,298
TURNER
  T B 179,182,184,185,186,188
  T B, MD 179,184,185,187

UNDERWOOD
  J W 11,12,15,323
  John W 8,9,10,12,13,14
  Julia V 8,9,10,11,12,13,14
  Vermell................................... 10,13,14
  Vermelle..................... 8,9,11,12,13,15
  Vernelle...15

VARNER
  T T................... 41,42,265,266,310,311
VAUGHAN
  Susan 88
  Susie.....................................88,90,91,93
VON KELLER
  F B..217
  F B, MD 217
VON KELLER
  F P..219
  Frederick P, MD..........................218

WALL

Index

Ida L 62,63,65
Ida Lee 61,62
Martha Eloise 61,62,63,65
Matha Eloise 64
Mrs Thos B 63
Thomas B 61,62,63,64,65
Thos B 62
Tom 299,300
WALLACE
   H L 135,136
   Harold 218
WALLS
   Jess 139
   T J 140,142,143
   Thomas J 144
   Thomas J, Jr 140
WALSH
   Geo W 24
WALSHE
   Geo W 25,26
WARD
   C B 39,306,310,311,312
   Curys B 314
   Cyrus B 312,313,314,315,316
   Freida I 78,79
   G H 62
   Helen I 78,79
   Jefferson D 78,79
   Lena Ola 310,312,313,314,315,316
   Nealia 312
   Nealie 312,314,315,316
   Nelia 313
WATSON
   Adam 80,81
   Mary 165
WELCH
   David Reagan 45,46,48,49,51
   J S 295
   J S, MD 295
   Lula M 45,46,47,48,49,50
   Pauline 45,47,48,50,51
   R A 51
   Robert A 45,46,47,48,49,50
WELLS
   A J 113
WEST
   W L 76,77

WESTON
   Mary 162,163,164,165,166,168,169
   Mitchel 162,163
   Mitchell 97,98,99,100,104,105,106,
   164,166,167,168,169
   Sarah 97,98,99,104,105,162,163,
   164,166,167,168,169
WHALEN
   Nealie 310,311
WHISTLER
   Swkey 96,97
WHITE
   Myron 266
WIGGINS
   J L 215
WILKETT
   Mrs N J 274
   N J 282
WILKINS
   Jim 214
WILLIAMS
   J E 217
   John 73,74,85
   Sarah 233
   Turner 286,287
WILLKETT
   Mrs M J 276,282
   Mrs N J 157,160
   N J 160,161,274,275
   Nancy J 158,159
WILSON
   E W 138
   Mary 23,24,25,26
   S W 136,137
   S W, MD 136,137
WILTON
   G C, MD 113
   G C, MF 114
WINSTON
   Annie 291
   S P 291
   S P, MD 291
WOOD
   C B 40
WOODSON
   B D 2,3
   B D, MD 3

Index

E B... 4
WRIGHT
 Louisa.....................74,75,76
 T L................................. 114
 Watson...........................73,74

YANDELL
 J D................................46,47,48
YARBROUGH
 Jas...................................16,17
YOUNG
 J T.................................. 213

www.ingramcontent.com/pod-product-compliance
Lightning Source LLC
Chambersburg PA
CBHW020240030426
42336CB00010B/560